1984

"How Can You Defend Those People?"

OTHER BOOKS BY JAMES S. KUNEN

The Strawberry Statement
Standard Operating Procedure

"How Can You Defend Those People?"

The Making of a Criminal Lawyer

James S. Kunen

Random House · New York

*Grateful acknowledgment is made to the following for permission to reprint
previously published material:*

Chappell Music Co.: lyrics from *Don't You Want Me* by Jo Callis, Phil Oakey
and Adrian Wright. Copyright © 1982 Virgin Music Publishers Ltd. & Sound
Diagrams. Published in the U.S.A. by Virgin Music, Inc. (Chappell Music,
Administrator) and Warner Bros. Music. International Copyright Secured.
All rights reserved.

Young Lawyers Section, The Bar Association of the District of Columbia:
excerpts from *Criminal Jury Instructions, District of Columbia,* Third Edition.
Copyright © 1978 by the Young Lawyers Section of the Bar Association of the
District of Columbia. Reprinted with permission.

Library of Congress Cataloging in Publication Data

Kunen, James S., 1948–
"How can you defend those people?"
1. Kunen, James S., 1948–   .
2. Public defenders—United States—Biography.
I. Title.
KF373.K78A34   1983   345.73′01 [B]   82-42799
ISBN 0-394-41184-6   347.3051 [B]

Manufactured in the United States of America

2 4 6 8 9 7 5 3

FIRST EDITION

to the memory of
Steve Erhart, Larry Lane, and John Short,
three brave souls,

and

to Samuel and Eleanor Kunen,
my father and mother

REMEMBER THIS ⟍

BETTER THAT MANY GUILTY SHALL GO FREE
RATHER THAN ONE INNOCENT SHOULD SUFFER

We find in the rules laid down by the greatest English judges, who have been the brightest of mankind, [that] we are to look upon it as more beneficial that many guilty persons should escape unpunished than one innocent person should suffer. The reason is because it is of more importance to [the] community that innocence should be protected than it is that guilt should be punished, for guilt and crimes are so frequent in the world that all of them cannot be punished, and many times they happen in such a manner that it is not of much consequence to the public whether they are punished or not. But when innocence itself is brought to the bar and condemned, especially to die, the subject will exclaim, "It is immaterial to me whether I behave well or ill, for virtue itself is no security." And if such a sentiment as this should take place in the mind of the subject there would be an end to all security whatsoever.

—John Adams*

If you have just come from page 158, please return to page 158. Otherwise, please turn the page and continue.

---

* Adams's final argument in defense of the British soldiers accused of committing murders at the Boston Massacre. See *Legal Papers of John Adams,* L. Kinvin Wroth and Hiller B. Zobel, editors (Cambridge, Mass.: Harvard University Press, 1965), volume 3, p. 242.

ACKNOWLEDGMENTS

I wish to express my appreciation to Marjorie Grant Whiting, my landlady, without whose generosity this book could not have been written; and to Rob Cowley, my editor, for his assistance and support.

INTRODUCTION

"How can you defend those people?" is a question frequently put to criminal defense attorneys, often in a tone suggesting that it is not so much a question as a demand for an apology, as though a defense attorney needs to justify his work, in a way that a prosecutor doesn't. Because the question presumes that "those people" accused of crimes are guilty, and that people who are guilty of crimes ought not to be defended, it reflects a profound misunderstanding of our criminal justice system and the defense attorney's role in it. It is, therefore, a question that should be answered. This book attempts to answer it, by explaining the systemic function of the defense attorney and suggesting some of the personal factors that motivate, and enable, a person to perform the defender's role.

I don't hold myself out as an expert on either jurisprudence or trial technique. But I do know as much as anyone about *becoming* a defense attorney, getting to *be* one—and acquiring the attitudes peculiar to that line of work. After practicing as a student in New York City's criminal court, I worked for two and a half years as a staff attorney at the Public Defender Service for the District of Columbia, where I represented about one hundred fifty clients, half of them juveniles, half adults, on charges ranging from disorderly conduct to murder. I had nine juvenile trials, seven of which ended in guilty verdicts, and ten adult jury trials, only three of which ended in guilty verdicts (five were acquittals, two were mistrials).

My clients were fairly typical of what people think of when they think of criminal defendants. They weren't corporations, or the officers of corporations, who calculatingly sent people to their deaths in faulty automobiles; they weren't urbane conservative intellectuals caught with a hand in the company till. They were poor people in the inner city, and they were virtually all black, because, in Washington, virtually all poor people in the inner city are black; and those who were guilty had committed crimes in the street, because they didn't have any better place to commit them. The cases I describe are not extraordinary; they typify what goes on in criminal court every day.

The incidents I discuss are based on actual cases. Sentences in quotation marks are taken from contemporaneous notes. To protect the anonymity of my clients and avoid violating the trust they put in the confidentiality of the lawyer-client relationship, I have changed names, descriptions, places, dates, and some telltale details of certain events. The names of judges, other attorneys, witnesses, police, and investigators have also been changed, where necessary, so that there is no reference point from which even the most enterprising and perverted journalist could hope to trace the actual identity of my clients. As a result of these changes, one reads of incidents occurring at places where they did not really happen. There has, to my knowledge, for instance, never been a fatal shooting at the Bolling Air Force Base headquarters building.

The attorney's obligation of confidentiality is a sacred obligation, honored through history, which dwarfs me and my purposes; and there would be no excuse for violating it. I have not violated it. Nonetheless, I acknowledge some misgivings about *using* my clients' confidences for this book. But, for example, psychiatrists publish papers about their patients' secret fears and dreams. If every confidence, however disguised, never left the room in which it was uttered, no one would know anything about anything.

I went into the practice of law in the first place with the idea that I'd write about it. It would have been strange for me *not* to have had that idea. I think of writing about everything. I'm a writer.

I am also a lawyer (in two states, no less), although in order to write this book, I resigned my job as a public defender. Let me tell you about it . . .

"How Can You Defend Those People?"

§1-01

"THE ONLY TRUE PRINCIPLE OF HUMANITY IS JUSTICE. JUSTICE IS DENIED NO ONE," it says, the inscription carved in stone beside the north entrance to the Criminal Courts Building in Manhattan. One bright autumn morning not long ago, if you had passed those words, pushed through the famous revolving door, caught an elevator to the fourth floor, and walked down the sticky marble hallway until the cigarette butts on the floor got really thick, you'd have been at the Criminal Court, All Purpose Part 3; if you'd run your finger down the mimeographed calendar of that day's eighty cases Scotch-taped to the wall, you'd have found my name in the "attorney" column; and if you'd walked through the pair of swinging doors, you might have seen me, the curly-haired young man in the obviously new pin-striped suit, walking down the center aisle of the courtroom, calling the name of my client-of-the-day, as usual.

It was my third "first day" in court. The alleged pickpocket who was to have been the first client of my career had missed that opportunity. A fellow accused of running a gambling enterprise, three-card monte, on a public street, Forty-second, had likewise declined to take his chances in court. They had both probably elected the "Cleveland defense," which is asserted by boarding a bus to any city that is preoccupied with its own problems.

I paused at each wooden bench, dutiful and stoic, like a deacon with a collection plate, not really expecting much, when, suddenly, a woman touched her chest with her index finger and stood up. I had my first live client—oddly enough, a white, Jewish female, not your everyday customer in criminal court.

Judy Hoffman was a gum-cracking little eighteen-year-old in platform shoes, breathtakingly tight jeans, a slinky jersey, and pink sunglasses with a sequined star on the one lens that was not covered by her cascading brown hair. She would not have been mistaken for a Campfire Girl, but she was well within community standards of dress for criminal court. She was charged with "loitering for purposes of prostitution."

An attorney from the Legal Aid Society, which is paid by the city to represent criminal defendants who can't afford their own lawyers, had handled her arraignment, at which she had entered a not guilty plea. The case was then passed on to New York University Law School's criminal law clinic, to be handled by a third-year student (me), starting with that day's "status hearing," the proceeding at which the parties inform the judge whether there is to be a trial or a plea.*

I deepened my voice a little and very professionally invited Ms. Hoffman to follow me to the clinic's "interview room," a derelict alcove in the Legal Aid office. There I explained to her some of the advantages of being represented by a law student, as opposed to a lawyer—foremost among them being that we had fewer cases, hence more time—and secured her written permission to represent her. (Only one clinic client that year refused representation, noting, "If I'm going to a real jail, I want a real lawyer.")

I was explaining lawyer-client confidentiality and the importance of full disclosure, when Ms. Hoffman, needing no encouragement, launched into her story. She was angry.

It seems that on the night in question, after dinner at her cousin Marlene's house, Judy and her boyfriend had driven from their native Brooklyn to the Library disco at Fifty-eighth Street and Sixth Avenue in Manhattan. Before going off to look for a parking space, her boyfriend dropped her opposite the Library; she intended to buy cigarettes and call her sister. She had completed the first errand and was standing at a pay phone, digging through her pocketbook for a dime in order to accomplish the second, when a man in a three-piece suit asked her if she knew a woman named Mary. She said no, and was about to drop a dime into the phone, when a man in a green windbreaker came up behind her and told her she was under arrest.

"What do you mean?" she said. "Are you serious?"

He was serious, and told her to hand over her pocketbook. He put her into a car and sat down beside her. "You're a whore," he said.

"Don't call me that!"

His investigation of the pocketbook led to the discovery of four dollars and change, and an address book. He looked through the book. "There's nothing here," he said. "You got another address book?" He handed the

---

* The Sixth Amendment to the Constitution, binding on the federal courts, provides, "In all criminal prosecutions, the accused shall enjoy the right ... to have the Assistance of Counsel for his defence." In 1963 the United States Supreme Court, in Gideon v. Wainwright, 372 U.S. 335 (1963), held that the due process clause of the Fourteenth Amendment made obligatory upon the states the Sixth Amendment's right to counsel, and that the right was violated by a refusal to appoint counsel for an indigent defendant charged with a felony. In 1972 the Supreme Court held that "[without] a knowing and intelligent waiver, no person may be imprisoned for any offense, whether classified as petty, misdemeanor, or felony unless he was represented by counsel" (Argersinger v. Hamlin, 407 U.S. 25 [1972]).

purse to another plainclothesman as they drove to the 18th Precinct. "Here, maybe you can find something." At the station, she was booked, fingerprinted, and locked in a cell to await the arrival of a relative.

It was hard for me to believe that the police[man-is-my-friend] would arrest a young woman for *no reason at all,* but Ms. Hoffman's *indignation,* coupled with her lack of any prior arrests, persuaded me. Prostitutes are arrested, and fined, and released to be arrested and fined again, and again. Prostitutes without arrest records exist, but not for long—sort of like falling stars. Ms. Hoffman and I agreed that complete vindication was the only acceptable disposition of her case.

We made our way back down the piss-stained stairs to the courtroom, where we waited, and waited, and waited for the clerk to call our case.

The court reminded me of a package express terminal. Each defendant was a package. The prosecutor and defense counsel were shipping clerks, who argued perfunctorily over where the package should be shipped, then accepted the determination of the black-robed dispatcher. Papers were stamped and tossed in a wire basket. The package was removed. The next package was brought in.

Finally, after three and a half of the most boring hours of my life—up to that point—our case was called. Drawing shallow breaths, sweat trickling down my ribs, I strode forward, lifted and replaced the maroon felt rope dividing what now seemed like the pews from what now seemed like the altar, and approached the judge, a thin-lipped, bull-necked tough guy who looked like he smoked Camels at both ends.

"Let's get rid of this," the judge said. "Plead her guilty, and I'll let her go with a fine."

"She's not guilty, Your Honor."

The judge did not appear to hear me. The D.A. rolled his eyes.

"All right," the judge continued. "I'll take a disorderly conduct."

"No. She won't plead to anything," I insisted.

"C'mon," the judge said. "She has to plead to something—a dis con, no fine, she can walk out of here right now."

Things seemed to be going against me. Then I was seized by inspiration. "But Your Honor," I whispered intently, my eyes blazing into his, *"she's not a prostitute."*

"She's not?"

"No, Your Honor, she's not."

"Oh well, in that case, she can go. Case dismissed."

My legal career's happy start was ascribable in part to my passion for justice, in part to my gift for the felicitous phrase, and in the remaining ninety-eight parts to luck. I had been able to make reference—"She's not a prostitute"—to the world outside the courtroom, where Ms. Hoffman either *was* or *was not* a prostitute, depending upon what she did for money; as opposed to the world *of* the courtroom, where she was either *guilty* or *not guilty* of being a prostitute, depending upon the evidence that the prosecution would be able to introduce. In doing so, I was, all unwitting, "playing up the justice angle," a tactic to which, I now know, one may not often have recourse.

§1-02

I had joined the NYU criminal law clinic because one of its instructors, Clint Levine, told me to.

I had already signed up for the juvenile court clinic when I encountered the strangely persuasive Mr. Levine as we waited for an elevator in the law school's marble and wood lobby. He appeared to be in his mid-thirties, with tousled red hair, rumpled tweed clothes, and a slightly mad pop to his eyes.

"What's this I hear about you taking the juvenile court clinic?" he asked, cocking his head to one side and gazing at me in amazement.

I didn't even know the man, but I felt compelled to explain myself. "I signed up for juvenile court because I used to work with delinquents as a counselor, and now I'd like to see what I could do for them as a lawyer."

Levine grabbed my shoulder and turned me into his sights. "That clinic's a waste of time," he said. "The criminal clinic is the *class* of the clinics. It's the one for you. Sign up for the criminal clinic—that's what *you* want to do." He followed this pronouncement with a prolonged stare, his bulging eyeballs gyroscopically stationary as he solemnly nodded yes, yes, yes.

I switched to the criminal clinic.

In contrast to the rest of the law school, the clinic was anything but academic. Rather than study the evolution of the principles of criminal law, we briskly familiarized ourselves with "the rules of playing ball in this particular ballpark," as Levine put it, and concentrated on developing "advocacy skills"—how to interview a client, conduct an investigation, negotiate with a prosecutor, examine a witness—things that lawyers *do*.

We spent the first two weeks learning to ask unambiguous questions:

"When you first saw the suspect, how far was the suspect from the front door of the bank?"

"How far were you from the front door of the bank when you first saw the suspect?"

"What was the suspect doing when you first saw him?"

"And what were you doing as the suspect was firing at you?"

The idea was to place everything precisely in space and time—always a challenge. We practiced asking questions for about forty hours. We took turns playing the roles of D.A., witness, defense attorney, judge. We watched others do it. We watched ourselves do it on TV. We dreamed about it.

Then we were thrown into court—the shallow end, misdemeanors, but well over our heads, all the same.

§1-03

Arguably, all criminals are losers, for their line of work involves periodic incarceration as a cost of doing business. Most people find this cost utterly unacceptable when weighed against the rewards of the criminal trade, and therefore choose other job options. One would expect, therefore, that those who are professional criminals must have no attractive career alternatives, and this is generally the case. ("You can be on welfare, you can sell drugs, or you can steal," one drug salesman told me.) Criminals are uneducated and unskilled.* Society has no use for them, nor they for it.

Aspects of the trade that are viewed negatively by those who eschew it are actually sources of gratification, a form of nonmonetary compensation, for some of its practitioners. The physical danger is a thrill that makes the psychically numb feel alive. Violence against others can be an eloquent expression of otherwise inarticulable rage. That it is almost universally considered immoral for an individual to take by force another in-

* In the District of Columbia in 1978—the most recent year for which detailed data have been published—among adults arrested for serious crimes whose employment status was known, 57 percent were unemployed. Of those arrestees who were employed, 30 percent held unskilled service jobs; only 10 percent held "white collar" jobs. (*Crime and Justice Profile: The Nation's Capital,* Office of Criminal Justice Plans and Analysis, Government of the District of Columbia [Washington, D.C.: October 1979], pp. 82–83.)

dividual's property is recognized by most criminals, but not dwelt upon. Immorality is another cost of doing business—sometimes a considerable cost, in terms of the toll it exacts on one's relationship to God and man and one's self—but a cost incurred only once. You cross the moral line with your first crime, and thenceforth *are* a criminal. The cost may be spread over years—amortized—but the actual investment of self is made in one lump.

Criminals, in any case, like baseball players, are not much given to introspection. I once asked a professional right-fielder what it was like to be a ballplayer, and he said, "I don't know. I've never been anything else." Most criminals could say the same thing.

("Did you say anything to the police?" I asked a teen-ager arrested on his tenth petit larceny charge.

("The cops asked me why I kept stealing," he replied, "and I said it was like a habit.")

If criminals are losers, misdemeanants are losers' losers. A lawbreaker with any initiative at all will commit felonies, like burglary, robbery, or the sale of substantial quantities of valuable drugs—crimes that are worth years and years in prison. Misdemeanants steal sums rendered inconsequential by inflation, or possess barely enough drugs for themselves, or just *bother* people. Many don't really *commit* crimes so much as stumble over the law. Helpless and hapless, they are easy arrests for the police.

In New York City, misdemeanors—crimes punishable by no more than one year in jail—are almost legal. The government, awash in serious crime, does not have the resources to try petty offenders, nor the jail space to lock them up. In Manhattan criminal court in 1980, 67,365 misdemeanor cases were filed, and 386 came to trial.[1] The rest were disposed of by plea offers the defendants couldn't refuse, or they were dismissed. Since, as third-year law students, we would represent only misdemeanor defendants, our job consisted almost entirely of plea bargaining.

Charles Pinckney was charged with public lewdness (exposing himself to a teen-aged girl) and assault (kicking her in the face), the crimes allegedly having occurred at the shelter for runaways where the two were residing. Since he had no local address, he was required to post bail to ensure his appearance at trial. Since he had no money, he might remain locked up for several months awaiting trial, unless he pled guilty to something first.

I clanked down the steel stairs to the holding pens beneath the courtroom. Before I reached the floor, I met the odor: ten men to a cell. I called out my client's name. He walked up to the bars. I stuck my hand through and shook his. (Good move, I thought, shows you respect him.)

Charles Pinckney was nineteen, five foot five, 150 pounds, black, from Buffalo, unemployed. (Date of birth, height, weight, race, home address, occupation—these were the bureaucratically manageable characteristics by which defendants were known to the police, the courts, and me.) The bruises on his face resulted from the events surrounding his arrest, but his missing front tooth antedated it. There was a certain vagueness about him; he'd smile at odd times. He seemed removed from himself, and from everybody and everything, as though his life were a dream to him, not a good one, and unaccountable forces swept over him.

He admitted to me that he had kicked the girl, but denied exposing himself to her. In fact, he said, he kicked her because she went to the staff and falsely accused him of exposing himself, after they had argued over a cigarette.

Ten minutes after I met him we pled guilty to attempted assault. In exchange for the plea, the judge released him to await his sentencing, which would be in six weeks, to allow time for a pre-sentence investigation by the probation department, and promised that he'd get no more than thirty days in jail.

As I walked Pinckney across the street to the probation department for his pre-sentence interview, I urged him to return in six weeks, for not to do so would be another crime. It struck me that I sounded like a servant of the system, as I was urging his cooperation with it, so I reminded him that I worked for *him*.

"C'mon, you work for the judge," he said.

"No, I work for you. Except you don't have the money to pay me, so the government pays me." (Actually, nobody paid me.)

As we crossed Lafayette Street, he asked, out of nowhere, "How do you know how I feel?"

"I don't. All I know is what you tell me."

We walked on in silence. Then, as we got on the elevator at 50 Lafayette, he said, "All you wealthy people . . ." and smiled, looked at the floor, shook his head.

"What about us wealthy people?" I asked. "We don't know how it is?"

He laughed. "How's it feel to have all that money?"

I thought of saying I didn't have that much money. "It feels lucky," I said.

Charles Pinckney did not show up for sentencing.

§1-04

I had been engaged in misdemeanor practice for a couple of months, when I looked at the people arriving at court one morning—the usual folks in vinyl coats, wearing knit caps although it was warm out (why *do* they wear those caps?)—and instead of feeling *alive*, involved in the elemental struggles of the world, I felt dragged down, depressed. The people all looked poor and worn-out. And the courthouse was poor and worn-out, too. And the whole city.

My client that day, accused of possession of marijuana, and a hypodermic needle, and a gravity knife, and of disorderly conduct, had not shown up. After waiting two hours, I wanted to have the case called so I could go back to school for my 11:30 class with Professor Norman Dorsen, the president of the American Civil Liberties Union. I wanted to sit in a soft leather chair in an elegant seminar room, under the wise and wealthy oil-paint eyes of prominent dead lawyers, and listen to a lecture on constitutional rights. But a Legal Aid lawyer whom I asked told me that one never gives up on a client's coming until noon, or even after lunch, at 2:00. I waited until 11:40 before informing the clerk that I was "ready." The case was called immediately, and a warrant was issued for my client's arrest.

I had, of course, spent some time studying the facts and law of this fellow's case. Although he had never met me, his failure to appear evinced a lack of confidence in my skill, and I resented it. I was also annoyed by his stupidity. We had grounds for a motion to suppress the evidence as the fruit of an illegal search, so there was a good chance that the government, rather than litigate the motion, would have settled for a plea to disorderly conduct. Instead, the jerk was a fugitive; the next time he was arrested—and there would be a next time—he would stay in jail.

Heading back to school, I squeezed onto a subway car and saw there were seats in the next car. I bravely walked, while the train was in motion, from one car to the next. My foot slid—shit! Shit on the floor of the IRT car. Under the knowing and sympathetic gazes of my fellow riders, I scraped my foot ineffectually, sat down in the stench, and rode in the stench the next ten minutes, my woolen suit absorbing the odor, I knew. The car was filthy, scarcely an inch not smeared with ugly, indecipherable graffiti, sprayed scars over seats, windows, maps, everything, the floor thick with dirt, the car thick with people breathing one another's breath, and breathing dogshit, too, this time. I told myself the ride was an experience.

I knew better than to expect bright lights and tinsel when I signed up to work in criminal court. I was ready for the cases to be routine, for the clients to be uncooperative. I was ready for anything. But I wasn't ready for *nothing*—clients not showing up, cases not being called, hours spent in courtrooms staring at the backs of lawyers whispering at the bench, with nothing for me to listen to but my stomach growling for lunch. It was getting hard to get up for the game.

§1-05

A winter afternoon at New York Criminal Court:

I bundled up and stepped outside into the ice-clawed wind, which street people call "the hawk." I had reached the sidewalk in front of the courthouse when I saw a man fall on his face and stay there.

Another passer-by and I rushed to him. The other guy rolled him over on his back. He was white, about forty-five, unshaven, fat. Looked like he could have been a messenger. He had a bag full of papers, which a lady picked up—to make sure they weren't stolen, she said.

He lay stiff, spread-eagled, heaving and drawing in hard breaths, which clicked through the blood in his nose. We figured he was having a fit. I put his yellow and brown knit cap, which had fallen off, under his head; thought I'd hold him still if he started rolling around; didn't know what else to do. Then it occurred to me, "This is in front of criminal court; I'll run in and get a cop; he'll know what to do." As I ran into the courthouse, I was thinking, "Here's the big defense attorney, and when there's trouble, he's glad there are cops around."

I rushed to the complaint room, where a dozen cops in plain clothes— all big stocky guys in lumberjack shirts—were sitting around on plastic chairs. "A man's collapsed on the sidewalk," I said. One languidly folded up the *Daily News* and started to get up. Another grunted, "Call nine-one-one." The first settled back into his seat, reopened the paper, and resumed his reading.

"I thought this would be faster," I said. I saw a phone on the desk in the front of the room and walked toward it.

"There's pay phones in the hall," the cop who'd told me to dial 911 said, just as I started to pick up the phone on the desk.

Amazed, I rushed to the pay phones. First phone—no tone. On the second phone, I dialed 911. A woman answered unintelligibly. I asked, "Is this nine-one-one?" She said yes. I said, "A man's collapsed on the sidewalk in front of 100 Centre Street. He may be having a fit. Send an ambulance."

I went back outside. The man was on his back, stone still, his eyes wide. He didn't appear to be breathing. I looked at him—dirty, blood in his nose and mouth—and was thinking I didn't really want to give him mouth-to-mouth resuscitation, when a stocky young court guard came running out, ripped open the man's shirt, and started giving him cardio-pulmonary resuscitation, hands crossed over the center of his pale, hairy chest: *One-two-three-four-five. One-two-three-four-five.*

The guard put a white handkerchief over the man's mouth and nose; a light ring of saliva and blood spots came through it. He blew into the man's mouth, then looked up and said, "He's got fluid in his lungs." He went back to massage. *One-two-three-four-five. One-two-three-four-five.*

A skinny street dude was saying, "He's gone. If only these people knew what to do before. These people were standing around and no one knew what to do."

As the guard pushed on his chest, the man's hands and feet twitched. Otherwise, no motion.

A uniformed cop arrived. He picked up the man's hand, opened the clenched fingers and let them go a couple of times. Each time the fingers sprang closed again. The cop examined the fingernails for some sign. He depressed the flesh of the thumb. The indentation remained.

An ambulance arrived from Beekman Downtown Hospital, one half mile away. Twenty minutes had passed. The ambulance men took out a litter and shoved the man into the back of the orange and white van. They drove away.

I knew then, and learned later, that the man was dead. I didn't feel too upset, just thinking, "Well, this is city life." But later I was quite shaken. It wasn't so much the dying man's blue-gray face, nor my own ineffectuality, nor even the failure of the cops in court to help. It was that *one* cop who *started* to get up and then sat down when the other said, "Call nine-one-one." Peer-group pressure. Cops are like that.

§1-06

"That's really disgusting," Professor Henry Goldman said when I told him about the cops' inaction. "That may actually be against the law."

Every Tuesday night we met for an hour with Henry for the "Professional Responsibility" segment (one credit) of the clinical program.

"The law school comes upon a problem, it makes a course out of it," he had explained at our first session. "It used to be 'poverty,' so we had 'The Law and Poverty.' Now, after Watergate, it's 'professional responsibility,' so there's a 'Professional Responsibility' course."

(I couldn't help thinking of crusty old Professor Herbert Peterfreund's mockery of liberal-artsy courses: "People don't seem to realize this is a *professional* school," he told us in evidence class. "They think they're still in college. I don't understand it. They take courses like *Botany* and the Law, *Women* and the Law, *The Law* and the Law. They debate whether the common law exists on the moon." He shook his bald head in wonderment. "You've *got* to *learn* the *fundamentals!*")

The urbane but earnest Goldman hoped that as we sat around his den-like office, we would put some real effort into examining ethical questions, even though his course was ungraded. Despite, or because of, our enthusiastic consumption of the wine he provided, we actually did attain at least a rudimentary level of self-awareness, undoubtedly a precondition for moral consciousness, a state of mind for which lawyers are not known.

"The American Bar Association's *Code of Professional Responsibility* is not a particularly useful guide for conduct," Henry said at the outset. "Most of the concern in the *Code* has to do with billing practices. My concerns are lawyer-client, lawyer-system, and lawyer-society relationships. And the answers lie within each person, as to what he thinks is right and what's not right. It comes down to how you feel. . . . The materials for this course are you."

We had begun by discussing our reasons for wanting to go into criminal defense work. "To help people," one woman suggested. I countered that if we really wanted to help people, wouldn't we go into welfare rights or mental patients' rights or tenants' rights or something? I proposed vicarious criminality as our prime mover. Other suggestions included the cineromantic thrill of being involved with cops and robbers; the challenge of pitting your wits against the massed forces of the state; the saintly feeling of standing with the reviled and friendless; the intensity of dealing with people in crisis; and the necessity of defending liberty by making the state prove its case before putting *anyone* (THIS MEANS YOU) in prison.

I might have added that my father was a successful small-town lawyer. (Of course, he became a lawyer back in the days when one said "doctors and lawyers" in the same breath, before lawyers had permeated society and become *common*—nothing recedes like success.*) So, for me, becoming a lawyer was always something to be done or not done, something to be considered.

I had no interest in, or talent for—which is much the same thing—fighting for IBM to get the billion instead of Xerox. Nor did I particularly want to devote myself to winning the money or children for one spouse rather than the other; or ensuring that the bin of bolts was delivered at the agreed-upon price; or preserving the estate of the rich departed from the designs of the tax man. I suppose I could have gotten into avenging accident victims—and oh, that money!—but only criminal law offered the chance to visit the underworld, know intimately the secrets of life invoked by that magic three-word incantation, sex-and-violence . . . and return to tell about it. For reasons psychological, political, or both, being a prosecutor did not appeal to me, so criminal defense was the only way to go.

As the weeks passed, we moved from such general considerations to specific situations as they arose.

"I have a real ethical problem for us," a student began, on this particular December night. In addition to handling misdemeanor cases, we assisted our instructors in representing felony defendants. This student had been helping Clint Levine defend a Mr. McDaniel, who was a co-defendant with a Mr. Ries in a liquor store robbery. The prosecution had a very strong case against Ries, but practically no evidence against McDaniel. If Ries pled guilty, McDaniel would be tried alone and have a good chance of beating the rap. But Ries insisted on going to trial; he and McDaniel were going to be tried together, and McDaniel would likely be found guilty by association.

Suddenly Ries comes into court beaten to a pulp and says he's changed his mind; he wants to plead guilty. And Clint knows that McDaniel beat Ries up. Question: Should Clint tell the judge?

Henry dusted off the *Code of Professional Responsibility*.

One section said that a lawyer must *not* reveal anything his client tells

* There were over 600,000 lawyers in the United States in 1980, up from 355,000 in 1970 (private conversation, Barbara Curran, American Bar Foundation, June 9, 1983).

him in confidence (which is how Clint learned that McDaniel beat up Ries*). But another section said that a lawyer *must* inform the court if he knows of a fraud about to be perpetrated upon it.

"Does it say which section supersedes which?" I asked.

"No, it just leaves both hanging out there," Henry replied.

A discussion ensued. "No, no, you don't reveal what your client's told you," one student insisted.

"But what if, for instance, your client told you he had tampered with the jury?" Henry wanted to know.

"Now, there, I would tell," I said, "because my duty to my client does not include becoming a criminal; and who could go through the charade of dramatically summing up before a jury he knows his client has bought?"

Henry discovered he'd been reading from the 1970 *Code of Professional Responsibility.* Checking the 1977 *Code,* he found that lawyer-client confidentiality takes precedence over the duty to reveal fraud, or so it seemed, according to his best efforts at statutory construction. The relative weight and meaning of everything depends on the order of presentation and whether or not paragraphs are indented.

Just then Clint walked in. Someone asked him what he would do in the hypothetical situation where your client tells you the jury is in the bag.

"You can't discuss moral issues in a vacuum," Clint said. "You need a factual basis. If there were jury tampering, you'd never know about it unless you were the kind of lawyer who was in on it from the git-go."

As for the situation with Ries, Clint said he thought everything worked out fine. "Ries was going to lose anyway. Why drag McDaniel down with him? Ries is the one who got McDaniel involved in the crime, and Ries is the one who was stupid enough to get caught with the stolen bottles of liquor. When Ries decided to plead guilty, he made the right decision."

But what about the fact he was beaten up?

"The fight didn't coerce him," Clint explained. "It caused him to reconsider his position, and he did, and he came to the right decision. People get angry. They fight. This is human life we're dealing with."

---

* The *Code* (Ethical Consideration 4-1) does permit a lawyer to discuss confidential information with other lawyers in his own firm. The clinic was incorporated as a law firm; thus, we were able ethically to discuss these matters.

§1-07

I was doing great. I was really rolling.

After six months in the clinic, I was starting to feel like a lawyer, although I'd never had a trial. *My* clients didn't *need* trials. We won big in plea bargaining.

Abdul Dhabour (formerly Earl Johnson), a slight, young black man in white robes and a turban, had been selling incense and handing out literature on Forty-second Street near Times Square, for the benefit of his mosque. The way he told it, he was talking with a "brother" who had made a donation, when a cop named Mike and his partner told him to "Move it!"

"Mike pushed me into an alley. I was scared they'd kill me," Abdul recounted, his gold earring flickering in the fluorescent light of our interview room. "But the brother followed. Mike took the incense out of the brother's hand and put it in mine. He said, 'Give him his money back.' So I did. Mike pushed the brother away. Then he slapped me in the mouth. The big one jabbed me in the stomach with his stick. I said I was sorry.

"They told me to leave and keep off Forty-second Street. But out on the street, I saw my mouth was bleeding, and I got mad. I told them they had no right. A crowd gathered, and Mike grabbed me and said, 'You are under arrest.' Mike and the other cop took me into a pizza shop and called a car. While we were waiting, Mike hit me once or twice. He said, 'You're a smartass fucker, a scumbag with a dress on!' They put me in a car and drove me down the West Side Highway to the precinct. They beat me with a club on the way. I was taken to court. I pleaded not guilty. And they told me to come back today."

Abdul was charged with harassment, disturbing the peace, and resisting arrest. He wanted to plead guilty and get it over with, which was all right with me, if that's what he wanted, but it wasn't all right with Maggie Bensfield, my clinic supervisor. She led us out into the corridor, into the haze of cigarette smoke curling under the yellowed fluorescent fixtures. The clickety-clack of hookers' heels echoed down the hall like train wheels on a track.

"The cops had no right to beat you up, and you had every right to pass out your literature," Maggie said, sounding angry at *Abdul*. "If you plead guilty, the cops'll think they're the Kings of Forty-second Street, and they can do what they want with you. But if you stand up and fight, maybe they'll lay off you."

Abdul thought possibly the opposite would happen, that the cops would really "get on his case" if he made them come into court; but he thought most likely the cops would be totally unaffected by anything that happened in court, and life on Forty-second Street would go on as before.

After Maggie's pep talk Abdul still wanted to cop a plea, but he did agree, seemingly to please Maggie, that if his guilty plea was going to carry a fine, then that would be too much to bear, and he'd fight the case.

I explained to him that if he pled guilty, he'd have to do an allocution, "admitting" the allegations on the record—yes, I punched the cop; yes, I did this; yes, I did that.

"Yeah, sure, I'll do that," he said with a shrug. For him this was no problem, because he never had any expectation of justice. He wasn't looking for justice. The court was to him a sham from beginning to end, and he was ready to play along so he could get out as quickly as possible.

Before the judge took the bench, I went up to the assistant D.A., Larry Giannotto, a tall, skinny guy, moustached, hippish looking—a reasonable man, from whom I'd gotten good dispositions before.

"Let's clear up the congested court calendar," I said. "This case is complete bullshit. This is the First Amendment."

When I mentioned the First Amendment, Giannotto looked at me as though I had just farted, loudly.

"Give me an A.C.D.,"* I said.

Giannotto replied that the complaint alleged that my client had been fighting with someone when the cops arrived. He said he wouldn't give me the A.C.D. if there'd been fighting. He wanted a guilty plea to harassment in exchange for dropping the more serious charge, resisting arrest.

"One thing for you to consider," I suggested, "is that the group he belongs to is a pacifist group, and if he engaged in fighting, they'd take away his turban." A little denigration of the client sometimes helps.

Just then I remembered that I'd spent two hours the day before looking up cases. I sat down in the front row of the court and went over them, picking out a few that I would mention. I'd been thinking that I tended to talk like a tobacco auctioneer to judges, because I felt as though they were looking at a clock above and behind my head, and that they gave

---

* Adjournment in contemplation of dismissal, an arrangement pursuant to which no plea is entered and no finding regarding the defendant's guilt is made, but, rather, the case is set aside for a time and is then dismissed if the defendant has stayed out of further trouble.

me about one minute, which was, in fact, the case. But that day I decided I was going to speak slowly and deliberately, and I was going to say everything I had to say, and that was all there was to it.

Our case was called. I approached the bench with the D.A. I didn't wait for him to say anything, nor did I say anything to him.

I put on my phone company voice—gentle but firm, patient but almost at the end of patience—and addressed the maternal figure of the judge. "Your Honor, I cannot in good conscience recommend to my client that he accept anything more than an A.C.D. He's charged with harassment. Harassment means annoying someone to the point where that person is likely to respond violently. Whom did he harass? Mr. Dhabour belongs to a disciplined pacifist mosque and would be expelled if he engaged in fighting, and, in fact, if you'll look at his record, you'll see that he hasn't been in any trouble during the years that he's been a member of that mosque, except four years ago he put a slug into a token machine."

"And was convicted of *assault* for that?" the judge interjected.

My heart sank; maybe I hadn't looked at his record closely enough. But I checked it and explained, "The assault was six years ago, Your Honor." She nodded, and I continued. "Now, Your Honor, I could cite chapter and verse, but that would be redundant. You know the law." I said that to make time to look down my list of cases, which I think the judge could see upside down was a list of cases, and I began reading from it. "Your Honor, as I'm sure that of course you know, vulgar language directed solely at a police officer does not constitute disturbance of the peace. Disturbance of the peace has to be an annoyance of a substantial segment of the public. And the mere collection of a small crowd on Forty-second Street, where the sidewalk is twenty feet wide—*that* isn't disturbance of the peace.

"This case involves a systematic and continuing pattern of harassment of this group as they attempt to exercise their First Amendment rights. And as for resisting arrest, not holding out your hands to be cuffed as you're being placed under an unauthorized, illegal arrest is not resisting arrest."

And so forth.

The judge, who'd been nodding silently as she listened, asked the D.A., "What is your position?" And the D.A. said, to my surprise and delight, "We are willing to offer an A.C.D."

As I was shaking Abdul's hand, Maggie came out and demanded, "How did you *do* that?"

First of all, I was *insistent*. That was the way it had to be. I would accept nothing else. In this case, the judge and the D.A. probably thought, "If it's *that* important to you, okay," because they didn't care about it that much. But it's amazing what can be accomplished by sheer will. Call it "the Levine effect." I once saw a judge rule certain evidence admissible, and Clint Levine walked up to the bench, and literally *laid his hands on the judge,* and said, "No, We're not going to do that, Judge. We're not going to let that in." And the judge *changed his ruling.*

My other technique was to cram into that two-minute talk (and two minutes is an eternity, talking up at a harried judge)—I was a real spell-binder, that day—cram into those two minutes as many buzzwords as I possibly could. It's like playing pinball. A buzzword is a hit. *First Amendment context* B-ding! *Continuing pattern of harassment* B-ding! B-ding! Chicka-chicka-chicka-chicka. *Arbitrary and discriminatory* B-ding! *Client is employed* B-ding! B-ding! Chicka-chicka-chicka BONG! Free game.

That day I was a real pinball wizard. And Abdul Dhabour was the happier for it.

I remember thinking as I left the courtroom, "I love this. I feel terrific. I'm going to have to remember this for the next time I feel terrible."

§1-08

The next time I felt terrible was a few days later, as I was sitting in the NYU law library trying to write a brief for the Carney case, one of the two felony cases I was working on with Clint Levine.

Carney had been charged with felony-murder, under a statute which holds that *every* participant in a felony can be found guilty of murder if anyone is killed in the course of the commission of the felony.

Carney, like many a wrongdoer, did what he did because he felt he had been wronged. He got a friend to hold up Carney's neighbor, who, Carney felt, owed him eighty-five dollars. Unbeknownst to Carney, who was keeping watch outside the neighbor's apartment house while his friend lay in wait inside, his friend was carrying a gun, and killed the man with it.

Carney's original lawyer, whom we'd replaced, didn't explain to him that he had a defense to felony-murder if he did not know or have reason to know that his friend was armed. So Carney, thinking that he had no defense, pled guilty and was sentenced to a minimum of fifteen years, and a maximum of life, in prison.

Carney escaped and made his way to Indiana, where he married and started a family. After three years someone informed on him, and he was apprehended. He was convicted of escaping from prison, and sentenced to two years, which would run concurrently with the fifteen-year murder sentence. At twenty-seven, his second life was over.

Fifty friends, neighbors, co-workers, and employers from Indiana wrote the New York authorities pleading for Carney's release. "A man so good can't possibly be so bad," one writer noted. Apparently, besides caring for his own family, Carney made a practice of feeding and sheltering hitch-hikers and drifters.

"I thought only hippies and eccentric billionaires did that," I said to Levine.

"And saints," Levine said.

"Now there's a defense: 'But Your Honor, my client is a saint!' "

"It's hard to prove," Levine said.

In fact, Carney was just a hapless little white guy. He didn't have anything that could be called an opinion about anything—he didn't know enough. He just lived from day to day. He used to think that the Jews had done him in, and he asked for a non-Jewish lawyer, but he got us, and he got over it.

We were trying to get his guilty plea vacated so he could have a trial on the murder charge. (He'd have to do the two years for escape no matter what.) Courts are very reluctant to let people withdraw their guilty pleas because that's what half the people in prison would like to do—upon reflection they're sorry they didn't risk a trial, which they imagine they might have won. There was a conflict between the state's interest in having guilty pleas stick and Carney's interest in having a trial. (Of course, Carney started out with more than "an interest" in having a trial; he started out with a *right* to a trial, which, because it is a right, overcomes any mere interest of the state. But the state argued that he had voluntarily given up that right forever by pleading.)

The appellate court would resolve the conflict by reference to the resolutions of past conflicts, just as future conflicts would be resolved by reference to the present one. I thus found myself smack in the middle of the endless process of defining principles by which the right and wrong of *every* situation can be fixed, which is the ongoing enterprise of the law— ongoing and endless, because there is always some play, there is never a perfect fit, between a general principle and a specific situation, indeed, between any words (which are all general) and the world (specificity itself).

Some people *like* doing legal research. Some people like handling snakes. The two activities struck me as similar. I was presenting the argument in my brief that Carney's plea was not "knowing and voluntary" (as it had to be, to be valid), because he had had ineffective assistance of counsel.

An appellate lawyer must construct and rebut arguments within a self-referential system comprising *all* the legal arguments and resolutions that have preceded his. He has to retrace everyone else's steps before he can take a single step of his own. A great appellate lawyer must possess that combination of discipline and inspiration, of compulsiveness and creativity, which is popularly associated with the scientist. I don't be that way.

Trying to pin down what constitutes "ineffective assistance of counsel," I read case A. The decision in case A held that the issue had been settled in cases B and C. I looked up case B. Case B cited cases C, D, and E. I looked for case C. It wasn't on the shelf. This was not unusual. On each of the thirty-eight long tables in the reading room sat a little sign saying, "Be considerate of your fellow students. Please reshelve your books." And on each of the thirty-eight tables sat dozens of books, used and abandoned by—whom?

I had my suspicions. On those occasions when duress or necessity drove me to the library, I noticed that certain individuals were *always* there. They did strange, incomprehensible things with index cards and multiple colored pens; they chatted with one another; they ate crumbly food; they aired out their socks; they *lived* there, and knew where every book was, and had no need of systematic shelving, having little systems of their own.

As I walked slowly from table to table looking for case C, tilting my head from one shoulder to the other as I tried to read the bindings of the horizontal books, I thought the little signs should have said, "Reshelve your books or DIE," an injunction I would have been happy to enforce. I never found case C.

I looked up D. It said E, F, and G were dispositive. After walking around with my nose parallel to the floor for half an hour, I found case E on a table. It said F and G *seemed* to support each other, but didn't really, in light of case H.

I looked up case H. It didn't seem to have anything to do with "ineffective assistance of counsel." I went back to case F. It said that a good overview of the issues could be found in a legal encyclopedia. I got that, and found that it had been revised since case F was written. I looked up the new encyclopedia article. It said the real lowdown on the subject would be found in case A.

The room started to spin. I went crying to a friend, a law review type more ardent and adept than I at research, and asked if I was doing something wrong. "That's the law," he said. "You pursue it far enough, you go right up your own asshole."

In the apparently pivotal decision, the court said, "We used to say counsel was ineffective when he rendered the trial a farce and a mockery of justice. Now we say the trial is a farce and a mockery of justice when counsel is ineffective." On such distinctions the freedom of Mr. Carney would hinge.

The Law, with all its hypertechnical petty arcane bullshit, sometimes struck me as sheer madness, particularly on a sunny Saturday afternoon. But maybe it's not madness, I told myself. It just *seems* like madness to me, because it is unrelentingly rational, rigorously logical, punctiliously exact, whereas I'm inclined to look at the Big Picture and rely on an intuitive sense of what's fair. Anyway, bad as this is for me, I reminded myself, Carney has it a lot worse, sitting out on Rikers Island. I tried to remember that Carney was a nice guy, and I was trying to get him out of prison. I spent the better part of two weeks in the library and found four or five cases where nice guys had been let out of prison under similar circumstances.

The court of appeals was not persuaded. It held that the facts of Carney's case differed, in small but significant ways, from the facts of the cases we cited, so that his case could properly reach a different result. He had to do his fifteen years.

From the probation department's pre-sentence report to Carney's trial judge:

The defendant plans to spend his [mandatory] 15-year (minimum) period in jail profitably. He enjoys writing poetry. The subject matter of his poetry generally involves material dealing with love or sadness. He states he hopes to pursue a college education and study psychology as well as law. The defendant's motivation for studying psychology is his own curiosity as to "why people do the things they do."

In summing up his involvement in the instant offense, the defendant states that he realizes he "indirectly" did kill the deceased and he "now has to pay for his crime." He states he is not a criminal, and never will be. He describes his involvement in the instant offense as "a nightmare."

The defendant states he does not blame anyone involved in apprehending him and feels all, including the detectives involved in the investigation did their jobs. He states he is looking forward to 15 years hence when he might be considered for parole. He states he plans to make a life for himself, when he is released from prison and feels that the only one he has to face once he is released to the community, is the Lord, for his involvement in the instant offense.

The defendant generally impressed as a sincere, somewhat, however, misguided youth who did not impress this writer as a dangerous individual.

§1-09

The other felony on which I was working for Levine was the Case of the Hasidic Armed Robbers.

One Sunday afternoon a Hasidic camera importer was visited in his lower Broadway office by two young men in Hasidic garb, who asked in Yiddish for charity, then whipped sawed-off shotguns out from under their black coats and relieved him of a brown paper bag containing $10,000 in cash, he said. Two days later, at a delicatessen in Brooklyn, he thought he recognized one of the robbers. That suspect, a twenty-year-old hulking teddy bear of a man, named Izzy, was arrested and became our client. His best friend was also charged.

Working as Clint's investigator, I traipsed around lower Broadway, the Forty-seventh Street diamond district, and the Williamsburg section of Brooklyn, trying to sort out the connections between the victim, the suspects, the Hasidic vigilante organization, and other parties, interested and disinterested, all of whom seemed to be cousins, in-laws, or both. Our theory was that Izzy and his friend were being scapegoated because of their reputation in the Hasidic community as rebels who behaved outrageously, going to movies and driving around in cars.

I learned the true meaning of the word "cold" that January, hanging around outside Williamsburg's Roberto Clemente housing project, where the East River served as strop for the razor wind, waiting for midnight and the return of my "sources" from worship.

Izzy was a volunteer auxiliary policeman and liked to think he was a good friend of a couple of real cops, Officer Dick Rodriguez and his partner, Officer Joseph Lear.

I went out to the 90th Precinct one night to interview Lear and Rodriguez about whether they could be character witnesses and testify about Izzy's reputation for truth and veracity, and for peacefulness. We walked across the street to a fast-food chicken place, where we sat talking over tepid cups of vile coffee.

Lear and Rodriguez were both, basically, assholes. They were cool, and very concerned with being cool, and they'd put on sort of black, or "street," accents, and they tried to act tough. I suppose they were tough. Rodriguez sported a bouffant of hot-combed black hair. He wore a diamond pinkie ring on his left hand, and on the fourth finger of his right, an enormous gold ring set with about thirty tiny diamonds. Lear's hair was prematurely gray, and his teeth stood out like those of a skeleton. They both had enormous bellies hanging over their black leather garrison belts.

"Izzy couldn't have done it," Lear said. "One—he's honest and up-standing; two—he hasn't got the balls."

Rodriguez, commenting on my necktie, which had a scales-of-justice motif, launched into a little rap about the court system which would de-cide Izzy's fate. It was his habit to launch into little raps about himself, and about what he's like, and about how he does things, and what he knows, and what the Hasidic community is really like, and what cops are really like, and what the courts are really like, what everything is really like.

What he said about the courts was, "It's a game. It's a game they play with your ass."

"It's chess," Lear interjected, "and you're the pawn."

Rodriguez explained that truth has nothing to do with the outcome of the trial; that there are a lot of innocent people in jail; that all that counts is how you play the game, whether you can win.

Rodriguez said that all the other cops hated Lear and himself, and, by association, didn't like Izzy too much. The reason they hated him and Lear was that they had put "bad cops" in jail and were considered rats. "So either we're good guys who put bad guys in jail, or we're bad guys because we put cops in jail. It depends on how you look at it. What do you think?" Rodriguez asked me.

I surprised myself by saying, "I don't think anybody's a bad guy or a good guy. I don't think of people as bad guys or good guys." I said this coolly, expressionlessly, as though to say, "I've been around. I don't think that way anymore."

Afterward I thought, "What's become of me? I'm changing faster than I realized. I *am* in that game he referred to. I'm in it to win. It's a matter of indifference to me whether my client's guilty or not." I had thought that was because I was committed to the adversary system, and to doing my job well; but that night I was beginning to think maybe I'd become amoral.

Upon reflection I decided I was just trying to sound cool to the cop, trying to go along with his rap.

A year later, after I had graduated from law school and moved away, I heard that Izzy and his co-defendant were acquitted, Clint Levine having successfully mounted a defense of misidentification.

I remembered what Izzy's father had said. I was having a glass of coffee at Izzy's family's small walk-up apartment one night during my winter of investigation, when his father came in, stomping the snow from his galoshes. He extended a great, meaty hand to shake mine. He was a watch repairman, and I wondered how he did that fine work with such big hands. His black overcoat and black lamb's wool hat framed a face as translucently white as paper. Izzy's father had a pot belly, big ears, and a big nose, but he was an exceptionally handsome man, owing to the strength and harmony of his features, the clarity of his eyes, the calmness of his bearing. He was a concentration camp survivor.

"If you could find out what the true story is," Izzy's father said to me, after my role had been explained, "I would give you such a good present."

"We'll probably never find out what the true story is," I replied, "but I do think that we can get Izzy acquitted—that's the main thing."

"Not for me," the old man said. "For me the main thing is to find out what the true story is."

§1-10

As for the rest of law school, other than the clinic, there really isn't much to say. School is school. You sit in chairs that are attached to the floor. You write down what the teacher says (or borrow the notes of someone who did). When the time comes, you memorize it and spit it back out.

Law school classrooms are perhaps a bit more arid than those devoted to other disciplines. In three years of discussions, I can't recall any mention of a *feeling*. But that figures, law *being* the utterly abstract, ineffable, absolute rationality which is at once the object sought and the method of seeking.

Law school is *not,* contrary to the mystification heaped around it by people who have done time there, difficult. *Boring* would be a better word, but not tremendously or profoundly boring, just boring in the ordinary, everyday sense, which leaves room for the occasional peak of interest by which the broad valleys of torpor are defined.

Those big books you see law students carrying around, which contain the greatest hits of centuries of appellate decisions from throughout the English-speaking world, read like a meticulously kept journal of human experience, written by a diarist whose only interest was *trouble. Every-*

thing happens. People shoot at A and hit B. They shoot people simultaneously being shot by other people. They shoot people who are already dead. People get drunk on purpose and do things by accident. They get drunk by accident and do things on purpose. Doctors butcher their patients. Butchers doctor their meat. Cars blow up, planes fall down, ships sink. Mice fall into soda bottles, children into wells. God acts.

No one seems to suffer in all these tales of woe, the pain having disappeared with the people who felt it. One gets the impression that human life is like nothing so much as an unending Saturday morning cartoon— *woops! pow! oof!*

The law student has to complete a certain number of tasks—the foremost being to look both ways, and stay alive for three years—and then he is through. Sometimes law school reminded me of one of those "strategy" games. The directions are in simple, straightforward English—3,700 pages of it. Anyone can play. But you have to *want* to.

In the process, through exposure and repetition, you do learn some things, primarily lingo. One day, in the midst of an afternoon of intense study of New York procedure, for my last exam of my last year, I was standing in the basement of NYU's Bobst Library, at a pay phone, when I overheard a fellow talking at the pay phone beside me.

The guy was apparently trying to get permission to use a university theater to shoot a film scene in. He said, "It's been allowed before."

Precedent, I thought.

He said, "I see, so if it's okay with Mr. Hughes, it's okay with Mrs. Costello."

Agency relationship, I thought.

He said, "I'm an NYU student."

Entitlement of status, membership in a class, I thought.

I was perceiving things as a lawyer, things which everybody perceives anyway, but which they are perhaps not so aware of, because they don't have names for the concepts.

I recall a Professor Greenberger, in first-year contracts, saying that our society's concept of *justice* is exactly what any three-year-old thinks justice is: the most sophisticated of litigants just wants to be treated *the same as everybody else.*

It was also Professor Greenberger who said, "Justice? What do I know about justice? I'm talking about the law."

He was joking.

§1-11

Everything I had done in law school, and, in retrospect, much of what I had done before, was done with a view to landing a job as a public defender—an attorney paid by the government to represent criminal defendants who can't afford their own lawyers. I'd been a counselor in a group home for juvenile delinquents; I'd worked as an investigator and law clerk for a Legal Aid attorney; I'd immersed myself in the criminal clinic. A public defender was all I wanted to be.

It is one of the great glories of our nation that we recognize the right of every defendant to be represented by counsel, and that the government provides an attorney for every defendant who cannot afford one, even though we *know* that the defense of their rights will result in some of the guilty going free. We mean to protect the rights not only of the wrongly accused but of the guilty themselves. That's the nature of rights—you don't have to earn them or deserve them; you *have* them. Although fundamental rights can never be taken away—they are "inalienable"—governments, more often than not, refuse to recognize them, and violate them. This propensity of governments must be guarded against. If the rights of the least deserving and most detested individual are not held inviolable, then no one's are, because in that case rights are being treated as privileges. Unlike rights, privileges are given, and can be withdrawn.

I had to make a living. How better than by defending our rights?

I was hired by the Public Defender Service for the District of Columbia, which was established by Congress in 1970 to represent indigent criminal defendants (and juvenile offenders) in the city of Washington.

My girlfriend Jan Drews and I got married and drove over the George Washington Bridge to start a new life in America.

§1-12

There remained the matter of the bar exam.

After three years of law school, you are more or less prepared to begin to prepare for the ritual hazing known as the bar exam, for which you have to know all the law you ever (or never) knew, all at the same time.

Fortunately, several commercial outfits have acquired a certain familiarity with each state's examinations, which they will convey to you in the form of lectures and outlines for a couple of hundred bucks. All you have to do is memorize.

I spent six full weeks of my life memorizing, and only memorizing. In an odd way, it was an almost pleasant experience, like eating endlessly without ever getting full. I spent day after day putting things in, and putting things in, and putting things into my head. No one disturbed me, no one asked anything of me, because everyone knew I was *studying for the bar*. My life was sublimely peaceful, my self was entirely centered, I had but *one thing* to do: memorize. Jan observed that she had never seen me happier.

I went into the exam armed with a technique suggested by the late Professor Stuart Stiller in one of the bar review lectures I'd seen on videotape. He said that you couldn't and wouldn't know everything, and when confronted with a question about the rule against perpetuities, or bills of lading, or any other area of the law that you didn't know and didn't want to know, you should simply say "Kiss my ass" and proceed to the next question. I endured two days in a hot, crowded room, saying "Kiss my ass" as necessary, and the bar exam was behind me.

§2-01

I reported for work along with thirteen other novices at the Public
Defender Service for the District of Columbia the autumn after my graduation. That seven of us were female, two black, and one Mexican-
American, was the result of an effort to change the composition of the office, whose other forty lawyers were predominantly young white men.*
Through no fault of mine, we did little to alleviate the disproportionate
representation of brilliant law review editors and judges' clerks (two from
the U.S. Supreme Court, in 1981) who were drawn to P.D.S. by its reputation for idealism and high professional standards, and the opportunity
it afforded to gain litigation experience. At a firm you start in the library;
at most prosecutors' offices you work on parts of cases, assembly-line
style. At P.D.S. you handled your own cases, from soup to nuts.

(P.D.S. was also one of the few places where you could do good and do
well at the same time. We got $19,300 a year to start, better than half
what you'd get paid to die slowly, writing memos as an associate at Pig
and Swine on Wall Street. Several hundred applicants had vied for our
jobs.)

The Public Defender Service was located in the former Superior
Courthouse, an ionic porticoed temple to the Dignity of the Law, which
had recently been succeeded by a poured concrete monument to the Efficiency of the Law, one myth giving way to another as times changed. We
were on the first floor, which in a more candid age was called the basement. It was a basement steeped in history, however. Our offices used to
be cells for nineteenth-century prisoners, not a few of whom were hanged
on our lovely front lawn, now graced by a touchingly small and awkward
statue of Abraham Lincoln—the oldest in America—erected by the local
citizenry soon after his death and placed at our building because it was
there that he signed the Emancipation Proclamation. The statue's pedes-
tal now bore an extra inscription: "Nana Premptu Is Coming."

It was easy to recognize the new people, who were all dressed to the

---

* Nationwide, in 1982, 33 percent of the law school graduates were women, up from 8
percent in 1972. Eight percent of 1982 law graduates were minorities, up from about 6
percent in 1975. (Private conversation, Kathleen Grove, office of the consultant on
legal education, American Bar Association, July 13, 1983.)

nines, ready to walk six blocks up the hill and argue in front of the Su-
premes at a moment's notice, whereas the experienced attorneys favored
dungarees out of court. We met in the "meeting room," an industrial-
carpeted warren decorated with stacked-up Xerox paper and a legless
pink sofa that must have been discarded by some fraternity.

We were greeted by Taylor Harrison, who in his full beard and long
hair looked like nothing so much as a Hell's Angel, but was in fact one of
the most experienced P.D.S. attorneys.

"The notion offends lay people that a defendant is caught with his
pants down stuffing a baby down the Disposall, and we defend him, and
consider it our duty to defend him, and in fact enjoy it," Harrison said,
kicking off two and a half days of lectures on legal ethics.

There is no stronger example of the power of an adjective to modify a
noun than the use of the word *legal* before the word *ethics*. The primary
requirement of legal ethics is loyalty to the client: "The duty of a lawyer,
both to his client and to the legal system, is to represent his client zea-
lously within the bounds of the law. . . . While serving as advocate, a lawyer should resolve in favor of his client doubts as to the bounds of the
law" (A.B.A., *Code of Professional Responsibility*, Ethical Considerations
7-1, 7-3).*

This duty gives rise to ethical demands that are practically the inverse
of what is commonly understood to be ethical. If the truth is that his client committed the crime, the defense attorney's job is to keep the truth
from coming out, or to keep the jury from recognizing it if it does. It is
unethical to hold back any effort, to do the job with less than all one's
"zeal." The lawyer who refuses to represent a child-molester for "ethical
reasons" does so not because he cannot in good conscience try to get the
guy off, but because he cannot in good conscience *not* try to get the guy
off.

I asked the director of P.D.S. why we were spending so much time on
ethics. "Is this a post-Watergate concern?"

"No," he said. "It's because judges like to attack your 'ethics' when
you're pushing hard to give your client a vigorous defense. If you're well-
schooled in legal ethics, you know where you stand, and you can resist
intimidation."

After the director left the room, another attorney gave a revisionist
view: "His concern is to make a record, so he can always say, 'We train all
of our attorneys to be ethical.' "

---

* The *Code*'s Ethical Considerations are "aspirational in character," as opposed to its
Disciplinary Rules, which are "mandatory in character."

Reasonable minds can differ about what is ethical. What is meant by "resolve in favor of his client doubts as to the bounds of the law"? If *you* were in trouble, what would you want your lawyer to do to get you out of it? Anything? Everything? Anything and everything? Many practitioners find guidance in a venerable maxim of the profession: "If someone goes to jail after the trial, make sure it's your client and not you."

"If you can give the impression that you know what you're doing," one attorney said, "then the best way is to do things improperly—go ahead and read aloud from inadmissible documents, wave your photos around in front of the jury. If you sound like you know what you're talking about, the judge will defer to you. Or, if you get caught at it, you can drift back into doing things right."

There were murmurs from the novices that such conduct would be something less than professional.

"I'd be all in favor of playing by the rules if I started out with the same number of cards as the government," the attorney continued, "but usually they've got fifty cards, and I've got two. We each play two cards, then where am I? You can put on a defense that will win the praise of the judge, or you can put on a defense that will win the trial."

§2-02

I left for a weekend in New York, where Jan was still packing up our stuff for the permanent move to D.C. As soon as I got on the train, I commenced reading and drinking, drinking and reading. I was examining the brochures of the various insurance plans that were available to me as a government employee. I had set myself that task for the trip. It's the sort of task a responsible person is never without. One's ability to handle such tasks is undoubtedly the true measure of success in this life. I found the brochures incomprehensible. I was going to pick the plan that my knowledgeable friends said I should pick. But it was essential that I at least look over the info. Gather data. Proceed in a rational manner.

At Philadelphia I made my way to the bar car once more. On my way back, my passage between cars was blocked by a young man who stood directly in front of me and held his hand up like a cop stopping traffic. He was unsteady on his feet, and his eyes were fixed straight ahead in a glazed stare. I wanted nothing to do with him. I walked straight ahead, but he didn't get out of the way. His palm hit my chest. "You don't want to do that," I said gruffly, and he turned aside as I pushed on. These drunks.

After I had regained my seat, I noticed that a couple of conductors were conferring and gesturing toward the space between cars occupied by the young man, and I heard one passenger say to another, "They're going to arrest him in New York." I got up.

"Are you feeling all right?" I asked the boy between cars.

"No. My mother's sleeping all the time. Are you a clone, or are you natural?"

"I'm natural. How about you?" I thought he was speaking metaphorically.

"I was touched two days ago."

He stuck his finger into my drink, then into his mouth.

"Ooh, that makes me feel sick," he said, and spat on the floor.

"You'd probably feel better if you could sit down, wouldn't you?"

"Yes."

We found a pair of seats. He started spitting on the floor again. "You can't be doing that," I said. "There are some things people just don't like, and spitting on the floor is one of them."

He was a solidly built twenty-year-old, a dark-haired boy a couple of inches shorter than my five feet eleven. He was wearing a clean white T-shirt and paint-spattered dungarees. His hands were also spattered with paint.

He was talking about points, lines, theorems. Everything turned to light, he said. His mother was sleeping, and he couldn't wake her up.

"Do you think my mother killed herself?"

"I don't know. I don't know your mother."

I asked him his name, which was Ron, and wrote down his address and phone number, in case he flipped out altogether. And I asked him if he had taken a pill, or failed to take a pill he usually took. He said no.

"Have we come to Philadelphia yet?" Ron asked. I said we had passed Philadelphia; Philadelphia was behind us, and we were moving toward New York. I asked him where he got on.

"Philadelphia," he said. "Can I look into your eyes?"

"Sure, go ahead," I said.

He leaned over so that his face was directly in front of mine, three inches away—big brown eyes, no pupils that you'd notice, just brown irises straining forward in a wide circle of white. A long, long time I let him stare.

"Can I take your hand?" he said.

"Sure." He clasped my hand in both of his, raised it and kissed it gently. He buried his face in my shoulder, muttering mathematical formulas. I looked at the back of the seat in front of me. I didn't mind anything too much. I was done with my first week of work, my heart was pumping beer and Scotch, and I was on my way to see my wife.

Ron spent a long time looking at his reflection in the window, trying to work through his Problem: "Convex, invex, reflex, duplex, preflex . . ." He made a square with his thumbs and index fingers, and rotated it clockwise, superimposing it on the geometry of space. "Four times four times four times four . . . I bet you're really good at math, aren't you?" he said.

"No. I'm a lawyer. You sound like you studied math?"

"No. It frightened me," he said. "I never dreamed in my earliest day that it would happen this fast. How many of you are there?"

"How many of whom?"

"Of you doctors. Ten? A million?"

I was about to say "enough," when Ron grabbed my arm and said, "No! Don't tell me! It *would* go fast, though. When it gets smaller, it goes fast. It's all proportional."

He told me he'd once been in Bellevue, New York's psychiatric hospital. I said I'd take him there when we reached New York.

"*Would* you? Oh, thank you! At the hospital will they give me Thorazine?"

"Would you like that?"

"Yes."

"Then I'm sure they'll give you Thorazine, if that's what you need."

He often looked at his left hand, then at his right, while thinking aloud: this, that, one, two, if, then—holding his hands up now as balance pans, now as points of reference. I thought I understood the duality he was chasing, the feeling of *getting it,* but "it" being just a bit too fast for you; every "it" reveals itself to be *not* "it," but then *contains* "it" after all, and *that's* "it," but that's *not* "it" . . .

When we got to New York, I told Ron to stick with me. As we left the train and went upstairs in the crowd, he walked in my footsteps, with his hands clasping my waist.

"Do you have anything against the police?" I asked. He said no.

We went up to a cop. "Ron, here, is confused and upset," I said, "incoherent, in fact, and I don't think we can handle fighting for a cab."

"What's the trouble?" the cop asked Ron. "Are you depressed?"

"Depressed? Yes. Very depressed," Ron said. The cop went out to the street with us, picked out a cab, leaned in the window, said something to the cab driver, and gestured for us to get in.

"What part of Bellevue?" the cab driver asked.

"Psychiatric."

Ron was talking about theorems when the cabbie said to me, "I said to the cop, 'Is he bleeding?' 'cause we don't have to take 'em if they're bleeding. Nobody cleans up after 'em. Ends up we have to clean it up ourselves. We don't have to take 'em."

"Well, nobody's bleeding here," I said. "We're both fine."

We arrived at Bellevue and went in the main entrance, Ron holding my hand as we walked. We were told that psychiatric was up at Twenty-ninth Street. We had to go out and walk up First Avenue.

Outside, on First Avenue, Ron said, "It's great to be in the hospital. Is Hitler alive?"

"No, he's dead."

"They killed him?"

"He killed himself, actually."

"Was that because he was so wicked?"

"Yes."

"All the Germans are wicked, aren't they?"

"All the Germans are over in Germany."

"They *are*?" Ron heaved a sigh of relief. "Do you think we could be friends?"

"Sure," I lied.

"We could go in and out together?" Ron asked. I assumed he meant through the warp and woof of time and space. I said, "Sure."

"Could I go home with you? Please. Just for one meal—it would mean so much to me."

"I don't think it would be a good idea, Ron, because I'm not a doctor. I couldn't give you Thorazine."

"Oh." He nodded acceptance and seemed to forget about it. He seemed to forget about everything as soon as we said it, until we came around to it the next time.

"Why did all the people fuck up in the beginning?" he asked the air in front of him. "Was it because of the theorems?"

I asked at the psychiatric admissions desk when we could see the nurse that the signs told us to wait for.

"Sit down and she'll come to you," the lady behind the front desk said.

"How long might that be?"

"I don't know."

"Could you give me an idea?"

"No."

"I mean, is it like one-half hour, or three hours?"

"It could be one-half hour. It could be three hours."

Ron and I sat down on yellow Fiberglas seats. An old crone with matted hair, clutching a blanket around her, sat down beside Ron. She started yelling and bouncing in her chair.

"Wait here, Ron," I said. I walked over to the cop who was sitting against the opposite wall. He was talking with a battered young woman whose husband was inside.

"Do you go around naked a lot?" the cop asked her.

"Well," she responded, "we're comfortable with our bodies, you know, but this was unusual, for him to assume the fetal position on the floor."

"Officer Ryan," I began, reading his nameplate, "I just met this young man—"

"Can't help you. I'm here on another case."

I went up to a fat nurse who was interviewing someone at a desk in the middle of a corridor. "I'm being a good Samaritan," I said, "but there's a limit." I started to explain, but she said I'd have to wait.

"You made the decision to get involved," she said.

I went back and sat with Ron. I neatly wrote out his name and address, so I could give it to the nurse, and handed Ron a copy, telling him to keep it in his pocket in case he got confused. "Here, here's two dollars, so you can buy candy and stuff. It's always better to have a little money than no money, don't you think?" He smiled and nodded, shoving the money, unfolded, into his pocket.

"Now, Ron, my job is done," I said, putting my hand on his shoulder. "I've done everything I can for you. My wife is waiting for me at home."

"Who's next?" the fat nurse called.

I took Ron to her. As she led him down the long corridor, I called out, "Goodbye." He didn't answer.

Outside, walking up First Avenue to the bus stop, I could hear the old woman screaming inside.

§2-03

D.A.'s and cops and judges came in to help with our training. Introducing Richard Locke, a senior attorney in the Criminal Trial Section of the U.S. attorney's office—which prosecutes all felonies and most misdemeanors in the District of Columbia, because the District is a creature of the federal government—P.D.S. attorney Taylor Harrison said, "Mutual respect

and professionalism are essential to the operation of *the system.*" (My ital-
ics. If I ever had any doubt whom I worked for, all I had to do was look at
the imprints on my pens: "Skilcraft–U.S. Government." We were paid
out of the federal court budget.)

"If you have a client who you believe is innocent," Harrison continued,
"and you can back that with some facts, you can discuss it with Richard,
and he'll consider dropping the case."

He would consider dropping the case because, by definition, "the responsibility of a public prosecutor differs from that of the usual advocate:
his duty is to seek justice, not merely to convict" (A.B.A., *Code of Professional Responsibility,* Ethical Consideration 7-13).

I found it a vaguely amusing idea, going up to a prosecutor and saying,
"Time out. This one is *really* innocent." It was Clint Levine, my NYU
instructor, who used to call such appeals "playing up the justice angle."

"When you don't believe your client is innocent," I had asked Levine,
"do you omit that pitch?"

"Yes," he said.

"Then doesn't that signal something to the D.A.?"

"It doesn't matter," he said. "Guilt or innocence is completely irrelevant. What matters is what the D.A. can prove."

Locke was perfectly cast for his role. Every pinstripe in his charcoal
suit was perpendicular to the ground, so straight, tall, and elegant was he,
the incarnation of the moral authority of the state, every kink pressed out
of his body by the rigors of the courts—criminal and tennis.

One of the more self-righteous members of our group asked Locke
whether he *liked* putting people in prison.

"You take a case like a mother beating her baby to death with a hair-
brush—it's a consummate human tragedy," he replied. "I'm just glad I
can be an objective bystander, and do my job, and go home and have a
cold beer. I don't feel good to see her get time, but I wouldn't feel that
justice wasn't done.

"I treat the defendant as a human being, with more respect than he
gave his victim, and I do my job. And if I do it well, he serves time, and I
wish him well, and hope when he comes out he'll have learned his lesson.
Now, maybe that's insane, but I've been doing this for several years."

I went over to police headquarters to pick up a homicide detective who
was to lecture us. Under the glass on his desktop, along with snapshots of
his family, was a picture of a severed hand in a cardboard box. Another
detective had the same picture on his desk.

* * *

"It's a mistake to call yourselves advocates. You're salesmen," we were told by one judge. "You've got to know your product, and you've got to know the territory.

"Don't go before me at the end of the day. And Friday afternoon is a poor time to have anybody sentenced."

Leroy Nesbitt, a defense attorney famous in Washington for his flamboyance and his winning record, gave a sort of closing sermon at the end of the six-week training program. He said the government would trash the Constitution altogether, were it not for the defense bar. We were "sentinels on the frontier of freedom," he said.

This was good news, because I had just read about two men who had broken into a house and raped the wife and stabbed the husband. I wasn't sure I would be really interested in helping out guys like that.

Nesbitt reminded me that defense lawyers are the true conservatives, defenders of the Constitution, of law and order. Without defense lawyers, there'd be no rule of law, no limit at all to what the government did. Governments have a demonstrated tendency to lock people up. You have to draw the line way out there, at the least sympathetic defendant, so the government doesn't even come close to taking you.

I was ready to report for duty on the frontier.

§2-04

I had yet to be sworn in to the bar, so I spent some time as an observer/go-fer at P.D.S. trials, including the murder trial of "former Washington abortionist Dr. Robert J. Sherman," as the newspapers called that notorious obstetrician-gynecologist.

The government alleged—in the language of court, "the government" means "the prosecution," although the public defender and the judge also work for the government, a fact of which defendants are acutely aware—the government alleged that Dr. Sherman, a white, had purposely performed incomplete abortions at his clinic, so that his (mostly black) patients would have to come back for a follow-up dilation and curettage, so that he could charge them for an extra visit and make more money. For the same reason—greed—he was alleged to have reused unsterile disposable plastic instruments, thrown away urine samples he was charging pa-

tients for testing, and employed a nurse's aide with a ninth-grade education to perform cryosurgery. One of his abortion patients, a black sixteen-year-old girl, had died four days after being treated by him. Dr.
Sherman was indicted for second-degree murder,* on the theory that his
"reckless treatment . . . motivated by his malicious and overriding interest
in making money," caused infection of the uterus, severe blood poison-
ing, shock, and death. He was also charged with twenty-six counts of perjury relating to the incident in testimony before the grand jury, before the
D.C. Commission on Licensure to Practice the Healing Arts, and in a
civil suit.

Bob Muse, Dr. Sherman's P.D.S. defense attorney,† maintained that if
Dr. Sherman had run an appendectomy clinic and performed 10,000 ap-
pendectomies, and one patient died, he wouldn't have been charged with
murder. In fact, the defense was unable to find a single prior case in
which a practicing physician in the District of Columbia had been
charged with murder based on evidence of a pattern of reckless behavior.

"The murder charge is the community's way of venting its tension
about the whole question of abortion," Muse told me.

The Sherman case was a perfect example of what my job was all about:
defending a despised individual from the wrath of the community. If anyone needed defending, Dr. Sherman did.‡

Wigmore's *Evidence,* the Anglo-Saxon Talmud on which all lawyers
rely, describes the criminal trial as an "antiphonal drama." The prosecution puts on its case first because it has the burden of proof. Until the
prosecution presents its evidence, the defendant has no reason to present
his evidence: he starts off presumed innocent, and would be content to
stay that way. Generally, the defense answers the government's case with
a case of its own. Then the government gets a chance to present a rebuttal
to the defense's answer.

At first I got all my information about the Sherman trial from the
newspaper, and the newspaper was merely repeating what was going on
in the courtroom, and what was going on in the courtroom was the prosecution's case—one side of the story. But it was the only side I was hear-

---

* In Washington an accidental killing constitutes murder in the second degree if it results from conduct so reckless as to manifest "malice," that is, a depravity of mind and
wanton disregard of human life. An accidental killing constitutes manslaughter if it
results from conduct that is reckless, but not *so* reckless as to manifest "malice."
† As a result of litigation and other matters related to his practice, Dr. Sherman's financial circumstances had deteriorated to the point where he qualified as indigent.
‡ "One of the highest services the lawyer can render to society is to appear in court on
behalf of clients whose causes are in disfavor with the general public" (Professional
Responsibility: Report of the Joint Conference," *American Bar Association Journal,*
vol. 44, December 1958, p. 1216).

ing. And somehow the fact that the information was *alleged* rather than proven seemed a formalistic technicality of which I was aware, but in which I did not really believe.

When I started attending the trial, the jury appeared to me to be biding its time impatiently, waiting for its chance to condemn the pale, sweaty old man sitting at the defense table. Witness after witness testified about being rushed through incomplete abortion procedures without counseling before, anesthesia during, or more than five minutes in the recovery room after. One recalled Dr. Sherman's handing her a green plastic garbage bag and suggesting that when her body eventually expelled the fetus, she should catch it in the bag and throw it into the Chesapeake Bay. A medical expert told the jury that yes, he did have an opinion about the practice of doing incomplete suction-aspiration abortions: "It's *barbaric.*" When the mother of the dead girl testified, jurors wept.

The defense moved that the case be dismissed on the basis of prosecutorial misconduct. Two defense witnesses claimed that they had been telephoned by the *prosecutors themselves* and discouraged from testifying. Other defense witnesses reported intimidating phone calls from the police. The judge reprimanded the prosecutors for "demonstrating extremely poor judgment" in taking actions that "have perhaps made more difficult an already difficult defense task," but denied the motion.

It was the defense's turn.

Suddenly I heard about a whole different Dr. Sherman. A parade of patients told about Dr. Sherman, whose clinic was immaculately clean; Dr. Sherman, who never rushed me, who always took the time to explain in words I could understand what he was doing and why; Dr. Sherman, who came to the hospital at three in the morning to be at my bedside when I went into labor, who delivered my first child and my first grandchild; Dr. Sherman, who was really more than a doctor to me; Dr. Sherman, my friend.

Then came the government's rebuttal case, and a patient testified that Dr. Sherman's procedure room was small and shabby, with blood and trash on the floor, and the windows were so dirty she couldn't see out of them. She seemed honest. The defense witnesses seemed honest. What was going on?

Whatever it was, it goes on at every trial. Conflicting testimony may be attributable to the psychology of perception, or the nature of reality, or simply the fact that people lie. Lawyers sum up this and other mysteries with a shrug-your-shoulders, toss-your-hands-in-the-air phrase: "reasonable minds can differ."

*   *   *

A trial is supposed to impose order on conflict, pull beyond-the-bounds behavior back into the realm of rationality. It's a constant struggle, chaining down passions with procedure, and the Sherman trial, which throughout its seven weeks had been straining the bonds, finally broke out and wasn't a trial anymore.

On the morning set for final arguments, one juror had approached the court stenographer, burst into tears, and said, "I can't take it anymore. I've been getting threatening phone calls for five days, saying I better vote 'guilty.' " She was brought to the judge's chambers.

The prosecution moved that she be excused from the jury, to be replaced by one of the alternate jurors who sit through the trial for just such an eventuality. The defense agreed reluctantly, since she was their favorite, having waved and smiled one day, and having been overheard to say that the prosecutors needed to go back to law school.

As she got up to leave, she said, "Your Honor, there's something I've got to tell you. That man is never going to get a fair trial." On the first day of the trial, she said, one of the jurors looked at Dr. Sherman and muttered, "Murderer, murderer." After the first defense witness testified, she overheard one of the other jurors saying, "This is all bull. Let's deliberate for three and a half hours to make it look good, and then convict." And the jury, contrary to the judge's instructions, had been following the case in the press.

Upon hearing all this, Dr. Sherman complained of chest pains and collapsed. He was rushed to a hospital.

The jurors were brought one at a time to the judge's chambers and asked whether they had received any phone calls about the case, and whether they had already decided on a verdict. They all said no, no. The judge ordered the jury sequestered for the remainder of the trial.

Gary Kohlman, who was in charge of the P.D.S. training program, told me I could make myself useful by researching the law on mistrials. I said I thought the only question was one of fact: was the juror telling the truth about the other jurors' violation of their duty not to decide the case until all the evidence was in?

"You'd think so, by common sense," Kohlman said, "but common sense isn't controlling. You've got to throw a few cases at the judge."

Muse asked me to have a memorandum of law in support of a motion for mistrial *typed* in four hours. First I ran over to the five-and-ten to buy the candles Jan had asked me to get for our housewarming party that night. Of course, it was absurd for me to do my errands when a man was depending on me for his freedom. But there was going to be that kernel of absurdity in my life as long as I was a defense attorney. Either that, or I would have no life.

I tried to stay calm by reminding myself that the idea of these trial memos is really not to persuade the judge, who knows all the law he wants to know and is going to do whatever he wants to do, but merely to make a record of having raised certain arguments, in order to preserve issues for appellate review.

I cranked something out, just in time: 1) The shock waves from the impact of the improper attempt to influence a juror cannot be contained. The examination of each juror was itself a disturbing influence. Blah. Blah. Blah. *Citation.* 2) Premature jury deliberation requires a mistrial. "By due process of law is meant 'a law which hears before it condemns, which proceeds upon inquiry, and renders judgment only after trial.'" *Citation.* Etc. Etc. Respectfully submitted . . .

Muse wanted a mistrial because he believed that the jury really had been prejudiced. In addition, at a retrial he would face no surprises, and might be able to contradict the prosecution's witnesses with the transcripts of their testimony at the first trial. A mistrial might also give him the leverage to get a plea bargain under which "there'd be a substantial likelihood the doctor would stay on the street," as it would cost the government tens of thousands of dollars to retry the case.

(It occurred to me that "on the street" is a strange place for a middle-class person to want to stay, but because most defendants hang out there, it's become a term of the trade for "not in jail." When you think about being in jail, you realize how important being on the street is. Whatever you want to do, and wherever you want to go, you have to start on a street.)

Tests completed over the next several days indicated that Dr. Sherman had suffered angina, not a heart attack, so he could return and face the music. But the music had become so dissonant it was beyond orchestration. The judge said that, in questioning the jurors, he found no facts to support the allegations that they had violated the court's instructions not to reach conclusions about the case, but he feared his questioning itself had pierced the secrecy of the jury, "clouding the fundamental fairness" of the deliberative process. Also, the prolonged delay would render it difficult for the jury to remember the evidence, and they might be distracted by the pressing need to do their Christmas shopping. He declared a mistrial.

The government announced its intention to prosecute again.

§2-05

As I emerged from the Metro at Eighteenth and I Streets to go to my swearing-in to the bar, the sun was a cold white disk in a steel sky. At 9:57 A.M. I took the aisle seat of the fourth row of the left-hand section of Constitution Hall. High above me, gold stars glinted on the blue ceiling. It was a very impressive setting, which lent a sense of occasion to the occasion. I clutched the handouts I'd picked up at the registration desk: an issue of *District Lawyer* magazine and a copy of the *Code of Professional Responsibility*.

At 10:00 A.M., exactly on schedule, a man cried, "Oyez, oyez, oyez, the court is now in session. God save the United States and this honorable court." Flashbulbs popped, bing bing bing.

A man in the front row was recognized by the chair to make a motion that the applicants on the list be admitted to the Bar of the District of Columbia Court of Appeals. "The court will grant your motion," the judge, a woman, replied.

"As the saying goes," the judge told us, "you have arrived. Each of you is now a member, for good or bad, of what is probably the second oldest profession in the world. The actors among you will probably be trial lawyers or politicians. . . . We hope not to see too much of you. We're buried in suits. Everybody sues everybody. A person in Colorado tried to collect one million dollars from the sheriff for letting him escape. A Redskins fan sued the NFL over an official's call in a Cardinals game. A young man sued his parents for three hundred fifty thousand dollars for raising him improperly. Please restrain litigation. . . . Don't become pompous, rapacious, cynical, or intolerant—words the public uses, and even the Supreme Court has used, about us. . . . I'm not asking you not to make enormous sums of money—that is your American heritage. Just do it with the *Code of Professional Responsibility* in one hand. The court will now adjourn."

When I got outside, the sun was shining brilliantly in a cloudless sky. It was warm.

§3-01

I went down the escalator to the basement of the courthouse, walked through a metal detector, the keys in my pocket triggering an alarm to which no one paid any attention—I was a lawyer—signed in at the marshals' desk, pushed open an orange steel door, which closed behind me, and entered the lockup's interview area, a seventy-foot-long room divided lengthwise by a cinder-block wall from the floor to a waist-high steel counter, and by an iron screen from the counter to the ceiling. The quietly whooshing ventilation system effectively blended the odors of sweat and iron into that admixture which is the unmistakable smell of men in cages.

Behind the screen were twenty juveniles who had been arrested in the past twenty-four hours—the adults would be brought in later. Some of the older and larger boys were sleeping on the counter. Others sat on the floor along the back wall. As lawyers drifted in on my side of the screen, the kids began to stir. "You my lawyer? Hey, where's my lawyer? Tell my lawyer to get down here!" A general cacophony built up as the boys began to shout, play, show off. A lot of them knew one another.

I was embarking, that January morning, on what would be my life's labor for the coming year—defending juvenile "respondents" accused of committing crimes.* We started out representing juveniles in family court because their trials are simpler than those of adults, since juveniles do not have the right to trial by jury; and, arguably, the stakes are lower: no matter what the offense, the worst that can happen to a juvenile in family court is incarceration until the age of twenty-one. (In Washington, anyone under eighteen is a juvenile, but those between sixteen and eighteen who are charged with serious offenses can, at the discretion of the U.S. attorney, be tried as adults in criminal court and sent to adult prison.) Juveniles' trials are often presided over by novice or retired judges; they are prosecuted by the city's assistant corporation counsels, who are generally less impressive than the assistant U.S. attorneys who prosecute adults. Family court is called "kiddie court" for more than one reason.

---

* Juveniles are "respondents," not "defendants." They don't have "trials," but "fact-finding hearings"; they aren't found "guilty," but "involved"; they aren't given "sentences," but "dispositions." The distinctions are purely semantic, lingering traces of the idealistic past when family court was conceived as an institution concerned with the "care" of "children."

I sat down on a steel stool bolted to the floor and laid out a notebook and a list of questions on the counter. Names were scratched into the orange metal counter on the other side of the screen, crude combinations of small and capital letters spelling out "The LAy," "EuGeNE aS SHOrTy," "siR ANtoNio SE76," "CriCKet," MouSE."

"Wyatt Clayton!" I shouted. "Wyatt Clayton?"

"Over here, man," a tough-looking guy lying at the end of the counter shouted. He slowly rose and ambled over to me.

We sat facing each other through the rust-colored screen. Other boys crowded around.

"Excuse me, guys," I said. "Do you think you could give us a little privacy? Thank you." The boys backed away.

"Wyatt, my name's Jim Kunen. I'm a lawyer with the Public Defender Service. Here's one of my cards." I pushed it through the inch-high slot at the base of the screen. "You're charged with armed robbery. I'll be your lawyer, if you want one. You want a lawyer?"

"Yeah."

No one ever said no. When you're locked inside, you can't help yourself. Somebody on the outside *might* help you. Can't hurt.

"Good. Okay. Now, as your lawyer, I work for you. You're the boss. Whatever you want, that's what I'll try to get. Like, you want to stay in jail, I'll try to help you stay in jail. You want to get out, I'll try to get you out. What do you want, in or out?"

"I want to get out," Wyatt said patiently.

"Fine. I figured you would. That's what we'll try to do. Now I've got to ask you some questions so I'll know what to say to the judge to try to convince him to let you out today. Is your correct name Wyatt Clayton?"

"Yes."

"You live with your mother, Jean Patterson?"

"Yes."

(I seldom had occasion to ask anything about a kid's father, whose address was usually marked "unknown" on the police forms.)

Wyatt verified that he had been born in D.C.; was, despite his moustache, just fifteen years old; was in the ninth grade, five foot seven, 150 pounds, dark-complected; and had lived with his mother and four brothers in the same publicly subsidized apartment for eight years.

The diamond-shaped apertures of the screen were having a bizarre effect on my vision. If I tried to look *through* the screen and focus on Wyatt, the iron lines doubled and began a blurry, circular dance. If I looked *at* the screen, it seemed to zoom forward to within an inch of my face, and Wyatt, now four-eyed, floated in shimmering space, as though the inhabitant of another dimension. This was one of those problems that have no solution.

"You ever been arrested before?" I asked Wyatt.

"Just one time."

"What for?"

"I was with some boys that took a lady's purse."

"When was that?"

"Hmm." Wyatt stroked his chin thoughtfully. "I don't know. Must have been 'round about September, October, sometime around then."

"What happened to the case?"

"They dropped it, I think. I got to come back to court this month."

"Wait a minute. If they dropped it, why do you have to come back to court?"

"The judge told me to."

Juveniles generally understood very little of what went on in court, unless their lawyers took pains to explain it to them.

"Who's your lawyer on that case?"

Wyatt closed his heavy-lidded eyes, frowned, shook his head. "Damn! What *is* her name? I can't think of it right now. She's a white lady—wears glasses, I think."

"Don't worry about it. I can look that up," I half-shouted to him. Other lawyers had occupied the other eleven stools and were conducting interviews side-by-side, fragments of conversations richocheting off the cinder-block walls: "Any weapons on you?" . . . "I was going to the john" . . . "knife" . . . "You want to go out to California?" . . . "Anybody could have dropped the TV in the alley" . . . "surety bond" . . . "Was that in this court or the big court?" . . . "Will you have any relatives here?" . . . "979-2086" . . . "What do you want to do?" As counterpoint, shouts echoed from somewhere deep inside the lock-up: "Hey, muhfuh! Hey, muhfuh!"*

I pressed on, explaining to Wyatt that on that day the judge wasn't going to decide whether he was guilty or not, but only whether he could be trusted to return for his trial or had to be locked up until then, which could be several months.

"So what the judge wants to hear is that you have something you have to show up at every week, like you're on a team, or in a band, or in the Boy Scouts."

* For an interesting discussion of the psychological implications of the expression "motherfucker" (and comparable insults in sixty-six languages), see Edgar A. Gregerson, "Sexual Linguistics," *Annals New York Academy of Sciences,* vol. 327 (*Language, Sex, and Gender*), 1979.

I never did find a Boy Scout in the lockup. (Or a varsity athlete.) Wyatt had held the same job for three years, though—selling newspapers on a street corner.

"One more thing, Wyatt. It says here that the police say that you robbed someone with a gun."

Wyatt leaned back, vainly looked to his left and his right for someone to back him up, and raised his hands in surrender. "Man, I don't know nothing *about* that."

"Okay. That's cool. Neither do I. I don't think we ought to talk about it right now, anyway, with all these people around. But what did the police tell you? Did they say why they arrested *you,* instead of, say, me?"

"They called me up and said this girl picked out my picture and said I robbed her. So me and my mother went down to the police station. And they *arrested* me." He was still wide-eyed with amazement.

"You turned yourself in? That's very good. That's great. That'll help convince the judge to let you out. Did you say anything to the police?"

"I said I didn't do it, because I *didn't.*"

"Okay, now listen. From now on, no matter what anybody promises you, or no matter what they threaten you with, all you say is, 'I'm sorry, my lawyer told me not to talk about it.' You got that?"

"Yeah."

"All right. Let's hear it. Pretend I'm a cop, and I say, 'Wyatt, just tell me what happened, and I'll make sure you get off.' Now, what do you say?"

"I'm sorry, my lawyer told me not to talk about it."

"That's it. Good. A lot of people think that if they don't talk, they'll get into more trouble. That's wrong. *Talking* gets you into trouble. No one ever got into trouble by keeping his mouth shut. So keep your mouth shut. Breathe through your nose. Now, I haven't got all day, so just pretend I sat here for ten hours and told you that a thousand times."

As I gathered my notes together to clear the deck for the next client, Wyatt stared through the screen at my wrist.

"Omega," he said.

"Rennie Jefferson!" I shouted. "Rennie Jefferson? ... Rennie, my name's Jim Kunen. I'm a lawyer ..."

I found out from the computer printouts in the juvenile clerk's office that Wyatt Clayton had been charged with robbery (pocketbook snatch) just a few months before, had pled guilty to the lesser included offense of petit larceny,* and was scheduled to come in for sentencing in that case in a week. His current arrest for armed robbery was his only other charge.

I took a seat in Judge Richard Quinn's courtroom and waited for my cases to be called.

Judge Quinn was an embittered fifty-year-old who exhibited rather extreme mood swings. When he was in a bad, or normal, mood, he would ferociously lash out at defendants and their attorneys, simply for *being* defendants and their attorneys. He did, however, on those rare days when he was in a good mood, display a certain intelligence and humanity. It was the existence of this stifled sensitivity that prompts me to use the word "embittered" to describe him. Maybe he was a sensitive man turned mean by years of exposure to brutality and suffering in an inner-city court. Or maybe he was just a mean son of a bitch. I couldn't tell.

Judge Quinn wore his black robe in such a way that his white collar looked like a priest's, and he had a priest's pallid complexion. The only color in his face was a small red triangle on each cheekbone. He had small eyes, small ears, a small nose, and his mouth was a downturned lipless slit that barely moved when he spoke, perhaps accounting for his Cagneyesque gangster pronunciation, which I otherwise might have suspected was put on. What vitality he had was all in his big, athletic hands, which had a seemingly endless list of personal tasks to attend to. His thumb grazed one cheek, his index finger the other, as though checking how close his shave was. (Not very.) His index finger scratched his sideburns. (Scratching the top of his head was his gold-ringed fourth finger's job.) Sometimes his nose needed support, which was provided by his finger as joist transferring the weight to the cheekbone via the thumb. Sometimes his nose needed other services.

His handling of the cases before mine was not encouraging. Upon being told that the trial date he had set for two black respondents was Lincoln's Birthday, he chuckled and mumbled audibly, "Lincoln's Birthday—that's ironic." When a lawyer argued that his client should be released to his mother, who was in court, Judge Quinn said, "I don't think much of your client, and I don't think much of his mother, either." He locked up a kid for violating a condition of his pretrial release—"no further arrests." The defense attorney, a quiet but courageous fellow, stood with his hands clasped in front of him, examining the tabletop. "Well,

* Larceny is a wrongful taking. Robbery is a wrongful taking *from* the immediate actual possession of another *person*. Larceny of property worth less than a certain amount ($100, in Washington) is petit larceny; of more valuable property—grand larceny.

Your Honor," he said, "unless he's guilty of the crime, being arrested really isn't something he's responsible for."

"The presumption of innocence is a legal fiction!" Judge Quinn shot back. "He's guilty! He knows he's guilty, and I know he's guilty!"

I composed a rejoinder to have ready should the judge ever *dare* say such a thing about a client of mine: "Your Honor, are you saying that my client's guilt is a foregone conclusion, that everything from here on out is a charade?" Because that's what the client must have been hearing, and that's what he'd think of the whole system. Judges like Quinn were tremendously destructive to the law and order of the system, which lawyers like me tried to preserve.

(On being told of my planned retort, an older defense attorney said, "In fact, what the client's probably thinking is, 'Who is this man? How can he possibly know already that I did it? I just got through convincing my lawyer that I didn't do it.' ")

Juveniles do not have a right to bail. The judge can order them detained pending trial if he has grounds to believe they will not show up for trial or are a danger to themselves or others.

I argued that Wyatt should be released because in his past dealings with the court, he had never failed to appear; he was in school, and had a job; his mother would keep an eye on him; and he could be adequately supervised by the probation department's "home detention program," under which he'd be checked three times a day to make sure he was in school or in his house, and nowhere else. "Your Honor," I concluded, "Wyatt is *eager* to come to trial, because he steadfastly maintains his innocence."

"You know," Judge Quinn responded, looking past Wyatt and me to the courtroom in general, "I've been to lots of fish markets, and the signs I see always say 'Fresh Fish.' I've yet to see a sign that says 'Stale Fish.' " His upper lip rose slightly, exposing his teeth in a mirthless smile.

The fraudulence of fishmongers notwithstanding, Judge Quinn released Wyatt Clayton to home detention until trial.

Rennie Jefferson, my other client that morning, was eleven years old, but looked like the cutest eight-year-old you ever saw. He'd been picked up on a custody order (juvenile arrest warrant) for having failed to appear at a probation review two months earlier. He'd been charged with burglary during the summer, pled guilty to unlawful entry, and been put on probation. He told me that he had actually come to court when he was supposed to, but then had turned and run because he was afraid he'd be locked up.

Judge Quinn ordered Rennie detained overnight so that he could be brought before Judge Wexler, who had sentenced him and therefore was responsible for reviewing his probation, in the morning.

I followed him back to the lockup behind the courtroom, where he sobbed quietly. The other, older boys backed against the wall to leave him alone as best they could in the five-by-eight-foot cell.

"Do you feel like a bird in a cage?" I asked.

He shook his head no.

"Do you feel like a boy in jail?"

He nodded yes.

I told him I would be in court the next morning to argue for his release.

The next morning I found his mother, a rotund woman in a worn-out cloth coat, outside Judge Wexler's chambers. We went over what the judge would want to hear, what she should say, what I would say. I was confident we could get Rennie released. All he'd ever done was one crime, and in three months of probation he'd been in no trouble, although he was flunking everything in school and seldom kept his appointments with his probation officer.

Just then, the private attorney who had been appointed by the court to represent Rennie in his original burglary case arrived, a bald man with hair flying in random directions over his ears. He hadn't shaved in two days. He was wearing a ratty tweed overcoat, and red and gold checked pants tucked into black army boots. This was Mr. Wickersham. He would have made a charming Royal Doulton figurine, but it was extremely unsettling to have him as your lawyer.

I had to defer to Mr. Wickersham. It was his case. I explained to him what had happened, and what we were planning to say: "Obeys his mother, goes to school, keeps curfew, no trouble with the law." I asked if I could observe the hearing.

"Certainly," Mr. Wickersham said as he fumbled through his briefcase, looking for Rennie's file.

We went in. I sat down at the opposite end of the table from Judge Wexler, an intense woman who seemed to think that everybody in the world was a member of her own family, so disappointed in them was she. Mr. Wickersham sat by the judge. Rennie sat by me.

"Sit by your lawyer," the judge said. Rennie moved to Mr. Wickersham's side. Mr. Wickersham did not look at him.

"I've seen his probation report. It's a very bad report," Mr. Wickersham said. That was all he said.

Mrs. Jefferson leaned over to me and whispered, "I don't like him. He never says anything."

The judge decided she wanted a full probation review. The probation officer was on vacation, and since Rennie couldn't be trusted to come in, he would have to be locked up for a week. Rennie pulled his sweater up over his eyes to hide his tears. He had learned a lesson: he was right to run away the first time—you come to court, you go to jail.

After the hearing, Rennie's mother asked me to take Mr. Wickersham's place. I explained that her request involved a sensitive area of legal ethics: thou shalt not take another lawyer's client without the approval of the other lawyer.* Mrs. Jefferson would have to write a letter to Mr. Wickersham asking him to withdraw—she had asked him twice already—and send a copy to the judge, with a cover letter asking that a new lawyer be appointed. But she had to make it clear that she was not trying to "pick and choose."

The court won't let an indigent client dump his assigned counsel just because he happens to think the lawyer's doing a lousy job. Half of the defendants have lawyers who *are* doing a lousy job, and the other half might ask for new counsel just to delay their trials. The calendar won't move *at all.* Beggars can't be choosers.

Mrs. Jefferson would have to say Rennie needed a new lawyer because he *couldn't communicate* (buzzwords, B-ding! B-ding!) with Mr. Wickersham. That would give the judge a palatable reason to appoint new counsel. I typed out the letters for Mrs. Jefferson.

Later that morning I found myself standing in a men's room beside none other than Mr. Wickersham. I told him that Mrs. Jefferson was unhappy with him, and that I had suggested she take it up with him.

"I can't get off the case," he said with a shake. "I need the money."

Mr. Wickersham was one of the private attorneys who put themselves on a list from which the judges appoint counsel for three quarters of the indigent criminal defendants (and juvenile respondents) in D.C., the Public Defender Service representing the remainder. (This is the reverse of the ratio in most cities, but Washington is not most cities. For one thing, 37,000 lawyers are members of the D.C. Bar, 13,000 of them actively engaged in private practice. The entire state of California, with thirty times the population of Washington, has 72,000 lawyers.) About two hundred attorneys accepted such appointments regularly. Many of them were young attorneys just starting out, or old attorneys fading out, or incompetent attorneys hanging on. Some of them were diligent and capable, but the amount they were paid by the court was totally inadequate to support proper preparation of a case. They were theoretically entitled to $30 for each hour spent in front of a judge, and $20 an hour for out-

* Ethical Consideration 2-30.

of-court work, the total compensation not to exceed $400 for a misdemeanor or $1,000 for a felony. Trial judges could get authorization from the chief judge to pay over the limit for a long trial. They could also decide arbitrarily to pay less than what the lawyer billed. The lawyers never knew what they were going to get paid and had to wait anywhere from three weeks to eighteen months to get paid at all. Only a couple of dozen earned the $27,000 per year which was the maximum the court would pay until 1981, when the limit was raised to $42,000, a level attained by only three or four.

Public defenders, on the other hand, work for a salary and therefore have no economic motivation to stint on the number of hours devoted to a particular case. In some cities, public defenders are so overburdened that this economic factor has no practical effect, since they haven't enough time to do *anything*. At New York City's Legal Aid Society, for example, criminal defense attorneys each often have from seventy to a hundred active cases—one of the reasons they went on strike in 1982. But the Public Defender Service for the District of Columbia, which has been declared an "exemplary" defender office and held out as a national model by the Law Enforcement Assistance Administration, handles manageable case loads, about thirty-five active cases per attorney, with the politically touchy result that its indigent clients often get better representation than the unrich nonpoor can afford.

Ironically, many defendants prefer private attorneys to public defenders, on the theory that anything "public," like public transportation or public schools, must be crummy. (An extreme example of this image problem prevails in New York, where, in the argot of the street, Legal Aid attorneys are called "Leeg-*aides*" and are widely thought to be something less than full-fledged professionals in their field, like teachers' aides or nurses' aides.)

Private attorneys paid by the court, though at least not "public," suffered along with public defenders from the stigma of representing their clients at little or no cost to them. (Indigent defendants found to be not utterly destitute were required to contribute at most $300 toward the cost of their defense. If they could afford more, they had to get their own lawyers.) If you get what you pay for, how good can a free attorney be?

Rennie Jefferson never did get a new lawyer.

§3-02

The elderly black woman walked up to the bus stop on the corner of East-ern Avenue and Varnum Street with short, stiff steps, as though the Jan-uary cold had made her sticklike legs brittle. The sun had just sunk behind the white-columned Northeastern Presbyterian Church, casting a long shadow over the brown Plymouth sedan parked in front of it. Across the street, the silver coin-return lever on the Coke machine by the door of the Citadel gas station glinted in the day's last light, even as the illuminated plastic canopy over the pumps grew brighter against the fading lavender sky, its orange letters proclaiming DISCOUNT CIGA-RETTES SODA PET FOOD. The air was so clear that it looked to the two burly white men in the Plymouth as though they could reach out and touch the red knit cap on one of the boys who were running up behind the woman.

Sound, too, had a winter sharpness, the men in the car hearing with equal clarity the screech of starlings in the church steeple, the thup-dup, thup-dup of tires on the seams of the concrete avenue, and the old woman's cry for help when the boys grabbed her purse. One of the men reached through his window and attached a flashing red light to the car's roof. *Whoop! Oh wow! Oh wow! Oh wow!* . . .

I didn't see or hear any of this, of course.

Richard Joe Madison—the boy in the red hat—and his friend had made the mistake of attempting a purse snatch right in front of two plainclothes cops. Richard became my client and ended up pleading guilty to assault. A shy sixteen-year-old, blind in one eye, he never would have punched the lady if she hadn't refused to let go of her purse, or even then if he had thought for a second that she was a human being, who felt pain, like his mother.

His mother called me almost every day, always reminding me not to identify myself if someone else answered when I called back. She worked as a domestic for a rich family who would not have wanted crime-in-the-streets dusting their furniture. Her deep, strong voice faltered when she talked about Richard. She was concerned, she was saddened, and she was perplexed: Richard was a good boy. How could he do such bad things?

"Thoughtless," I said.

* * *

At the plea, Judge Quinn told Richard he was letting him out for now—he'd been detained for the month since his arrest—but his only chance to avoid getting locked up at sentencing was to go to school (which he hated, maybe because he was two years too old for the ninth grade, and was reading at the fourth-grade level), work at his part-time job, see his probation officer regularly, go to his tutoring program, avoid his past associates, and cooperate with his counselor at Washington Streetworks, the community-based counseling program in which I had enrolled him.

No sooner did Richard walk out of the courthouse than the probation officer who was to write his pre-sentence report told me that she was going to recommend that he be locked up "unless I hear all the right noises from him."

The "right noises" are to admit your guilt, take full responsibility, and say you are sorry.

"You have to make the right noises," I told Richard when I prepared him for his pre-sentence interview with the probation officer. "You shouldn't say anything that isn't true, but I'm sure you can say you're sorry and mean it, because you don't want to be locked up."

He said he understood.

§3-03

My wife Jan and I left our house at three o'clock in the afternoon one Saturday in my first winter as a public defender. We returned a few hours later. I was thinking, "We've got to clean this place up. It looks like it's been ransacked," when Jan shouted, "Jim, the stereo!" Burglarized. All of our negotiable instruments were gone—the stereo, the camera, the cassette recorder. Nothing else was taken—in and out quickly, that's the key to success in that business—and we were insured, but I felt like looking up "booby traps" in the Yellow Pages.

(It is fair to say we were unlucky. There were 16,260 burglaries reported in Washington in 1980, which is only about 26 for every 1,000 people. The average in twelve American cities of comparable size to Washington, in 1980, was 30 per 1,000 people. St. Louis had 45; Denver, 40; Oakland, 39; Boston, Cleveland, and Minneapolis, about 31; Milwaukee, only 15. Overall, Washington is not a particularly crime-ridden city, as American cities go, although many whites assume it is, simply because its population is 75 percent black, and years of racist demogoguery have forged an association in whites' minds between race and crime, which obscures the meaningful correlation between poverty and crime. Of the twelve cities, Washington ranked tenth in reported property crime and fifth in reported violent crime. St. Louis had the highest crime rate in both categories, Milwaukee the lowest.[1] Compared to other national capitals, Washington's property crime rate is moderate—lower than Paris's or Ottawa's; its violent crime rate astronomical.[2])

At work, everyone expressed sincere outrage that such a horrible thing had happened to us—"It's the idea of someone *invading your home*"— then went back to work defending alleged burglars, as did I.

Reginald Chatsworth Dickinson, a slight, stammering, fifteen-year-old burglar, studied the green industrial carpet on my office floor as he told me what he had told the police: he had successfully hit two houses in Georgetown (my neighborhood) before he was caught in a third.

I fought back the urge to ask him if he happened to have burglarized my house. Any suggestion that I identified with the victim—let alone that I *was* the victim—would taint the lawyer-client relationship. It was always a challenge to convince my clients that they could trust me. I was very good at it—maybe because I looked them in the eye, maybe because they *could* trust me. I did ask him about his *modus operandi,* and learned that he and an adult friend would knock on the front door of a house; if someone answered, they'd ask for "Tony." If no one answered, they'd go around back, put lots of adhesive tape on the windows to keep them from shattering noisily, and then smash them with a stick. *My* burglar had very neatly sawed out the wood between two windowpanes, lifted out the glass, and waltzed through. Satisfied that Reginald had not burglarized *me,* I didn't have to worry about any conflict of interest in representing him.

According to the police report, Reginald had stolen, among other things, a Canon camera (just like mine). I asked him if he still had any stolen property. He said he'd sold the last of it yesterday.

"Reginald, that's another crime!" I said, not quite accurately.* "You've got to stop doing this stuff."

He smiled. He had a beautiful smile. He tipped his head back slightly; his eyes sparkled. Then the smile vanished, and he returned to his stolid self.

---

* *Possessing* stolen property (if you know or should know it's stolen) is a crime in D.C., of which you can be convicted if, and only if, you are *not* convicted of stealing it; but *selling* the property is not a separate crime itself.

I was explaining to him that his trial would be in a couple of months, and that in the meantime he should refrain from ratting on himself to the police—"I'm sorry, my lawyer told me . . ."—when Tom King, the attorney with whom I shared an office, walked in. He'd just been to court to receive a jury verdict.

"How'd it go?" I asked.

He turned his thumbs down and frowned. "Guilty," he said.

Reginald slid down in his chair, his eyes wide with fear. "Was that *my* trial?" he asked.

"No, Reginald, that was somebody else's," I said. "Don't worry, you'll be *at* your trial."

§3-04

It was spring. A million daffodils* had risen to greet the shiny-haired high school girls, back, on their Gold Line buses, like a host of Persephones from the frozen West. As you crossed Indiana Avenue to the courthouse, you could smell their fragrances—the daffodils', the buses', the girls'—also the muddy Potomac and the tar streets heating up and the virgin grass and the tree buds bursting and, oh! it was great to be alive in the Nation's Capital!

The fragrance stopped at the courthouse door. I walked across the lobby to the information counter, to check what courtroom Judge Quinn was in, as I had to go to Richard Joe Madison's sentencing. On the black slate countertop sat four computer consoles with keyboards and video displays, but no operators. Behind the counter was a wall of glass, and behind the glass were thirty-two TV screens with two empty chairs in front of them. The TV screens showed pictures of closed doors and empty hallways. *What has befallen the crew of the starship* Superior Court? I found a mimeographed list of judges' assignments lying on the countertop and rushed off to face Judge Quinn.

For the tenth time that day, I mounted the gleaming stainless-steel escalator hissing skyward through the court's vast atrium. As the clattering conveyer bore me aloft, I felt like a pill, tack, nail, or nut, some such fungible item, at an unknown stage in the interminable process of my own manufacture.

* Actually, the National Park Service alone had two and a quarter million daffodils blooming in the Washington area in 1980.

As the appearance of a yellow line on the sinking step in front of me signaled the impending dissolution of the illusory step on which I was standing, the entire contraption stopped, all but sending me sprawling. How many times was I going to be the butt of this same joke?

The next flight up had also quit, so I had to climb it, noting, as I always did, with the same degree of surprise I always felt, that climbing a broken escalator is immeasurably more difficult than climbing a staircase that never *was* an escalator. Psychology may have something to do with this, but I believe it's mostly attributable to the greater depth (from front to back) of the mechanical steps.

I passed through two sets of doors into the courtroom, which, like all the other courtrooms, had no windows. A curved railing—the bar—separated rows of cushioned theater seats from the semicircular area where the judge and lawyers performed. A circle of spotlights on the ceiling poured random pools of intense brightness on the judge's right shoulder, the third seat from the left in the front row of the jury box, a spot on the beige-carpeted floor just in front of the defense table. It looked like a set for one of those boring plays where no one wears costumes and you see the stagehands working.

Richard Joe Madison, his mother, and the young woman who counseled him at Washington Streetworks were waiting for me. Richard looked the impeccable gentleman in his suit and tie, his short haircut and protruding ears accentuating the boyish look of his smooth-skinned face. He smiled self-consciously as his counselor reviewed the highlights of his progress, for me to relay to the judge.

It was a very confident attorney-client team that strode to the defense table when our case was called. I reemphasized to Judge Quinn what I had already reported to him in writing: Richard had fulfilled every condition that the judge had imposed at the time of his release. He'd been a well-behaved student at school and a terrific worker at his part-time job in the school library ("very helpful and dependable, easy-going and willing to do any task," wrote the librarian), kept all his probation appointments, studied with his tutor, stayed away from his old friends, and developed a close relationship with his counselor. Judge Quinn rested his cheekbone on the base of his thumb and drummed his fingers on the side of his head.

The representative sent up from the prosecutor's office spoke next, never taking his eyes off a note clipped to the case file on the table in front of him. He had no personal knowledge of the case. "The government feels," he read, "that although Richard may have done all of these things, he has not been *sincere*. He has done all of this just to avoid incarceration."

Judge Quinn felt for his Adam's apple; then, his eyes darting about the room, he pronounced sentence: Richard Joe Madison was to be committed for an indeterminate period to that institution which someone—an Orwellian fascist or utopian dreamer or both—had named "The Children's Center."

As the marshal led him away, Richard silently pulled off his wristwatch and handed it to his mother to keep.

When I set out on the long walk across the street back to the office, there'd been a subtle change in the weather. The spring colors had lost their intensity, as though the blood had drained from the face of the day.

I pulled open a little green door hidden under a staircase along one side of 451 Indiana Avenue, N.W., and hiked down the long, narrow, windowless corridor, its gracefully arched ceiling higher by half than the passage was wide. A bundle of cables ran along one wall, and steel plates in the floor concealed the source of a steamy smell, which, together with the peculiar dimensions of the hall, gave our building the ambience of a Victorian submarine. Crew members, obviously engaged in some desperate, labor-intensive enterprise, hurried in and out of little doorways on either side of the hallway. Phones rang everywhere.

Bang! A loose floorplate announced my arrival at my office. I sat down at my desk and began taking stock, as it were, of all my cases, noting their procedural status. I had to report my caseload monthly to the head of the P.D.S. Trial Division, who'd adjust the number of days you'd pick up new cases according to the number of cases you already had. While I was at it, I paid particular attention to the dates when I was supposed to appear in court. I went through my pocket calendar and checked the notations there against the notification slips the court had sent me, and then checked those against the entries on my case files. When I'd gone through my pocket calendar, I went through the court slips and checked to see if the noticed hearings were entered in the pocket calendar and on the case files. I also went through the case files and checked them against the pocket calendar and the notices. Then I made sure the entries on my wall calendar agreed with those on the court notices, the date book, and the case files. This exhaustive four-way fail-safe system was so enormously complicated that an occasional court date would snake its way through and surprise me. I was trying to tighten up.

My inventory verified what I already knew: an inordinate number of my clients were languishing behind bars. I took things one at a time, and I'd put one client out of my mind the moment I turned my attention to the next; and sometimes they'd all merge, and I'd forget them all, really, and just be pushing papers on my desk, trying to file things on time, keep on top of my calendar. But when I thought about it, there really *were* a lot of them locked up.

I picked up the phone—a man of action, I was always picking up the phone—and called the mother of the complainant in one of my robbery cases. My investigator had told me that this kid's mother wouldn't let the investigator interview her son. I was going to say things, *all of which would be true,* that I hoped would change the woman's mind.

(You try to get a signed statement from an opposing witness, so that if his testimony in court varies in any way from his original story—which it almost always does, memory being what it is—you can confront him with his "prior inconsistent statement," throwing his credibility into doubt.)

"My client is charged with stealing five dollars from your son," I began.

"No, it's not a question of just stealing," the woman's voice replied.

"Well, stealing by force and violence," I admitted. "The allegation is he threw him to the ground and hit him several times."

"I'm sorry it had to come to this," she said. She had a pretty woman's voice. "The man at the Safeway says they're having trouble with kids taking money from other kids all the time. The boy who did it is black. We're a black family. There comes a time when we have to stop letting things go. If he's guilty, he should be punished. Maybe it will do him good. Next time, he could use a knife. Or a policeman could shoot him. I wish he had a mother who would talk to him."

"I'll be talking to my client," I pointed out, "and if I had a written statement from your son, I'd be able to see the strength of the evidence, and I might advise my client to plead guilty."

"As far as answering questions about it, I'm not sure our boy should have to live through it again," she said.

"Good," I was thinking, "maybe he won't testify," when the woman mentioned that her husband was a former police officer. End of conversation.

An intelligent and compassionate woman, she was concerned for her son, and her community, and even for the boy who had attacked her son. Where did I fit into this?

Not only were virtually all of my clients black,* the great majority of the complainants were black, as were almost all the jurors. Even half the

---

* Of all people arrested in Washington in 1978, 94 percent were nonwhite (*Crime and Justice Profile: The Nation's Capital,* Office of Criminal Justice Plans and Analysis, Government of the District of Columbia [Washington, D.C.: October 1979], p. v). Of the 2,500 men imprisoned at D.C.'s Lorton Correctional Facility, there were usually less than two dozen whites (private conversation, Kirby Howlett, Esq., Public Defender Service, August 1982).

cops were black. The 25 percent of Washington's population that was white included practically no poor people or even working-class people, but was almost entirely middle class, like me, and lived mostly in one narrow sliver of town, which a colleague of mine dubbed "Caucasia." (The city as a whole he called "Johannesburg on the Potomac.") In a typical criminal case, the only whites involved were the defense attorney, the prosecutor, the judge, and maybe a cop—the four faces of "the authorities." Being a public defender did not necessarily make you a champion of the poor in the eyes of the poor. Some said we were elitists who exercised our principles (and egos) at the expense of the black community. When we put a client on the street, we didn't put him on *our* street.

I got a call from Yeats Moore's group home counselor, asking my help in dealing with a crisis situation.

Yeats had been arrested several months before, for smoking on a bus. It *is* against the law to smoke on a bus, but not just anybody could manage to get arrested for it. Yeats had what it takes. Yeats had an *attitude*.

I'm sure Yeats put on quite a show—waving a big fat jay around, blowing reefer smoke rings, laughing like the coolest dude alive, letting everybody know exactly *whose* bus they were on. He was wrong, as usual. This bus belonged to a "mod squad roller" (plainclothes cop), and Yeats's antics offended him. He arrested him simply for "smoking on a bus"—Yeats threw the herb out the window; and when he searched him—a cop is allowed to search you after he makes a legal arrest, because you could have a weapon or evidence on you—he found a hypodermic needle in Yeats's pocket. Yeats had ridden right into trouble *again:* count one—smoking on a Metrobus; count two—possession of implements of a crime (hypodermic needle). The syringe had traces in it of Bam, as phenmetrazine is called on the street. (Phenmetrazine, a powerful stimulant, is taken alone or in conjunction with heroin.) And Yeats had just gotten off probation for disorderly conduct three months before this arrest.

He was put back on probation, with the condition that he report regularly for drug testing. The first time he appeared for urinalysis at the Youth Abstinence Program, an attendant, who was reading a newspaper, told him to have a seat, and continued reading the paper. This infuriated Yeats. He left and never returned.

Everything infuriated Yeats Moore. Having violated a condition of his probation, he was put into a group home. Now his counselor there was calling me for help.

"Yeats won't go to school," the counselor said. "He won't go to the doctor for lice. He's cursed out everyone here except the cook, and that's only because her four huge sons are here all the time. He doesn't keep his curfew; he's been in fights; he told the head of residence to fuck herself. The chief of aftercare services for the whole city came to see him. Yeats told him to kiss his ass.

"Yeats is very disturbed. He needs evaluation."

The counselor wanted to know if I would cooperate by not opposing placement of Yeats for forty-five days at St. Elizabeths* psychiatric hospital—he was afraid of what might happen during a delay. I said I'd talk to Yeats about it.

I called up Yeats, who professed that he "didn't give a shit" where they put him.

"Good," I said. "So we'll let them put you in St. E's for a while. It'll be a nice vacation for you. The food's not bad. You'll enjoy the change." I meant it. I'd had kids in the evaluation program before. Yeats said he'd go quietly.

All that remained was for me to clear the plan with Yeats's other lawyer. (Many clients had more than one case, and more than one lawyer.) This other lawyer was not a slouch; he was a real go-getter. He fought for every right his clients had. "If they want to put him in St. E's," he said, "they can give us thirty days' notice and schedule a full hearing." Period. The man was an expert on the law. Yeats Moore wouldn't see a psychiatrist for a long time.

§3-05

The word for Cheryl Lee Harris was *formidable.* She was only fifteen, but looked much older. Intelligent, sophisticated, and self-possessed, she could look you in the eye and lie, and you'd never suspect a thing. She had the delicate wrists and elegant hands of an artist, and an artist's eye for clothes, and a face . . . She had *presence:* you wanted her to like you, and she did—she was a real sweetheart, very friendly. Of course, she *was* quite pretty, and I am inclined to ascribe all good qualities to pretty girls,

* A congressional clerk inadvertently left out the possessive apostrophe when a bill was finally passed giving the hospital its present name in 1916. The facility was originally called the Government Hospital for the Insane. It was used as a military hospital during the Civil War, and wounded Union soldiers demanded the name change because they didn't like it as an address. (Private conversation, Philip Baridon, Ph.D., Chief, Program Evaluation Branch, Forensic Division, St. Elizabeths Hospital, May 9, 1983.)

but *everybody* liked her. The detective liked her. The FBI men liked her. Even the teller she robbed at the bank liked her, as much as could be expected.

Cheryl, unarmed, had walked into a big bank in the middle of Washington, in the middle of the day, handed a teller a note ("This is a hold-up. Give me 20's, 50's, and 100's. Don't give me no funny money or you are dead") and walked out with $1,000, leaving behind her image on film.

Detectives, suspecting a gang that had used teen-agers as note-carriers in past robberies, showed Cheryl's picture around a neighborhood the gang was known to frequent. Someone recognized the picture and put a name on it. The detectives staked out Cheryl's house.

"You take a pretty picture, girl," one detective said as he grabbed her. Nobody loves a line like a cop.

Cheryl thus became one of the females who are the respondents in 15 percent of all cases referred to juvenile court. (Girls are the respondents in just 11 percent of cases involving acts against persons, such as assault and robbery, but 59 percent of "status offenses"—"beyond control," truancy, runaway.[1])

Cheryl had no prior record, and the judge had no factual basis on which to decide that she posed a danger to herself or others or was likely to flee, so he had to release her to await her trial.

We walked across the street to my office, where I set about taking pictures of her, to record what she looked like at around the time of the robbery—it might be a year before she would be tried. We went out into the parking lot in pursuit of enough light for the office's balky Polaroid. Cheryl stood, hands on hips, shoulders back, head tilted gracefully, the white kerchief around her head nicely accenting her white terry cloth V-neck top. The pictures showed a young woman looking at someone with a mixture of tolerance and amusement.

Back in the office, I sat down behind my big desk and cleared an area in the center of it large enough to accommodate the emblem of my profession (American equivalent of the British wig), a twelve-and-a-half-by-eight-and-a-half-inch yellow pad of paper.

"Tell me about your life in crime," I said.

Cheryl took a deep breath, blinked her memory into focus, and began: "Harry Smith is a professional bank robber. I was messing with this guy Tony, and Tony and Harry used to swing together real tough, so I knew Harry." She paused after each phrase, to give me time to write it down. "Harry approached me and asked me, was I about making money? I asked, doing what? He said, going into a bank. He told me how he'd do it:

I'd go into a bank with a note, and the lady would give me the money. So I said okay."

Harry's goal, of course, was to minimize his own risk by sending an agent into the bank, rather than venturing in himself. His problem—not uncommon in the world of banking—was, how do you get someone to take all the risk without demanding all the profit? His solution was to get kids to do it. Not only were kids easily manipulated by someone who was a bank robber with a *big car,* and a *gun,* and *drugs,* but they faced substantially less risk than an adult: Harry, if caught robbing a bank, would be looking at fifteen years, or up to life imprisonment if he were armed. As a juvenile, Cheryl could be incarcerated until she was twenty-one, but, as a practical matter, wouldn't do more than a year or two, tops. That kind of time she ought to be able to swallow with her mouth shut, particularly when snitching on Harry would make him *very angry.*

The juvenile messenger method promised to breathe new life into the bank robbery business, which had been showing a very poor return: on account of those little cameras on the walls, and because there are always plenty of witnesses, and because there aren't a whole lot of people in the field—bank robbery is a specialty, and the police know whom to look for—bank robbers are caught far more frequently than other criminals. The D.C. Metropolitan Police Department's annual "clearance rate" (number of cases closed as a percentage of number of new cases filed) for bank robbery runs around 85 percent, compared to under 30 percent for all robbery.[2] In United States district courts nationwide, in cases that proceeded to judgment, 1,362 bank robbery defendants were found guilty, and 22 not guilty, in 1980.[3] There were only 62 bank robberies in Washington in the year ending in September 1980, compared to 1,146 robberies at other commercial establishments, and the bank robberies netted an average of less than $1,000 each.[4] One of the robbery detectives handling Cheryl's case told me that the smarter robbers were switching to jewelry stores, where security was relatively lax, and you could steal a single watch worth a couple of thousand dollars.

Harry and Cheryl drove to the bank, where everything went as planned. Then they drove to a tourist home and split the money, and Cheryl caught a cab home.

"I got six hundred and thirty dollars," she said. "I spent it on clothes, and I gave my mother some—fifty dollars. I told her my boyfriend got his income tax refund."

She recounted how four detectives grabbed her and took her in a car with them. "They gave me their cards: Schwartz, Myles, Stanko, and Luchner. I was scared. They flashed this picture on me. I said, 'That's not me.' But Schwartz kept saying, 'You was very hard to catch up with.' They was joking with me. About a block and a half from the precinct, Stanko stopped the car and said, 'Go ahead, get out. You want to go?' I didn't move. He said, 'Now we *know* it's you, 'cause any innocent person would have jumped at the chance to go.' "

At the station, they handcuffed her to a desk and "pressed" her for a while, she said. Then Stanko took her into a separate room and quietly persuaded her that he was on her side, and she should confess to him, which she did. She'd been read her rights, and she told me that she had understood them.

"I think this is where I came in," I said.

We went over her personal info once more: her father had died when she was a little girl. She lived at home with her eleven-month-old daughter and her mother. She'd been dating the same twenty-one-year-old maintenance man for a year. She'd never been in trouble before, "except I was caught stealing crayons eight years ago."

A lot of important business was transacted in the courthouse hallways. I was approached, soon after picking up Cheryl's case, by Detective Stanko, a flinty, weatherbeaten man whom I did not know, but who had made it his business to know me. He wanted to do me a favor.

"This Harry Smith who sent your girl into the bank—he and his gang are going on trial for bank robbery and conspiracy in Big Court [U.S. district court] next month," he said. "You ought to contact the U.S. attorney. I think you might be able to get the charge against Cheryl dropped if she'd testify against Harry."

"Gee, that's a great idea!" I thought, but said, in the hard, savvy tone I always fell into when speaking to police, "I'm not sure we need a break. I mean, maybe she was forced into it. Maybe we can get over with a duress defense."*

"Forced? Sometimes they'd do that," he said. "One of them caught a kid who broke his car window with a rock and took him to two banks 'to get the money for it.' He put a gun to the head of another girl, and those kids got about twenty bucks to keep. But Cheryl—Cheryl went right along. And she got six hundred of the thousand-dollar take."

"Don't you think it would be dangerous for her to snitch?"

"She's not *snitching*," the detective said. "She's saving her ass. She can

* Generally, "duress" is a defense (although not to a murder charge) if the will of the accused was overborne at the time of the offense by threats of imminent death or serious bodily injury, so that the commission of the offense was not the voluntary act of the accused.

say we threatened to take her baby away. They'll understand." He looked me straight in the eye as he said this, the rhythm of his Chiclet-chewing steady. I couldn't tell if he was lying, mistaken, or a truth-telling Perfect Master of the ways of the street, about which I knew nothing.

The government would, of course, have to do something for Cheryl to induce her to cooperate against Smith. They could compel her to take the witness stand by subpoenaing her, but they couldn't make her talk. She could assert her Fifth Amendment* right not to testify, because anything she said pertaining to the robberies would tend to incriminate her.

I thought the government should drop all charges against Cheryl, since she would be risking her life by testifying. But after consulting the United States attorney's office, all the assistant corporation counsel prosecuting Cheryl's case offered in exchange for her testimony was a plea to the less serious charge of attempted robbery,† with a promise that he would not argue for incarceration.

I set up an appointment for Cheryl and me with the assistant U.S. attorneys prosecuting Harry Smith, hoping they would lean on the corporation counsel to give us a better deal once they appreciated Cheryl's value as a witness.

A week after Cheryl's arrest, a different teen-aged girl walked into the same bank as had Cheryl, handed a similar note to a teller, and walked out with another $1,000. This time the "funny money" worked, a package of red dye exploding as the girl left the bank. She dropped the money and ran, but was later caught, thanks to the bank surveillance pictures, and she told the police that *Cheryl* had written the note and told her what to do. Cheryl was charged with this second bank robbery, and a warrant was issued for her arrest.

Cheryl sauntered into my office, which was right across the street from police headquarters, a couple of days later. I suggested that she turn herself in, but I also let her know that if she chose to go home and lay low, she could turn herself in that Saturday to a reasonable judge, who might release her, rather than face the judge sitting that afternoon, Judge Wesson, who seldom released anyone. I was not counseling her to evade arrest, but merely advising her of the likely legal consequences of alternative courses of action, which is what a lawyer is for.

Cheryl came back Saturday and spent the entire day with the P.D.S.

* The Fifth Amendment provides, in relevant part, that no person "shall be compelled in any criminal case to be a witness against himself . . ."
† It is impossible to commit a robbery without *attempting* to commit a robbery. Thus, attempted robbery is a "lesser included offense" in robbery and may be pled to, even though the robbery was completed.

attorney on duty, trying to turn herself in. There's paperwork involved. By the time she was finally accepted into custody, it was too late for her to go before the judge, so she was locked up to await an initial hearing that Monday morning, before Judge Wesson, after all.

On Monday morning, but not as bright and early as I had planned, I called up the court official who oversees the assignment of indigent cases and asked that I be assigned to represent Cheryl on the second robbery charge. Too late. Her new case had already been assigned to a private attorney. She went before the judge and was on a bus to the Children's Center for pretrial detention before I had a chance to see her.

When she was delivered for our appointment with the U.S. attorney the following Friday, I met her in the lockup.

"Where were *you* Monday morning?" Cheryl asked, her tone indicating that she didn't expect much in the way of an answer.

"Listen," I said. "I think one of the reasons you like me is that I don't bullshit you. I fucked up. What can I say? I'm sorry."

Cheryl just looked at me for a moment. "It's all right," she said, her face softening.

(Her other lawyer let me do all the work on his case, anyway.)

I asked Cheryl if she was still sure she wanted to cooperate against the bank robbers. "Don't you think they might hurt you?"

She shrugged her shoulders. "I'm not afraid of Harry and them."

"Yeah, but you're just a dumb fifteen-year-old kid, and what do you know?"

"That's true," she said.

I went out to the marshals' desk and met the FBI man who had come to escort Cheryl to the U.S. attorney's office. (The FBI investigates bank robberies because theft of federally insured deposits is a federal offense.) He shook my hand and claimed that it was nice to meet me.

"Has the young lady arrived yet?" he asked, smiling the pleasant, cold smile of the Bureau. Like so many FBI men, he looked just like an FBI man; that is, he looked like a television actor who would be cast as an FBI man—handsome in an off-the-shelf, men's cologne sort of way. This odd quality of rigid self-imitation might have something to do with the fact that one out of eight FBI agents is an accountant: 982 *armed accountants.* Scary![5]

The marshal told the FBI man to turn in his weapon before he entered the lockup. He reached into the breast of his gray flannel suit jacket, pulled out a Clint Eastwood cannon, flipped the cylinder out, and dumped the bullets, each the size of a dill pickle, onto the counter with a clatter.

Citing their nebulous, ever-changing "regulations," the marshals refused to let Cheryl, the FBI man, and me use the back elevator, so we went up the public elevator, she in handcuffs, he in his suit. Only once we were under way did it hit me: "My God, this is *endangering* her, to be seen with an FBI man."

In the U.S. attorney's office we sat down with three FBI men, each bigger than the other, and two young women, the assistant U.S. attorneys who were prosecuting Harry Smith and his gang. The prosecutors promised that nothing Cheryl said in the meeting would ever be used against her, and that if they liked what they heard, they would renew their efforts on Cheryl's behalf with the corp. counsel.

Cheryl told what she knew about Harry. "Harry had his gun, weapon, pistol, piece, whatever," she began.

The biggest FBI man interrupted. "He's kind of strange, isn't he?"

"What do you mean?" Cheryl asked.

"He's a faggot, isn't he?"

Cheryl didn't deign to respond, but continued her narrative. She had an awesome memory for detail, and an IQ that wouldn't quit, and she was the most vivid of raconteurs—all this packaged into a voluptuous yet vulnerable fifteen-year-old who had been *taken advantage of.* She was the *perfect witness.*

I suggested to the prosecutors that they'd get what they paid for. They said they'd do what they could.

§3-06

Dr. Sherman pled guilty in April, four months after his abortion-murder mistrial, to twenty-five counts of perjury in exchange for the government's dismissal of the second-degree murder charge against him. He remained free pending sentence, when he'd face a maximum of ten years in prison for *each* of the twenty-five counts.

The prosecutor stated that the government entered the plea bargain because the deceased girl's mother expressed "a very strong preference not to undergo the anguish of another lengthy trial" and because conviction on the murder count "would not effect a significant difference in terms of the ultimate sentence the defendant would be exposed to."

Sherman's P.D.S. lawyer, Bob Muse, said the defense accepted the bargain because "for nearly four years my client has been living a virtual nightmare. He sought this agreement because he wanted to bring his life back to some sense of reality."

§3-07

I was on the phone to the corp. counsel, trying to negotiate a deal for Cheryl. I spent so much time on the telephone every day that I experienced inevitable moments of dissociation, during which I found myself sitting alone in a room with a black plastic dumbbell pressed against one ear, talking to the wall. But now I was wired right into the prosecutor. I was speaking deeply and strongly, in well-formed, highly controlled sentences. I sounded affable, while obviously just feigning affability, formal, lawyerly, masculine—I was doing very well, in short.

The prosecutor suggested that in return for Cheryl's cooperation against the adult bank robber Harry Smith, in addition to accepting a plea to a lesser offense in my bank robbery case and refraining from arguing for incarceration, he would also drop Cheryl's second bank robbery case altogether.

"That's not doing us a favor," I said, "because you can't prove the second case anyway." He had told me that his handwriting expert was not able to determine whether the block-printed note used by the girl in the second robbery had been written by Cheryl. "All you've got is the squeal of a co-respondent trying to get her own ass off the grill."

"We have other evidence," he said.

"Like what?"

"There are some things we're working on." He agreed that his offer would improve if the "other evidence" didn't come through.

I received a message that Cheryl had telephoned me from the Children's Center, where she was locked up awaiting trial, and that it was *urgent* that I call her right away.

After the usual half-hour on the phone, being transferred from "Administration" to "Control" to her "Cottage," I finally got through to Cheryl. "What's the emergency?" I asked.

"Tell my mother to bring me my Calvin Klein jeans," Cheryl said.

I put it on my list of things to do.

* * *

The mother of Richard Joe Madison, my first purse-snatch client, called to tell me that one of Richard's brothers had died. He died in a sewer in which he was working, overcome by leaking gas. She asked me to tell Richard, because she said she was not allowed to call him on the telephone, up at the Children's Center. It occurred to me to tell her that, of course, for such an emergency they *would* allow her to call through, but then I realized that she knew her experience better than I, and no doubt she would have been put through unendurable humiliation in the form of "verification" of who she was and what she was saying before she would ever have gotten Richard on the phone. So I said that I would tell him in person when I went up to the Children's Center in a couple of days on another matter.

(My waiting two days to deliver the message, which seemed reasonable at the time, in retrospect struck me as appalling, but perhaps *was* reasonable at the time, given my other obligations. It was not the sort of news to convey by phone, and I felt as though I couldn't drop everything every time one of my clients had a death in the family—which was quite often, as a result of violence, drugs, and disease.*)

Richard and I sat on opposite sides of a square linoleum table like they used to have in soda shops, in a tiny, windowless, airless room. "I have some bad news," I said. "Your brother Tom died in an accident. He was overcome by gas at work. They're sure it was painless. He just went to sleep."

Richard Joe Madison sat abruptly back as though pushed. A single tear rolled down his cheek. He silently wiped it away. "He been buried yet?" was all he said.

The answer was no. The next day I filed a standard "Motion for Release to Attend Funeral," which was routinely granted.

---

* The rate of tuberculosis among Washington children is four to five times higher than the national average and the infant mortality rate is double the national average (Phil Gailey and Warren Weaver, Jr., "Troubling Figures," New York *Times*, November 18, 1982, p. B-14).

§3-08

The cherry blossoms, their tragic beauty too delicate for this world, had come and gone, and were once again a memory. They were always a memory. Leaden air had stifled the spring breezes. The siege of summer was on.

"The evidence I hoped for is not coming together on Cheryl's bank robbery number two, and I think you correctly analyzed the effect of that on my leverage," the corp. counsel phoned to tell me.

He still refused to drop all Cheryl's charges, noting that to conclude such a deal before the trial of Harry Smith's bank robbery gang would render her testimony practically worthless. The defendants' attorneys could simply ask Cheryl, "What did you get in exchange for testifying?" and the answer would be, "They promised to throw out two bank robbery charges against me." The jury would discount everything she said. So we agreed not to reach an agreement. We decided to have "an understanding" that if she testified, he would "take into account" the fact that she had cooperated, when he dealt with her cases. That way he could do more for her after she testified than he was able to promise before.

Cheryl testified at Harry Smith's trial.

It is a lawyer's job to foresee all possible problems. But in this case, as so often happens, an unforeseen problem arose, creating the sort of dispute that is the forte of contract lawyers—an argument about what two parties *really* meant by what they didn't say about what they had never thought of. The jury in Harry Smith's case was not able to reach a verdict; a mistrial was declared; and a new trial date set. The corp. counsel and I disagreed about whether Cheryl's promise to testify applied to a second trial.

I was sitting on a hard metal chair in the corp. counsel's office, listening to him argue on the phone with the telephone company about his home phone bill, while Cheryl waited outside. Finally, he turned his attention to me. He said that Cheryl's promise to testify would not be fulfilled until she testified again.

"For more testimony, you'll have to promise me right now that you're going to drop all charges," I said. "I won't tell Cheryl anything other than that she'll get 'consideration,' so she can still be a perfectly good witness."

"You're holding me up, and I resent it," he said angrily. He insisted that if Cheryl did not testify again, he would not rest until she'd been convicted of two bank robberies and committed to the Children's Center. The deal had been a break in exchange for *cooperation,* and that meant whatever was necessary to help convict Harry and his gang.

I said the deal had been a break for *testifying,* which she had done. To go back on that was simply unfair.

"Like the man said, 'Life is unfair,' " the prosecutor said, alluding to an observation by then-President Carter.

"Maybe, but the question is, are *you* unfair?"

I said Cheryl wouldn't testify, so we might as well set a trial date for her. He said that he was tied up every day for two months, which meant that Cheryl would remain in custody for that period of time. I figured it didn't matter, because I had no intention of trying the case, a sure loser. I'd bluff him for a couple of days trying to get a better deal, and then plead her guilty to everything, if necessary, rather than leave her detained waiting for trial. My supervisor had assured me that she'd probably get probation, anyway. "All the judges are male chauvinists, including the women," he said. "They're not going to lock up a poor girl who's been exploited by these bad men who had her in their thrall."

I found Cheryl, dressed that day in a Grecian-looking lavender dress, holding court in the courthouse corridor with some of her many juvenile acquaintances. When I mentioned her remote trial date, her face turned ashen, even though I explained that it was all a bluff, meaningless.

"Relax," I said. "It'll all be over, one way or another, in a couple of days." She had a far-off look as she walked out the door.

Something told me to call the shelter house (where Cheryl had been moved to facilitate her trips to court) and explain to Cheryl that her situation had improved.

"She's not back yet," the voice on the other end said. "When did she get out of court?"

"Oh," I said. "I'm not sure. I didn't see her leave. I was tied up there all day. She should be back shortly."

"She said this morning if things didn't work out so she saw any prospect of getting free, she wasn't coming back," the voice said.

That evening Cheryl's mother called me up, crying. She'd received an anonymous call threatening Cheryl's life. Cheryl was not at her grandmother's, or at the shelter house, or at her girlfriend's. She must be up in the robbers' neighborhood, her mother said.

I said that I was sure that the threat was just talk, an attempt to intimi-date Cheryl. The robbers knew that if anyone touched her, they'd be in big trouble.

"I've known them to do it. They'll do it," she said.

What was I going to say—"No, you're wrong. I know more about your world than you do"?

I suggested she call the robbery squad. They'd know whom to keep an eye on, and they could try to find Cheryl and pick her up.

"Those prosecutors. They get her to cooperate by promising to let her go. Then she gets it in her head she's getting out," Mrs. Harris said through tears. "Then they go back on their word. They say they won't do anything for her, so she runs away, and now she's going to get killed for cooperating."

Over the next several days I was engaged in the unusual enterprise of pestering the police and FBI to find and arrest my client. This was proba-bly unethical, since the last indication from my client was that she did not want to be found, much less arrested, so I was acting as her adversary in-stead of her advocate. But, seeing as how she *was* a juvenile, and people apparently *were* out to kill her, I followed my own judgment. One tends to.

Cheryl showed up at my office a week later. Wherever she'd been, and whatever she'd been doing, something had led to her to decide she'd rather risk being locked up.

After signing a detailed "Memorandum of Agreement," specifying that she would testify truthfully "at the current trial and any ensuing trial(s) concerning the said robbery activities" of Harry Smith, Cheryl pled guilty to the lesser included offense of bank larceny in my case, and her second bank robbery case was dismissed. The corp. counsel, who had agreed to support Cheryl's release in the community pending sentence, and then to support a sentence of probation, interpreted "support" to mean "not op-pose" and said nothing when the judge said he guessed he better lock Cheryl up for the six weeks until her sentencing.

One of those occasionally manifest imperatives of justice—an Appeal to God, Don't Tread on Me!—suffused the courtroom and lifted me to my feet. I implored the judge to give heed to any remaining shred of de-cency in this vale of tears, and *at least* respect the right of Cheryl's inno-cent, unoffending infant to have her mother at home. Cheryl herself broke down into shuddering sobs as I invoked mercy for her baby. The judge saw it my way.

Across the street at Jaybird's restaurant afterward, Cheryl sat beside me at the bar, demurely sipping a lemonade as I celebrated her freedom with a beer. I asked her what her plans were, now that her bank-robbing days were through.

"I'm going to be an aerial physicist," she said.

Cheryl testified again at Harry Smith's second trial, at the conclusion of which he and two of his cohorts were sentenced to extensive periods in prison. Cheryl was put on probation, but within four months she was back in custody, charged with two more bank robberies. She was convicted of those and committed to the Children's Center, whence she escaped. She was a fugitive, wanted for yet another two bank robberies, last I heard.

I had been disappointed by Cheryl, and somewhat annoyed—all that work, and I might as well have stayed in bed. But mostly I was saddened. That girl had so much going for her.

§3-09

Most of my juvenile clients pled guilty to something. There was very little reason not to. If you went to trial, you were almost sure to lose, anyway. Unlike juries, which are unpredictable, a judge is going to convict if the evidence permits, and maybe even if it doesn't.

It really didn't make much difference what a juvenile pled to. Minor charges subjected him to precisely the same sentence as more serious charges—an indeterminate period of incarceration not to extend beyond his twenty-first birthday—and charges that were dismissed were still carried in his file and seen by the sentencing judge, who would often explicitly refer to them as the equivalent of convictions. But dismissal of charges at least kept the kid's record of *official* convictions shorter than your arm. And as part of the deal, the prosecutor usually agreed not to argue for incarceration (which, incidentally, meant that he didn't have to show up at the sentencing). That took a little pressure off the judge.

Pleading also suggested to the judge that the kid acknowledged his guilt, and it saved the hassle of a trial—a favor that the judge might take into account when deciding whether to lock him up. There wasn't room to lock up everybody, and the idea was to give the judge a means of sorting through the candidates that would be favorable to your client: "He pled, Your Honor." If pleading even marginally improved the client's chances of avoiding commitment to the Children's Center, I figured it was worth it.

Avoiding the Children's Center made sense. Little else did, in juvenile court. It was a self-contained, self-referential system, like a court held below deck in a rudderless ship—everything seemed orderly and purposeful until you stepped outside.

If I got a kid off, that victory was usually no triumph at all. I had simply ensured that there would be no intervention in his life, and he would go back to the same troubled family, in the same overcrowded house, and skip the same crummy school with the same delinquent peer group, until he got in trouble again, the only difference now being that he thought he could beat the system. The kid lost, and the community lost.

If I didn't get the kid off, the Juvenile Branch of the Division of Social Services of the Superior Court would prepare a pre-sentence report for the judge. The report, sometimes prepared with the help of specialists in medicine, psychology, and education, would detail the respondent's personal history from day one ("mother reports he was carried to term and developed normally"); describe his situation at home ("resides with his mother and four siblings in a three-bedroom subsidized National Capital Housing apartment, which appeared neat and adequately furnished") and at school ("reads at the fourth-grade level; was absent thirty-nine days last school year"); and recommend that the respondent be placed in "a structured, homelike setting with positive male role models, where he could benefit from psychological counseling, tutoring, and job training." No such facilities existed.

The judge could then put him on probation or commit him. If he was put on probation, he would be one of thirty to forty cases handled by his caseworker, who would be able to offer only minimal supervision.

If he was committed, unless he was one of the handful placed in a group home or a residential facility for the mentally handicapped or disturbed, he would go twenty-five miles up the road to Laurel, Maryland, to the Children's Center, an isolated collection of drab brick barracks operated by the Institutional Care Services Division of the Bureau of Youth Services of the Commission on Social Services (formerly the Social Rehabilitation Administration) of the Department of Human Services (formerly the Department of Human Resources) of the District of Columbia government.

Unless the committed child was among the 150 incarcerated in the Children's Center's maximum-security facility, Oak Hill, where he would have his own locked room, he would join the 280 or so juveniles at Cedar

Knoll, where, except in one maximum-security cottage, the inmates slept in large dormitory rooms holding fifteen to twenty-five beds. No counselor stayed in the dormitories at night. The doors to the dormitories were locked. He would face beatings and sexual abuse from the other juveniles, and could expect no protection from the staff. Indeed, according to a city council task force report, "The counselors ... themselves pose a threat to the health and well-being of youths at Cedar Knoll and Oak Hill."[1] Sexual abuses of juveniles by staff have been documented,[2] and beatings of the inmates by the staff were commonplace.[3] The "institutional counselors" who provided most of the care and supervision of the inmates were not required to have a high school diploma or any experience working with children. Cedar Knoll employed individuals who had themselves been inmates of the institution as little as three months before their hiring. After four days of training, they were put in charge of the kids. This was what the taxpayers got for $20,000 per incarcerated kid per year.

An inmate could readily obtain drugs from staff members, but he could not get adequate health care, counseling, education, or job training. At Oak Hill there were four "training programs": culinary (working in the kitchen); laundry (working in the laundry); maintenance (working on the grounds); and barbering.

He would, however, during the course of his indeterminate sentence, learn to think of himself as a criminal, and refine his criminal skills, and become adjusted to institutional life and, thus, maladjusted to life in the community. Finally, based on "no formally established or generally used or written criteria for the release of juveniles," after a period of time "based on neither rhyme nor reason,"[4] the inmate, now in all likelihood more dangerous than when he went in, would be unleashed on the community. The kid lost. The community lost.

I have never heard anyone, including the people who run it, claim that the Children's Center has a salutary effect on the children who pass through it. At best they are simply warehoused, and that not very well—escapes are common.

An average of 340 kids per year are committed to the care of the Commission on Social Services.[5] Over 1,200 are detained—locked up while awaiting trial or "disposition" (sentence).[6] Not surprisingly, no data are kept on the number of Children's Center graduates who go on to be convicted of crimes as adults—the figures would only make the taxpayers angry.

The stated goal of the juvenile court system is "care," not punishment. The law requires that "when a child is removed from his home the [court] will secure for him custody, care, and discipline as nearly as possible equivalent to that which should have been provided for him by his parents . . ."[7]

Giving young people "care" has tacitly been abandoned as the rationale for sending them up the road, replaced by the goal of getting them off the streets, on the assumption that the safety of the community will thus be enhanced, at least until their return.

Even that assumption is shaky. Before a new youth services commissioner, Jerome Miller, closed down the state's large "industrial schools" for delinquents in 1972, Massachusetts had a daily population of up to 2,000 incarcerated juveniles. There was no dramatic increase in juvenile violence when all but *100* were released or placed in small unlocked facilities[8]—this in a state with *eight times* the population of the District of Columbia.

Since my client's involvement with the system was a no-win situation for everyone, I viewed my representation of him as an end in itself. He would have a relationship with an adult who was honest with him, and with whom he could be honest. I figured that experience had some intrinsic value.

§3-10

Judge Whitter, one of several retired judges who heard cases to relieve the burden on the full-time judges, had no idea what was going on in his courtroom, and neither did anybody else. Dealing with him required a certain flexibility, but it also created opportunities—he was manipulable.

I appeared before him with Reginald Chatsworth Dickinson, who, slow to realize that burglary was not his calling, had been arrested again in another Georgetown house. (An alarm went off, but he thought it was next door.) He had pled guilty to one burglary in exchange for the dismissal of the other—"one-for-one," a standard deal—and was to be sentenced.

Judge Whitter sat on the bench like a toad on a log. He appeared to have no neck, his head, the size and shape of an antique football, resting directly atop his round body. His lips were the same parchment color as his skin, leaving his face almost featureless except for the black frames of his gogglelike eyeglasses, which were half an inch lower on one side than

the other, like a permanently tilted scale of justice. He was reading, obviously for the first time, a motion that had just been argued to him for
half an hour. The white paper was reflected in his glasses, rendering them
the color of fishbellies. He had two silver-white disks of dead fishbelly
where his eyes should have been.

The judge took off his glasses and held them up toward the ceiling at
arm's length, focusing a yellow spot of light on his cheek. He beckoned
with a pudgy finger to the young woman bailiff and handed the glasses to
her. "Clean them," he said.

For Reginald's sentencing I'd decided to try the "Tan His Hide"
speech, which I'd heard about over a beer at Jaybird's. It was supposed to
be very effective with Judge Whitter. I ran through the scenario with
Reginald in the lockup behind the courtroom first, then came out and
went over it with his bleary-eyed mother, who was never far from tears
over Reginald, for whose troubles she felt responsible. It must have been
confusing for her to hear her son's attorney say, "As I've explained to
Reginald, I'm going to say some things that sound as though I'm against
him, but that's only because that's what the judge wants to hear. Pay no
attention." I would have had to be extraordinarily persuasive to get a
mother to believe what I said to her and disregard what I said to the
judge, a person so well situated that he literally sat several feet above everyone else's head. But no matter. She had no choice. Anyway, her alco-
holism had left her unable to understand much of anything, hard as she
tried.

"Your Honor, Reginald Dickinson is one of the sorriest characters I've
ever represented," I began, casting a withering glance at Reginald, who
looked properly abashed. "He doesn't deserve another chance. He
doesn't deserve anything. And I know his folks feel the same way about
him, Your Honor." I had the judge's attention now. "In fact, if for any
reason you *do* let him go home today, they're going to TAN HIS HIDE!
Which is exactly what he needs."

Judge Whitter, unable to resist the prospect of some old-fashioned discipline, put Reginald on probation. No Children's Center for Mr. Dickinson this time.

I made it back to my office in time for a client conference with Ricky
Melville and his stepfather. Ricky, a lean, pretty fourteen-year-old, was
charged with simple assault, based on a complaint arising out of a fight in
school.

"School fight" was one of my favorite buzz-phrases, conjuring up, as it
did, a Norman Rockwell image of rasslin' in the schoolyard—"boys will
be boys"—rather than the reign of terror prevailing in the corridors and

stairwells of some of our urban public schools. But in this instance, my investigation showed it was a fair description of what had happened. Ricky had never been in trouble before, and had been at most a peripheral participant in this particular melee, which involved a dozen boys on both sides, triggered by someone's insulting someone else's jacket.

From the lawyer's point of view, such minor, first offender cases fall into the category of nifnaf shit, busywork lacking the drama of "heavy" charges. But it could be argued that they are the most important cases, because they determine whether a kid is drawn into the system and swept up in its inexorable tide. As I explained to Ricky, "This may seem like a silly charge, but it's no joke. If you bring your witnesses down, the government will probably drop the charge, and everything will be fine. If you don't, you'll be found guilty, you'll be put on probation, you'll spit on the sidewalk sometime and you'll be revoked, you'll be sent to the Children's Center, and your whole life will go down the tubes. It's that simple."

§3-11

Eric Webster, four-foot-eight, seventy pounds, twelve years old, was a crook. He thought what was bad about wrongdoing was that you got in trouble for it, sometimes, if you got caught.

He did get caught, acting as the lookout for some older boys who snatched a purse. (He said he was "just playing.") And, after I got him released to await trial, he was caught again, this time helping some older kids pull a daylight burglary. The burglary was successful. The big kids were successful. But a neighbor had recognized Eric.

A Detective Salt had dropped by Eric's house shortly after the burglary. Eric's aunt had tried to stop him from questioning Eric. She said he would not talk without a lawyer. But when she left the room to call me, Eric's grandmother encouraged him to make a clean breast of it. ("Eric's grandmother gets nervous around police," his aunt explained.)

Eric had given Detective Salt the nicknames of a half dozen accomplices, and the streets they lived on. As is common in his society, even among close friends, he didn't know their last names. Last names weren't used, perhaps as a hedge against inquiries by the authorities, perhaps for other reasons. Now the detective wanted Eric to come down to the station and ride around with him, pointing out their houses.

Eric's aunt brought him to my office. I asked her to wait outside. Eric sat down opposite me, his sneakered feet swinging back and forth above the floor. (His sneakers were immaculately white, as though fresh from the box. In fact they were several months old, but Eric cleaned them every night with a bar of soap and a toothbrush.)

"You remember how everything you tell me is a secret?" I asked.

"Yes."

"Then we don't have to go all over that again. So, did you do this burglary?"

Eric took a deep breath and told me that he had stuck his arm through the mail slot in the door of the house and opened the door, and he and six other kids went in. He said he did not want to snitch on the others. He was afraid of what they would do to him.

I called Detective Salt and told him that Eric had no information to share, so I would bring him to the station only if he was going to be arrested. The detective said that, as a matter of fact, he had just gotten a custody order for Eric.

I drove Eric and his aunt down to the police station in my new Mustang (later stolen) through searing sun-bleached boulevards that reminded me of Florida, L.A., or Mexico, and reminded Eric of nothing, since they were all he had ever known. I think that the simple fact of never leaving the city must be one of the most insupportable conditions of poverty, but I wouldn't know.

Eric's aunt lectured him as we drove: Eric goes along and helps the big boys; he gets in trouble; they get the money. "They say there were color TVs and all sorts of stereo equipment stolen, and Eric hasn't got a dime to show for it," she said. Eric sat silently in the back seat.

His aunt talked about her daughter, who was in the hospital. She'd come out of a two-month coma and was beginning to talk, but she remained paralyzed on the left side. I asked what her illness was. Eric's aunt explained that her daughter was beaten up by a guy "she used to mess with, but she stopped messing with him." He beat her up with his fists. The doctor at the emergency room thought she had been hit by a car.

At the police station, as we waited for the detective to see us, Eric sat with his face between his updrawn knees and his hands over his head. Detective Salt, a fortyish, overweight man with an acne-scarred face and short, wet-looking hair, greeted each of us politely. There was something seamy about him, perhaps from the spiritual residue of doing society's dirty work, or maybe from the physical residue of spending too much time in police cars, which are eaten in and slept in and aren't that clean.

He took me aside and said he would like Eric to give him a written statement to "firm up" what he'd already told him, and to ride around pointing out perpetrators' houses. He hoped to do that right away, while there was still a chance to recover some of the property. I refused both requests, as my client did not want to cooperate with the police. Salt remained affable. What was it to him? He understood my job, and he brought all the passion to his own that one would expect from someone working on his eighteen-thousandth burglary investigation. For my part, as I stood there obstructing the search for somebody's property, I felt as though I were preventing the recovery of my own.*

Eric pled guilty to the burglary in exchange for the dismissal of the pocketbook snatch, and was put on probation.

§3-12

"Perry Mason didn't win those cases. Paul Drake won those cases," old Professor Peterfreund of NYU used to say. The case of Wyatt Clayton, my first client, proved how right he was.

Wyatt Clayton's day in court on his Christmastime robbery charges finally arrived in the dead of summer, after five continuances. As it turned out, he was charged with *two* separate gunpoint holdups, of a young woman and her brother, and the facts were complex enough for me to request two continuances for "continuing investigation" by the defense, which were granted because there were no available trial judges, anyway. The third continuance I obtained by throwing myself on the mercy of the prosecutor when I discovered, the day before the trial, that it was scheduled for the next day. I had written it in my datebook, but I hadn't *looked* in my datebook. The prosecutor agreed not to oppose my request for a continuance (thus assuring it would be granted), because he was a nice fellow, and because he generally preferred doing nothing to doing his job. The fourth continuance was necessitated by the defense attorney's broken leg. The fifth was requested by the prosecutor so he could take his vacation. Altogether, seven months had passed since Wyatt had allegedly

---

* In Washington, about 6 percent of property stolen in burglaries is recovered. In 1979, $5,482,858 worth of property was reported stolen in burglaries; $317,274 worth was recovered. (*Crime and Arrest Profile, The Nation's Capital, 1979*, Office of Criminal Justice Plans and Analysis, Government of the District of Columbia [Washington, D.C.: October 1980], table 14, p. 97.)

pulled the holdups—not an unusual delay. In the meantime, he had been sentenced to probation for a prior pocketbook snatch and had made a "satisfactory adjustment," according to the probation officer.

Ernie Savage, my investigator, had used those months to amass a huge amount of material, taking written statements from the complainants five different times. Ernie believed in Wyatt's innocence, which made me think him naïve.

Ernie was one of the college students who did unpaid "internships" at various institutions in Washington. Those who worked at the Public Defender Service were a varied lot. Some were primarily interested in getting away from college; others, like Ernie, wanted mainly to get into law school. But all had chosen to tramp the dark streets of the city when they could have been relaxing by some congressman's Xerox machine, and I admired them for it.

From the piles of yellow paper Ernie kept putting on my desk, I learned that complainant Marilyn Tracy was a twenty-year-old active in the Explorers, a volunteer auxiliary police program for teen-agers. Three years before, she had been named Explorer "Teen of the Year," presumably for exhibiting the sort of virtues that win one that sort of award. Her career as a would-be cop waved just the shadow of a red flag at me as I went over her story. I had done a brief stint as an auxiliary policeman in New York—strictly out of curiosity—and had found, not surprisingly, I suppose, that a lot of people who walk around the streets at night dressed up to look like cops tend to exhibit personality problems marked by an unhealthy respect for authority, and a need to pretend that they are it.

Marilyn told Ernie that on a Friday night in December, at between 10:00 and 10:15 P.M. (she had just looked at a clock in a grocery store), she was walking past an alley near her home when she heard what sounded like a backfire. Just then, a medium-blue 1974 Mustang Mach I with black paint on the back and a long whip antenna on the front passenger side roared out of the alley, almost hitting her. She saw four boys in the car. She "didn't get a good look" at the two in the back seat, one of whom she later identified as Wyatt, but she "knew" they were two kids who hung out at a corner in her neighborhood. (Wyatt lived across the river on the other side of town.)

After the car screeched away, Marilyn's brother ran out of the alley and told her that one of the boys had gotten out of the car and held him up at gunpoint. When her brother had turned to look for the license of the fleeing car, he was shot at, the bullet passing through his hat, she said.

The day after her brother was robbed, Marilyn said, she got off a bus at quarter to three in the afternoon and was walking past the same alley when the same car pulled out and stopped in front of her on Belmont Street. The same four boys were in it. The two in the back seat got out. "You got any money?" one of them demanded.

"I do, but you're not getting it," she said.

"Oh, yeah? That's what you think," he said, and stuck a gun in her ribs.

The gun "looked like a .25 caliber automatic, the kind you put the clip in the bottom," Marilyn's written statement continued. "The barrel was black and the handle was silver. I said to him, 'You think that gun scares me? I'm going to die from something, whether it's cancer or by you shooting me.' Right after this, I heard the gun click."

The gunman reached in Marilyn's pocket and took out two dollars. "That's all the money you have?" he asked.

"That's all you see, ain't it?" she replied.

"You have more heart than your little brother does," the gunman responded.

Meanwhile, the second boy, who was supposed to be Wyatt Clayton, was "just standing there," pounding his fist into the palm of his hand. He was about eighteen years old, about five foot nine, 150 to 160 pounds, with a slight mustache—a pretty fair description of Wyatt, who was fifteen, but looked older.

After "two or three minutes," the robbers drove off, and Marilyn called the police, who arrived at "about 3:03 P.M."

Eleven days later, Marilyn went down to the *modus operandi* section of police headquarters and looked at 140 full-length color slides of teenaged arrestees before selecting Wyatt Clayton as the boy who "just stood there." She did not see a picture of the gunman or the other two boys.

Twenty-seven days after the robbery, she picked out Wyatt Clayton from among eight young black men of similar height and build in a police lineup. Her brother did not identify anyone.

We had, of course, made a motion to suppress identification evidence—that is, to prohibit any mention at the trial of Marilyn's having picked out Wyatt's picture, or having identified him at the lineup—on the grounds that the photo identification was unreliable, because it was the product of "impermissibly suggestive" activity by the police, namely, showing Marilyn a group of pictures in which the only subject shown in handcuffs was Wyatt; and that Marilyn's lineup identification was unreliable, because it resulted from her unreliable choice of the photo. We also argued that no one else in the lineup looked very much like the described perpetrator, so that Wyatt "stood out" unfairly.

The judge denied our motion to suppress, as I expected he would—

defense attorneys joke that the only ID procedure that would be found impermissibly suggestive would be a lineup that looked like "six nuns and a refrigerator." But the hearing on the motion did give me an opportunity to question Marilyn under oath before the trial.

Up against this "Teen of the Year" with photographic memory, Wyatt was completely outclassed. He didn't remember much of what he was doing on the crucial Friday night and Saturday afternoon, and what could be reconstructed was better forgotten. He'd spent much of the time smoking marijuana and shooting craps with his friends.

Wyatt's mother was able to recall that she had seen Wyatt at home when she returned from grocery shopping at about 3:00 P.M. that Saturday (the time of Marilyn's robbery), but she was Wyatt's mother, and most judges probably shared my supervisor's view that "God put mothers on earth to lie for their children."

After many hours of going over their accounts with Wyatt and his friends, trying to get them to refresh one another's memories, I decided against an alibi defense. Alibi defenses in general are viewed with disfavor by defense attorneys. When you put one on, you are pitting the defendant's story against the complainant's story, and the fact-finder (judge or jury) will tend to reach a verdict based on the one that's more believable, regardless of how flawed it may be. It is better to pit the complainant's story against the standard of "proof beyond a reasonable doubt," which is tougher competition than an opposing story from the defense, unless it's an exceptionally good one. Wyatt's was not.

The other reason I decided to focus on picking apart Marilyn's story, rather than presenting Wyatt's, was that I did not believe Wyatt's. I didn't believe him because I considered him a deadbeat: he had failed to appear at about five appointments with me, which was three or four more than the average for my clients. And I didn't believe him because he had flunked a lie detector test, which I had him take in the first place only at the insistence of the lawyer on his prior purse-snatch case, who swore that she knew him well enough to know that he *couldn't* have been involved in an armed robbery.

Polygraph examination results are inadmissible as evidence in D.C. courts (and generally throughout the United States) because of the fear that juries would give them more weight than their reliability warrants.

Dr. Martin Orne, a professor of psychiatry at the University of Pennsylvania and an authority on the polygraph, has found that polygraph examiners vary greatly in their accuracy, and even the best are wrong 5 percent of the time.

Reliability aside, polygraphs offend our quasi-religious belief in adversarial examination of witnesses as the best means of finding the truth. Polygraphs *don't belong* in a court, any more than computers belong in a church. These are special preserves set aside for a particular kind of search for a particular kind of truth. NO MACHINES ALLOWED.

But when you have a client who really seems innocent, it can be helpful to have him tested. If he passes, you can bring the report, along with other exculpatory evidence, to the prosecutor and ask him to drop the case, lest an injustice be wrought by the vagaries of a trial. If the prosecutor refuses to drop the case, then you make a motion to the judge asking that polygraph results be admitted at trial. The judge always denies the motion, but it signals him that your client has passed a lie detector test, which is a useful thing to have the judge know.

I explained all this to Wyatt, assuring him that if he flunked the test, I would throw it away; no one would ever hear of it; and it would have absolutely no effect on my view of him or my efforts to get him off.

I hired a private polygraph examiner. (P.D.S. had limited funds for hiring experts. Appointed private attorneys could make a motion requesting funds from the court.)

The examiner first conducted an "acquaintance test." He told Wyatt to write down a number from thirty-one to thirty-nine, without showing it to him. He then instructed Wyatt to answer "No" to every question, and asked him, "Did you write the number twenty-nine? Did you write the number thirty? Did you write the number thirty-one?" and so on up to forty. Then, "Did you lie about a number on this test?" "Now answer truthfully," the examiner said, and repeated all the questions.

At the end of the series of questions, the examiner had identified the number Wyatt had written, and also identified the idiosyncratic changes in Wyatt's respiration, pulse rate, blood pressure, and galvanic skin response (the skin's resistance to an electrical current, which is affected by glandular secretions, particularly sweat) that accompanied deception. He told Wyatt his number, reinforcing Wyatt's respect for, and response to, the machine.

The examiner then asked Wyatt, "Were you involved in that Marilyn Tracy robbery?

"Were you involved in that Marilyn Tracy robbery on Saturday, 10 December, 1979?

"Did you ride in a Mustang automobile on Saturday, 10 December, 1979?

"Do you suspect someone by name of being involved in that Marilyn Tracy robbery?

"Do you know for sure someone by name who was involved in that Marilyn Tracy robbery?

"Were you in any way involved in that robbery?"

He went through the questions three times. Wyatt answered every question "No."

"Examinee's responses to the relevant questions regarding his knowing who was involved in the Marilyn Tracy robbery were indicative of deception," the examiner reported. "These test charts indicated further that he became so tense during the examination that normal reactions were diminished. This tenseness increased so rapidly during each test chart that instrument rebalancing procedures were required two or more times. In the opinion of the examiner, this is an indication of 'overall' deception to the remaining relevant questions. This testing precluded this examiner from clearing Wyatt Clayton of any involvement in the Marilyn Tracy robbery."

I knew that Wyatt, even if innocent, had every reason to be nervous, being questioned alone in a closed room by a middle-aged white ex-FBI agent, who put two rubber tubes around his chest, taped electrodes to his fingers, wrapped a blood-pressure cuff around his wrist, and hooked everything up to something electronic in a metal box. I knew that nervousness was supposed to be compensated for by "instrument rebalancing" and not throw off the test. I knew that the tests were far from perfect, and were inadmissible in evidence for good reason. What I did not know was that, having read a report of failure, I would be unable to disregard it.

After the test, I presumed Wyatt guilty, which is to say I viewed the evidence in the same light as would the judge and prosecutor. From a purely technical standpoint, this was a helpful attitude. It caused me to take a skeptical view of the defense case and to spot weaknesses in it. It's no good being the only one in the courtroom who really thinks that the *government* has the uphill battle (burden of proof).

As for motivation, apparent guilt cuts both ways. An obviously guilty client poses the greatest professional challenge. Winning an "impossible" case is a real feather in your cap. On the other hand, you feel less personal pressure: if you lose, at least justice wins. It's like walking a tightrope with a net. With an innocent client, there's no net. You *must* win. But if it's clear to you that your client is not guilty, chances are it's pretty clear to everyone else, too. *Anybody* can get an obviously innocent person off. There's no glory in that.

In any event, thanks to my investigator Ernie, I ultimately came around to thinking that Wyatt was *not* guilty, again.

Marilyn's brother told Ernie that although he didn't identify Wyatt at the lineup, "I could have, because Marilyn told me on the way down what he looked like." He also contradicted Marilyn's claim that a bullet had gone through his hat.

Marilyn had attempted to fabricate an identification by her brother and had invented a dramatic detail. When the complainant and defendant don't know each other, as opposed to when they are, say, rivals in love or dealers in dope, one doesn't expect to find this sort of *lying* in the complainant's account of the incident, and therefore one tends not to look for it. We began looking.

I called the prosecutor with a proposition: "If I can show you ten material* contradictions in Marilyn's statements, will you drop the case?"

If he didn't drop it, we were in trouble, because many of the contradictions involved Marilyn's accounts of events other than the robberies themselves, and it would be hard to get them into evidence in a coherent way, if at all. The judge would want to hear nothing beyond the "positive identification" by a "stranger-victim" with no reason for bias, and convict. The fact was that Marilyn identified Wyatt as her robber. The prosecution's theory was simple: Wyatt robbed her. The defense's theory was Byzantine: Marilyn was jealous of the attention her brother received because he was robbed; therefore, she pretended that she herself got robbed, made up a description of a robber, and picked out Wyatt's picture because he looked like the description she had made up, and, of course, selected him at the lineup because she recognized him from the picture she had picked.

The prosecutor said I should show him my evidence on the morning of the trial, and if the contradictions were really "material," he would drop the case. It was a high-risk proposition. If he didn't drop it, all I would succeed in doing would be to give away our defense.

I went in on Monday morning with my lists. Wyatt and his mother waited outside as I sat down with the prosecutor in his white wallboard cubicle. An easy-going forty-year-old, he was much too old for his job, knew it, and didn't care. The rat race was not for him. He paced himself, methodically chain-smoking Camels and Trues, alternately.

I placed my long yellow lists on the desktop facing him. Reading upside down, I pointed out each item as I explained it.

"Regarding the Friday night robbery of her brother," I began, "Marilyn said in her January statement that the robbers' car almost hit her, and

* Material: tending to prove or disprove a fact at issue in the case.

'I didn't get a good look at the two in the back.' But at the identification suppression hearing, she said she got 'a good look at them' for 'about maybe ten seconds' as the car sped past. She said the car came out of the alley backward; her brother said frontward. She said a bullet went through her brother's hat; he said it didn't. She gave three different versions of the first three digits of the car's license plate."

The prosecutor silently put red Xs on my list in the margin beside the bullet-through-the-hat and the direction the car traveled. He put a big red star beside the "ten-second look" at the speeding perpetrators in the back seat. The license plate he left alone. He crushed the life out of a Camel, lit a True, and invited me to continue.

"Regarding her own robbery on Saturday, she said in January that the gunman was wearing a *brown* jacket, 'about the same color as your [Ernie's] sweater.' But in February she gave Ernie a detailed account of a subsequent confrontation at which the robbers supposedly threatened her in front of a liquor store. She said the gunman 'had on the *same blue* jacket he had on at the robbery.' "

"Well, anybody can make a mistake about clothing," the prosecutor said.

"Of course, that's just it," I argued. "Anybody would say 'It might have been brown' or 'I think it was blue,' but she was *positive* it was *brown* when she was talking to Ernie in his brown sweater, and now she's *positive* it was *blue*. She's always positive."

The prosecutor seemed to mull that over as he smothered one cigarette in the ashes of another.

"Read on," I said. The context of these inconsistencies was more important than the inconsistencies themselves. Continuing her description of the February confrontation outside the liquor store, she had told Ernie, "He stood right in front of me and said, 'You go to court and you're going to end up dead.' I said, 'If you wanted to kill me, you would have done it the day you robbed me in the alley.' "

I told the prosecutor, "She said in January *she* was robbed *on Belmont Street*. Her *brother* was robbed in the alley!"

The prosecutor put a red X in the margin.

Her account of the liquor store scene continued: "He said, 'You still got a lot of heart, don't you?' And I said, 'Yes, and I'm going to die with a lot of heart, too.' At this point, an employee of the liquor store came out and said, 'Are you okay?' I said, 'Yes, I don't need no help with this little punk.' The gunman said, 'Girl, I am going to punch you in your face.' I told him if he did, he wouldn't live to tell about it."

"She's talking to a man with a gun?" I said to the prosecutor. "Where have you heard that kind of dialogue before? In her other statement. And where have you heard it before that? IN THE MOVIES! Nobody really talks like that to someone with a gun, at least no one who's alive now."

The prosecutor did not put his red pen to the paper, and turned the page.

In January Marilyn said the robbery took two or three minutes. At the identification suppression hearing in July, when she knew that her opportunity to observe the perpetrators was at issue, she said "five or six minutes." The prosecutor, knowing that the hardest thing to remember about events is their duration, was unimpressed.

Ernie had interviewed every employee of the liquor store, and none remembered the incident. That merited a red question mark in the margin. "They might not have wanted to get involved," he said.

"Or maybe it never happened," I suggested.

I directed his attention to Marilyn's account of yet another supposed encounter with the four perpetrators, this time at Thomas Circle, as she was jogging one night in March. The incident unfolded in a now-familiar pattern: One of the boys from the front seat got out and said, "Man, you're a hard-head. You're still going to court, aren't you!" A prostitute Marilyn knew from the area came over to offer help. Marilyn declined: "No, I don't need no help with them." The boys sped off, in the same car with the big antenna "on the driver's side."

"In January, she said the passenger side," I told the prosecutor. That didn't rate an X.

The next point did: Marilyn told Ernie that, after the March confrontation, she had called the police from a drugstore, and that an officer made an "incident report" about the threat. No such report existed.

I had saved the best stuff for last.

I showed the prosecutor a transcript of one seemingly minor and irrelevant inquiry at the identification suppression hearing.

Q. What's your educational background?
A. I will be starting back attending school in September.
Q. What school would that be?
A. Georgetown University Law School, Undergraduate Law School.
Q. Do you have any college up to this point: have you attended any college?
A. Yes.
Q. Where was that?
A. The school I just mentioned, Georgetown University.
Q. You were a student at Georgetown?
A. Yes.

Q. I see. When was that?
A. Last—the past year.

I laid a piece of paper on the desk in front of the prosecutor. "Read it and weep," I said. It was an affidavit Ernie had obtained from the registrar of Georgetown University stating that Marilyn Tracy was not and had never been a student at any division of the university—which was why, at Ernie's suggestion, I had asked her the question in the first place. "You've got a pathological liar on your hands," I said. "She lies even when she has no reason to."

"Do you have anything else?" the prosecutor asked.

I did. Marilyn had described to Ernie *three crimes,* other than the robberies, of which she had been the victim within the past year. The first was a simple assault. The second was an obstruction of justice by her assailant, when he approached her and said, "If I go back to jail, I'm going to kill you." Both cases had been dismissed by the U.S. attorney. The third was an attempted rape, which she escaped, telling her attacker, "If you want to rape me, you're going to have to kill me first," and then punching him in the eye and kicking him in the groin. She told Ernie she would soon be testifying at the man's trial. There was no such trial pending.

The prosecutor said he wanted to give Marilyn a chance to explain herself, and he asked me to wait outside. As I stood up to leave, I said, "One more thing: Marilyn told Ernie this morning that someone set fire to her car last night, to intimidate her. She said the fire department put it out. Why don't you check that out?"

I sat on a chair outside the prosecutor's office for three hours while he conferred with a police detective, then with Marilyn, then with Marilyn's brother, then with the detective again, and Marilyn again, around and around, verifying the contradictions I had pointed out, or resolving them. I watched the clock on the wall like a husband waiting for his wife to give birth—in the movies, or like an attorney waiting for a jury to come in with the verdict, also in the movies. Finally the prosecutor emerged and stated matter-of-factly as he walked straight by me, "We'll drop the case." Two armed robberies—poof, gone away.

With the boundless energy and dedication that only an unpaid volunteer could have, my investigator had blown the government's case out of the water.

I walked over to the waiting room where Wyatt Clayton and his mother had been sitting all morning. "They dropped the case," I said.

Wyatt went limp and slid down in his chair. "They dropped the charge?" he asked.

"Yes." I shook his hand. He smiled a smile I can still see. His mother dropped her head back against the wall and sighed.

Not long after, I ran into the prosecutor and asked what he had found out about the "firebombing" of Marilyn's car.

"We checked it out with the fire department," he said. "It really did happen." He looked at me blankly and I looked at him blankly, and we both shook our heads.

We would never know whether Wyatt Clayton had committed the crimes, but that was beside the point. The complaining witness had lied. She was not credible. In our world, that's what mattered.

Misidentification is a common phenomenon. Even as the Clayton case was unfolding, I had another juvenile client who was stopped one night by a scooter cop who had "monitored a lookout"—heard a description broadcast—for a black teen-aged boy in a striped jersey. The cop took him to the scene of a mugging, where he was "positively identified" by the white woman victim, who naturally *expected* him to be the perpetrator, since he had been captured by the police, and *wanted* him to be the perpetrator, so that he would be punished and kept from victimizing her again.

Novice that I was, I probably would have assumed he was guilty myself, were it not for the fact that he was an A student in high school and had never been arrested before. Those of us who can claim neither of these characteristics are reluctant to acknowledge that they correlate with innocence, but they do. When stopped, he was walking home from work at McDonald's—employment under the Golden Arches being another reliable indicator of rectitude—and his time card at work proved that he could not have committed the crime. The charges were eventually dropped.

Between this and the Clayton case, I was getting the idea that eyewitness identifications were grossly unreliable. I was right.

Experiments in behavioral psychology have shown that "accurate recall is the exception and not the rule."[1] Witnesses typically remember more than they actually observed, filling in gaps by "remembering" what they expected or wanted to see. Ten thousand partisan eyewitnesses at a baseball game can have an abiding moral conviction that they saw their man slide into home safely, while fans of the other team are just as certain that they saw him tagged out, though a dispassionate videotape shows nothing but a cloud of dust.

Witnesses are often more positive about the false details they have unwittingly invented than about those which are in fact true. To make matters worse, witnesses are tremendously suggestible. In an experiment by Dr. Elizabeth Loftus, twice as many witnesses remembered seeing (non-existent) shattered glass in a filmed automobile collision, when asked if they'd seen the cars "smash" together, as opposed to when they were asked if they'd seen the cars "hit."[2]

"Victims of assault are notoriously unreliable witnesses regarding the description of their assailants," G. A. Talland concludes, "but then so are onlookers who watched in safety."[3]

§3-13

Dr. Sherman was brought before Judge Ugast in July to be sentenced on the twenty-five counts of perjury to which he had pled guilty. Though the murder charge was dropped in the plea bargain, the judge could take it, and anything else about the defendant, into account in deciding what the sentence would be—anything from no sanction on up to 250 years in prison.

What went on in the courtroom—like much of what goes on in court-rooms—was pure ritual. The lawyers had already submitted their argu-ments to the judge in writing, and the judge had already made up his mind, before court was called to order. The impassioned calls for retribu-tion or mercy, from the prosecution and defense, respectively; the tear-choked plea of the humbled defendant; the Solomonic deliberation of the judge; were all parts of a drama played out for the community, but it was a drama for which the community had paid and to which it was entitled.

Sherman's lawyer Bob Muse argued that there was no need to lock the doctor up to deter others, nor in order to punish him. "His despicable, pa-thetic, tragic existence is deterrence enough to anyone who reads the papers." As for punishment, "He doesn't need to be locked up. His mis-ery will be with him forever." Muse asked for probation.

The prosecutor passed quickly from the perjuries themselves, which, she said, "represent only a small part of Dr. Sherman," to the more sordid activities of "this butcher." "Running his abortion mill over fifteen years, he's practiced cheap, cut-corners medicine, which resulted in the death of [the young girl]." She evoked again the image of a fetus-bearing garbage bag thrown into the Chesapeake; a woman "who was drugged and kept against her will in Dr. Sherman's clinic, and after three days had a fetus yanked from her womb"; a woman who was given an abortion without her knowledge, "and lives to this day with the grief of losing a baby she wanted." (I recalled Muse's telling me that the doctor was being scapegoated for performing abortions at all.) She adverted to his censure by a medical society, the revocation of his hospital privileges, his numerous malpractice suits. For this "merciless swindler dressed in a doctor's gown . . . worse than the usual vicious white-collar criminal," she asked five to fifteen years.

Muse got up again: "Your Honor, this man is the most battered, degraded man you'll ever see. In a sense, he's not worth the hypocrisy we're all indulging in."

This contest to see who could say the more damning things about the defendant typified the general scramble as the prosecution and defense tried to outmaneuver each other, a scramble that saw Muse contrast Dr. Sherman with his usual clients, whom he called "the dregs of society," only to have the prosecutor leap to their defense: "What he's talking about are disadvantaged young people from the ghetto. It would be an insult to the community to apply a double standard and not incarcerate him, as so many young people are incarcerated here every day."

Dr. Sherman put in a word for himself, sounding very pathetic. Pudgy and round and bald, he looked like a giant baby. "Judge Ugast, this is a very strange experience for me. I don't understand where I've been, where I am, or where I'm going. I don't understand what's happened. From a life of joy I've moved to a life of humiliation and destruction. I wake up in the middle of the night in a sweat from nightmares. No one can understand the pain, suffering"—he choked back tears—"remorse I feel." He went on to describe his humble beginnings in poverty, his unwavering dedication to medicine, and his hope that the judge would be guided by God. Since he denied any wrongdoing, it was unclear what he felt remorse about. It was apparent that he really *didn't* understand how he had come to judgment. There was something about life, something about causality and morality, that he just *didn't get.*

Judge Ugast called the sentencing decision the most difficult in his five years as a judge. He said he'd studied everything submitted—including more than a hundred letters in support of Dr. Sherman.

In a quiet, calm, friendly voice, he explained that perjury undermines the community's judicial system, and that, therefore, it was a serious offense and that, therefore, he was sentencing Dr. Sherman to from two and a half to seven and a half years in prison.

The judge later granted a defense motion to reduce Dr. Sherman's sentence because of his ill health, and he was paroled after serving fourteen months. Following his release from prison Dr. Sherman resumed the practice of medicine, in Brookline, Massachusetts. In April 1983, the Massachusetts Board of Registration of Medicine revoked his license.

§3-14

Reginald Chatsworth Dickinson, the Georgetown burglar, would sit in my office silently weeping. It was very hard for him to say things straight out, but by answering questions, usually with just a "Yes" or "No," he told me that his mother and her boyfriend were having drunken, violent fights, and he couldn't stand it. But in his sixteen years he'd never been away from home, and the idea of going to a foster home or shelter house of some sort—in the unlikely event that I could get him such a placement—frightened him. He didn't know what to do.

What he did do was commit still more burglaries. Soon after he was put on probation, he was arrested again. I couldn't keep him on the street this time. When the door of the lockup closed behind him, he cried. I don't think he was sorry he'd kept on breaking into houses. He was just sorry that he was locked up, and he probably thought that he didn't deserve it.

§4-01

I had been in business nine months before I had a trial. Most of my cases had been disposed of by pleas or were still in the pipeline, being continued from one trial date to the next, a month at a time, until they would be old enough to be at the head of the list for a trial judge, at which point, if the government's witnesses were still available, we would plead guilty to something. While cases aged, I would have them thoroughly investigated, so that I could explain to my client how his trial would probably go (badly), so that he could reach an informed decision about whether to plead (yes), and not feel that he was being sold down the river. Although it was not my department, I did feel that the likelihood of rehabilitation increased if the defendant felt he had been dealt with fairly by his lawyer and others in the system.

I finally went to trial when I got a client who had nothing to lose by having one. Roberto Lewis, sixteen, had pled guilty before, lots of times, for unauthorized use of vehicles and purse snatches, and had been committed to Oak Hill, the maximum-security juvenile facility. He was awaiting trial on outstanding charges of unauthorized use of a vehicle and carrying a pistol without a license, when he escaped. He remained at large for a year, until he was arrested in *another* stolen car. We were going to trial first on the old U.U.V. and C.P.W.L. case. No matter how it came out, Roberto wasn't coming out.

Roberto Lewis had some unappealing characteristics: a limp handshake; a hunched-over, shuffling walk; a habit of lolling his head from side to side and smiling at you-knew-not-what. The very fact that at sixteen he looked twenty-five was somehow disagreeable. But I liked Roberto because he was intelligent, affable, and responsive. He seemed to trust me right away, and to open up to me—he showed me portraits he had drawn of his girlfriend, a slow-witted young woman with thick eyeglasses who had met him just before his recapture. She sat in the back of the room whenever Roberto appeared in court. The drawings were very true to life.

In the case we were going to try, the police had found a pistol under the seat occupied by Roberto in a stolen car. He told me that he did not know that the car was stolen. Some friends of his had honked at him and offered him a ride. He got in the front seat; his three friends were in the back. The driver was a stranger who could have owned the car, for all Roberto knew. He noticed nothing suspicious about the car. The ignition had not been "popped"; the key was in it. When a police car began to chase them, a boy in the back seat threw a pistol into the front; it bounced off the dash and landed on the transmission hump, and the driver shoved it under the seat, under Roberto.

I went out with Bert Meyers, a gangly young man from Tennessee who was interning as an investigator while waiting for his country music career to take off, to find the boy who Roberto said had thrown the gun. We walked up three flights of unlit stairs in a housing project, knocked, and were admitted into an apartment by three teen-agers, who were sitting around in the dark smoking marijuana. I had some vague plan in mind to have the gunman, who had already pled guilty to U.U.V., and been on and off probation, testify that Roberto had been the last one to get into the car—just to corroborate some part of Roberto's story. (It is always helpful to have another witness corroborate *any* part, however, minor, of your client's story, to convey the idea that it is not made up out of whole cloth.) This plan of mine stopped making sense to me about the time the apartment door closed behind us and we found ourselves standing beyond the law with the gunman. Our plan didn't make much sense to him, either. He said he would be happy to help Roberto, so long as it did not involve going anywhere near the courthouse. My investigator and I were allowed to leave.

The only defense witness would be Roberto.

The night before his trial, I sat down with Roberto and went over his story. I read to him what he had told me originally. I then asked him questions designed to elicit that story at trial.

Rehearsing witnesses is not only proper, but absolutely necessary to effective representation. You are not allowed to use leading questions in the direct examination of your own witnesses, as you are in cross-examining "hostile" (adverse) witnesses. A leading question is one that suggests to the witness the answer that is desired. "You didn't know the driver, did you?" is leading. "Did you know the driver?" is arguably leading because it identifies a material fact and is answerable by "Yes" or "No." You're supposed to ask your witness something like, "Who was in the car?" If you haven't rehearsed, he won't know what you're getting at, and his story won't come out. As Clint Levine taught us at NYU, "On direct, you want him to respond to the question, to tell something, not just answer 'Yes' or 'No' to questions he doesn't understand—that's for cross-examination."

Before rehearsing your witness's testimony, it is proper to *prompt* him as to what the testimony should include. *He* doesn't know what's important; you're the lawyer. You have to explain the legal significance of certain facts. For example, if a defendant charged with burglary is asked by his lawyer simply, "What happened?" he is likely to omit the fact that he was drunk, since getting drunk is widely thought to be "bad." But if the lawyer says, "Burglary carries a sentence of up to thirty years. Unlawful entry carries a sentence of no more than six months. It's burglary if you go into the house *with the intent* to commit a crime inside. Otherwise it's unlawful entry. So if you were too drunk to be intending anything, it's unlawful entry. Now, what happened?" the client is likely to tell the truth about his drinking. Moreover, the client is now marginally closer to standing on the same footing as a John Mitchell or a Maurice Stans facing criminal charges. He knows all there is to know, and he should know no less.

(On the prosecution side, once apprised by the D.A. of the legal requirements for the admissibility of evidence, police are able to recall, with stunning consistency, that evidence seized by them was "dropped" by the defendant, or was "in plain view," rather than found in the course of an illegal search, which would cause the evidence to be thrown out of court.)

I reminded Roberto that he was guilty of unauthorized use of a vehicle only if he knew or should have known that the car was stolen. He was a quick study. He remembered to include the important points—about the key and not knowing the driver. But we ran into a problem about the gun.

"Okay. The police are chasing you. Then what happened?"

Roberto looked away and smiled, as though embarrassed.

"You know, about the gun," I prompted. "When I ask 'And then what happened?' that's when you tell about the guy in the back seat tossing the gun in front."

"I can't say that," Roberto said, shaking his head and smiling his sheepish smile.

"Why not?"

"The dude would kill me. He's always got a gun. I can't say he's got a gun."

"I see. That *is* a problem," I said. I paused for a moment, not so much thinking as letting something well up inside me. "Well, you know, Roberto, when I talked to you the first time and you told me about the gun, you'd just been arrested; you'd been up all night; you were in the lockup; you were probably tired and confused. Maybe you weren't thinking clearly? Maybe you remembered wrong? Maybe if you think about it now, you'll remember that you never knew anything about the gun? Maybe you don't know whose it was? Maybe you don't know where it came from? Maybe the first time you saw it was when the police took it from under the seat?"

Roberto closed his eyes, put his hand to his forehead, and thought for a moment. "Yeah, I don't know nothing about that gun."

"Fine," I said.

The *Code of Professional Responsibility* prohibits a lawyer from "participat[ing] in the creation or preservation of evidence when he knows or it is obvious that the evidence is false."[1] I didn't *know* what had happened with the gun in that car. Still, I felt a little queasy about possibly encouraging perjury, and said so, to another lawyer.

"If it makes you feel any better," he responded, "you probably aren't getting your client to lie. You're getting him to *stop* lying, or, at worst, to switch from one lie to another, if he chooses to do so."

The trial went rather well. The government attempted to introduce a bullet found wedged into the passenger's side of the front seat, where Roberto had been sitting, but I objected that I had never been told about it, in violation of the rule of discovery requiring the prosecution to disclose to the defense any physical evidence that it intends to introduce. The judge suppressed the bullet, in effect directing himself to forget about it. (This being a juvenile trial, there was no jury.) Roberto testified flawlessly, and the government couldn't rebut anything he said.

The government didn't prove to *my* satisfaction that Roberto knew the car was stolen, or that the gun was in it. The judge, however, perhaps relying on some sixth sense, found Roberto guilty of both charges.

Roberto was sent back to Oak Hill, where he would have remained anyway because of his prior convictions and pending charges.

I felt like a real lawyer. I had had a trial.

§4-02

To my dismay, my daily work did not immediately change to reflect my experience and stature. The next time I picked up cases, I was assigned one client who had been arrested for being a "fugitive from institution" and another arrested for "failure to appear" at a court hearing. A colleague asked me if I'd gotten anything interesting. "No, just more garbage," I said. It seemed I'd never get any murders, or even attempted murders.

It turned out that the fugitive from institution (Children's Detention Center, Milwaukee) was Patricia Dawn Princetter, a.k.a. Sandy Jones, a.k.a. Patricia Golden. I recognized her as the blond girl I had seen in court the previous week, when she had been picked up for streetwalking. She was to have been returned to Milwaukee, where she had been facing trial on other prostitution charges before she came to D.C.

Patricia told me that she *was* put on a plane to Milwaukee, but just before arrival she went into the plane's restroom, changed clothes, and put on a dark curly-haired wig. She walked off straight past the cops waiting to meet her and called her pimp from the airport. He put her on the next plane back to Washington. She was rearrested soon after.

To maintain absolute control over their "girls," pimps need to keep them away from friends and family. Also, when a girl gets arrested repeatedly in a given city, the pimp has to post higher and higher bail to get her back on the street. So pimps move their girls on "circuits" from city to city. Patricia was on "the Great Northern Route."

Patricia had recently turned fifteen.

She looked younger. At five foot three, ninety-eight pounds, with her button nose and pink lipstick smeared over her lips, she looked like a little girl playing house who had gotten into her mommy's makeup.

She was near tears in the cell. I asked if she wanted me to leave her alone for a minute. She said no, took a big sniffle, and got hold of herself.

We went in front of the judge, who ordered that she be returned to Milwaukee (again) within five days. Even as the judge was entering his order, someone from the United States attorney's office sidled up to Patricia and handed her a subpoena to appear the next day before the grand jury that was investigating pimping in Washington.

The Bicentennial celebration had prompted a lot of pimps to add Washington to their circuits. With the heightened competition in the prostitution industry came a rash of "loyalty"-enforcement violence by pimps against their girls, including three murders. The murderers were commonly known, but the cases against them were not provable in court because the prostitute witnesses were intimidated. A unit of six detectives and one assistant United States attorney was assigned full time to develop and present evidence of violations of D.C.'s "pandering" (pimping) law to the grand jury.

Four hundred women arrested on prostitution charges were interviewed. Although most professed love for their pimps and refused to say anything against them, the grand jury did learn that many women were being coerced into prostitution. Pimps commonly forced their girls into drug dependency, assaulted them, and took all their money so that they had no way to leave.

As she was led away to be taken to the Receiving Home, where juveniles detained for brief periods were held, Patricia asked me whether she should talk to the grand jury. Since I had no idea, I whispered to her that I would call her in the morning about that.

I sought advice from other P.D.S. attorneys. "Don't let her testify," one said. "She could be killed for informing on her pimp." My supervisor suggested that I find out what my *client* wanted to do.

I called her up. "If you testified, would your pimp beat you up?"

"Oh, no, he'd never hurt me. He'd have one of his friends do it."

It is in the nature of the English language that no amount of analysis of the preceding two sentences yields any basis for discerning whether Patricia was describing her pimp's habitual behavior in the past or predicting what it would be in the future, or both.

Patricia tended to be vague. And she happened to be dealing with me during one of the rare but not unheard-of periods when my mind was encircled by a wall of weariness that no amount of coffee could breach. All that was clear was that she wanted me to decide for her what to do—not an unreasonable desire, considering that I was bigger, older, better dressed, not locked up, paid to give advice, and presumably privy to arcane information about which she could not dare to guess.

I explained her situation and her choices. She could say she would plead the Fifth Amendment—refuse to testify because it could get her in trouble—and the prosecutor wouldn't even bother to bring her in to the grand jury. Or she could testify and in return get a letter from the U.S. attorney to the Milwaukee judge, recommending leniency for her.

"You're a pretty wild kid, right?" I asked. "Sometimes you do something one minute that you didn't think of the minute before? Am I right?"

"Yeah."

"Well, you better stop and think about this seriously. If you're ever coming back to Washington, you better not testify."

"Oh, no, I'm not coming back."

Assuming she really wasn't coming back to D.C., I figured the danger to her should be minimal. (Later it occurred to me that this made no sense, since her pimp's operation covered Milwaukee as well.) Anyway, *she* didn't seem to be frightened. I recommended that she testify. That's what she decided to do.

(This was bad advice. Testifying put her at some risk, whether minimal or not. And there was nothing in it for her. I can't imagine that the Milwaukee authorities would have viewed her as anything but a victim, whether she testified or not. My rage at the pimp distorted my judgment. Lawyers try to be emotionally detached *for a reason.*)

"I see you've dressed up for the occasion," I almost said when Patricia was delivered to testify the next afternoon. She was wearing what looked like a 1920's flapper dress: white satin, bare shoulders, fringe hanging down over the bust.

We sat down in Assistant U.S. Attorney Mary Cipriani's office with three cops: a black defensive tackle in a straw cap; a white yokel with Wildroot-pasted hair and buck teeth; and a mod squad roller named Flaherty. All three were wearing shoulder holsters with big gun butts sticking out. Flaherty, in his mid-thirties, with shoulder-length red-blond hair combed up and across a bald spot in front, and crinkly lines around his eyes from constant grinning, seemed to be the leader. He smiled as he talked to Patricia, as though we were all in this together. I felt an instant distrust of Flaherty. I didn't know who or what he really was.

These cops, three of six assigned full-time to the pimping investigation, were there to question Patricia while she waited her turn in front of the grand jury. Flaherty, who'd been sitting with his feet on the U.S. attorney's desk, leaned forward, pen to paper. He asked Patricia how she met her pimp.

"I met him at a bus stop."

"What'd he say?"

"He said, 'Come here.' "

"What did you say?"

"I said, 'No, you come here.' "

The pimp asked her to come home with him. She went.

"Why?"

"To see what he was about." When she got there, she met his ladies. "I knew right away he was a pimp."

"How'd you know?"

"The girls told me."

She lived with him for three weeks.

"Did you have sex with him?" Flaherty asked.

"Not during that time."

"Sounds like a very patient man."

"*I* was very patient." Patricia broke into uncontrollable giggles. "Stop looking at me!" she said. "Why are all of you looking at me?"

I was not. I was reading a newspaper clipping on the wall about a woman's life in a massage parlor.

"You feel like a *star*, huh?" Flaherty said.

"What?"

"You feel like a star. The spotlight is on you."

She just wanted people to stop looking at her. The black cop put his head down and stared at his lap. From time to time during the questioning, he sighed. Maybe he was just tired. Could he possibly still be touched by this? The other white cop sat looking at the ceiling.

Patricia came to Washington with her pimp, who got her a hotel room. He told her "not to mess with young dudes."

Flaherty asked her whether the pimp said not to turn dates with blacks. She said no, he didn't say that. Assistant U.S. Attorney Cipriani, who'd just walked in, looked at Flaherty quizzically. He said, "Well, we just had one in here the other day whose pimp told her not to turn dates with blacks."

He asked Patricia whether the pimp told her to use rubbers.

"Oh, I'd do that anyway, for my own self."

Her first night she made $200.

"How much did you make on average?"

No answer.

"Did you ever make two hundred fifty dollars?"

"Yes."

"Ever make less than two hundred dollars?"

"Yes, sometimes one hundred fifty."

"What was average?"

No answer. She didn't know what "average" meant.

"How much of the money did the pimp let you keep?"

"A half."

"He let you keep one hundred out of two hundred?"

"No, about fifty—for clothes, food, anything I wanted."

"That's more like a quarter, right?" Ms. Cipriani said.

Patricia smiled and giggled self-consciously. "Yes."

Cipriani figured Patricia worked thirty days at $200—that would be $6,000 she made.

It was time to go in to the grand jury. Patricia rose, smiled, took a deep breath. She was nervous. Opening night, school play. "Give 'em hell," I said.

The cops and I chatted about prostitution. "Washington is wide open," Flaherty said. "You can start in the prostitution business any time you want. In Chicago, for instance, you'd get constant hassles from organized crime, unless you knew somebody. In D.C., the only hassle you get, to the extent it is a hassle, is from the police."

In fifteen minutes, Patricia returned. Ms. Cipriani said she did fine.

Patricia said she wanted to talk to me. We stepped across the hall into an empty office.

"What's going to happen to me?"

"I don't know your record. I don't know how the Milwaukee courts work. So I can't say."

She looked at the floor.

"All right. Look. Here's what's going to happen. You're going to get on a plane to Milwaukee. You'll be picked up and taken to some kind of holding . . ."

"Detention Center."

"Right. You'll wait there until you come to trial."

"I couldn't stand it if it was like four weeks."

"Well, tell your Milwaukee lawyer that. I'd say you'll probably plead guilty to something."

"That's right."

"And there's no reason to delay that. Why wait? Plead guilty tomorrow. Then the judge will get a letter from the U.S. attorney here, saying you were helpful. And he'll figure, 'I guess she really wants to go straight.' And your lawyer will put together some kind of counseling program to help you. The judge will go along with it. No one wants to *punish* you. The judge will say [I shook my finger], 'Now listen here, young lady . . .'"

She smiled, giggled, shook her own finger. " 'Listen here,' " she imitated.

"But listen, there will be some bad times. You probably don't get along with your mother that well . . ."

"No, it was my father I had trouble with."

"But he's gone?"

"He's deceased."

"Well, you may find it difficult getting along at home after you've been out in the world. And it'll be hard sometimes at the Detention Center. But if you know there'll be hard times, and you expect them, then when they happen, it'll be just like watching an old movie."

She hugged herself and smiled, saying, "Oh, I expected this," practicing.

"Listen, you've had some interesting experiences."

She just looked at me.

"Well, it hasn't been dull, has it?"

"No," she admitted.

"Fine. You've had some interesting times. Now you can put it behind you and get on with your life, make some kind of life for yourself. Okay?"

"Okay," she said.

We went back across the hall. I insisted that she get her thirty-dollar witness fee, but Cipriani said it was too late and suggested I get it for her the next day.

"Do you trust me with your money?" I asked Patricia.

She smiled. "Sure, you're s'posed to be my lawyer. Do you have a dollar so I can get some cigarettes up the Receiving Home?" she asked tentatively. "Then you can take one dollar out of the thirty dollars you're getting for me."

I gave her a dollar.

I kept thinking of the last paragraph of the signed statement she gave the police when she was first arrested.

> Q. What do you want to do now?
> A. I want to get home and be with my mother, if that would ever be possible.

The grand jury indicted twenty men, including "Gizmo," "Delicious," "Reds," "Ricky Love," and "Scooby-doo," for violating the pandering law. Eleven pled guilty. One had his pimping case dismissed in return for a plea in another case. The cases of five others were dismissed because of the unavailability of witnesses. One defendant disappeared. The body of one, Scooby-doo, was found with barbells tied to it in a Florida bay. And one was found not guilty after trial.

In the summer of 1978, before the offensive against pimps, there were, by police estimate, 300 prostitutes on the streets of Washington in a typical twenty-four-hour period. A year later, after the indictments, that number had fallen to 200. Within a year after that, street prostitution had returned to its former level, according to the U.S. attorney's office.

§4-03

After nearly a year of handling juvenile cases, I began representing adults.

Roberto Lewis, whom I had unsuccessfully defended on a charge of carrying a pistol without a license, had immediately escaped (again) from Oak Hill. A few weeks later, the assistant corporation counsel who had beaten me at that juvenile trial stopped me in the hallway to share what he seemed to consider exciting and amusing news. Roberto had been arrested for first-degree murder with a handgun. If I had *won* the gun possession case, this would have been occasion for some soul-searching, but as it was, my principal reaction was excitement at the slight possibility that I could get to defend Roberto on the murder charge, which would be prosecuted "upstairs," in criminal court, before a jury. (The U.S. attorney had exercised his discretion to prosecute Roberto, who was now seventeen, as an adult.) I tore a small item noting the murder out of the newspaper. Perhaps there would be more to come.

I related the prosecutor's version of the murder to a couple of attorneys back at my office.

"Roberto comes up to a stranger on the street, pulls a gun, and says, 'Give me that camera.' And the guy says, 'No, you'll have to shoot me first.' So he shoots him."

"Well, the guy asked for it," one lawyer said.

"Hell yes, certainly," said the other.

We all laughed.

A private attorney was appointed to handle Roberto's murder case, but Roberto's mother called me to say that she didn't like him. He hadn't contacted her, and she didn't even know his name. She wanted *me* to try to take over the case.

I wrote letters for both Roberto and his mother, requesting the judge to appoint me in place of the current lawyer, who, in fact, had earned a reputation as perhaps the laziest, sleaziest, and most ineffective lawyer in the jurisdiction, which was not an easy title to hold.

My supervisor agreed to try to get me the case. I checked in with him one day to see if he'd made any progress. He said he'd been trying to reach the court-appointed lawyer, to convince him to withdraw, or at least accept our assistance.

"Here, I'll call him right now," he said, reaching for the phone. "This action shouldn't be taken to imply that I haven't been doing this right along," he hastened to add, in his lawyerly way.

"Is Mr. Sandstone there?" he said into the phone. "Oh. Well, would you tell him that—oh, you know it's me? And you *will* tell him I called? Okay. Thanks." He hung up and looked at me. "Every time I call, I get this woman who sounds like I've jarred her out of a narcotic stupor. She always tells me he's not there in such a way that it's perfectly obvious that he's sitting about six feet away from her with a needle hanging out of his arm."

I asked him to keep trying. If I could just get this case . . .

§4-04

It being October, Jan and I drove to the Maine Avenue waterfront to buy Chincoteague oysters. Oysters from that particular little Virginia bay are so far superior to ordinary oysters, so much firmer in texture and more delicate in taste, that it's not quite adequate to call them terrific oysters; they leave oysterness behind, transcend oysterdom entirely, and are really something different altogether: they are Chincoteagues.

For reasons having to do with their reproductive cycle and our calendar, you can eat Chincoteagues only in months whose names contain an R. September being the first such month after a four-month hiatus, it usually slips by before you have a chance to remember your old dining habits, and it's October when you head down to the fish pier.

As we drove along the Potomac, I pointed out two motor yachts tied alongside each other stem to stern, a configuration that struck me as vaguely obscene. But then, everything about yachts in the Potomac rubbed me the wrong way, and I noted with satisfaction that the self-satisfied fools aboard those boats had undoubtedly never been to the Maine Avenue fish market, which had not been declared chic by the Washington *Post* and therefore did not exist, so far as the great majority of white Washingtonians were concerned.

Jan and I enjoyed the poetry of the place:

Pruitts
Seafood Is the Best
We Carry a Line that Tops the Rest
Food Stamps Accepted

Seafood Delights
From Captain Whites

The fish were sold right off the decks of the half-dozen big boats tied up at the pier. They had every kind of fish imaginable, arranged in schools according to their kind, frozen in mid-swim atop oceans of ice, eyes wide with outrage, mouths downturned in anger: "Jumbo Croakers, Giant Blues, Large Butters, Boston Mackerel, Pan Trout, Red Snappers, White Bass, Spanish Mackerel, Fresh Pompanos"—one modifier per fish. It was an orderly world, except for the struggling masses of live blue-clawed crabs heaped in bushel baskets, which looked like crab hell. I asked one of the Virginia watermen how you could tell the males from the females, a necessary point of information for certain recipes, such as she-crab soup.

"Now, here's a female," he said, as he picked one up in his gloved hand and showed me its belly. "What's that blue marking look like to you?"

"The Capitol dome," I said. There was nothing else to say—it might as well have been a picture postcard.

"Right," the fisherman said approvingly. He tossed that one back and picked up a slightly larger crab. "Now, this one here's a male, see, and if you look at the blue mark on *his* belly . . ."

"Don't tell me it's the Washington Monument!" I said, but there it was, clear as life.

This is the sort of thing that makes Washington the symbolic capital of the nation, in my book. The fish pier itself is a triumph of imagery. None of those boats have put to sea in fifteen years. Early each morning, trucks pull up to the dock and unload the fish, which are then loaded onto the boats. But they are beyond doubt the freshest fish in Washington, you buy them right at the pier, and it *is* a fishing pier. See the boats? See the water?

Most people didn't know what I knew about one of the boats: it had been the scene, several years earlier, of a spectacular multiple-victim machete murder. I shared this info with Jan—she liked local color, too. Just about anywhere I went in Washington, I knew of some crime that had happened there. I moved about in a criminal landscape.

§4-05

You never see sentencings on Perry Mason, but most defendants do end up being sentenced, and it's at the sentencing stage that the lawyer gets his best opportunity to help these clients.*

Sentencing is the least just, most arbitrary stage of the criminal justice system. Different judges give widely varying sentences for the same offense; even the same judge gives different sentences for the same offense

---

* The whole famous murder "trial" of Leopold and Loeb consisted of the sentencing hearing, of several weeks' duration, which followed their pleas of guilty.

to different defendants; sometimes a trend sweeps through the courthouse and all the judges start hitting harder, as when a high-profile murder has aroused the community; at other times, they all lighten up—around Christmas, for instance.

I had one client who was sentenced to probation for shooting someone, whereas another client got nine years simply for *carrying* a pistol without a license. The client who got probation had lent some money to a friend so that he could "pay his rent," and shot him—not fatally—in anger when he learned that he had actually used the money to buy dope. The judge apparently shared my view that the shootee was the bad guy, and that the defendant, who had never been in trouble before and was a Vietnam veteran, was the good guy. (I thought, and judges seemed to agree, that the government owed at least one break to anyone who had served in Vietnam.) The fellow who got nine years had committed armed offenses in the past, and had the misfortune to be sentenced by a notoriously draconian judge. One client benefited from "judicial discretion"; the other suffered from it.

Some jurisdictions are experimenting with mandatory sentencing, whereby a specific offense carries a specific sentence, which judges have no power to vary. In addition to its obvious drawback—you can't fit the punishment to the criminal—mandatory sentencing causes systemic problems: defendants can't get a reduced sentence in exchange for pleading to certain offenses, so they insist on trials, jamming up the system; where the mandatory sentence is stiff, juries may refuse to convict. A compromise being considered is "presumptive" sentencing, whereby a certain penalty is automatic unless the judge gives a written reason for varying it.

Convicted criminals develop an extreme sensitivity to what is "fair," and a great deal of antisocial rage is attributable to one convict's watching another man convicted of the same offense walk out of prison years before he does. The situation is exacerbated by the parole system. In Washington, the judge explicitly states a minimum period to be served before parole eligibility, which cannot be more than one third of the maximum sentence, but can be less: people get sentences of "five to fifteen," of "five to twenty," or of "fifteen to life." Once the minimum time has been served, the prisoner's fate is in the hands of the parole board.

Parole was originally instituted as a liberal reform, to motivate rehabilitation, but in practice it is administered so inequitably—at the whim of unelected, inexpert parole boards—that prisoners themselves widely favor flat, determinate sentences, so that they would know in advance exactly how much time they had to do. Of course, restrictions on parole eliminate a valuable safety valve for alleviating prison overcrowding.

It's not surprising that there is so much debate about sentencing, because there is no general agreement about what incarceration is *for;* many inmates have never committed a violent crime, and those who have are often more dangerous when they come out than when they went in. Although the options are more limited in juvenile cases, the sentences are just as capricious. Amid all the confusion, one can state with confidence that absolutely anything can happen at sentencing.

Usually by the time of the sentencing hearing the judge has made up his mind, influenced, one hopes, by the memorandum the defense attorney has submitted recommending a particular program, other than incarceration, perfectly suited to his client's unique background and needs. Occasionally, however, particularly in run-of-the-mill cases to which he has not devoted a great deal of thought, the judge can be pushed to a desired decision by an effective presentation at the hearing itself.

Just before Thanksgiving, Leon Lincoln, one of my first juvenile clients, came before Judge McCord for sentencing on a shoplifting charge for which he'd been convicted at trial in August. Things didn't look too good for Leon. He was already on probation when he decided to help himself to a natty beige velour shirt at Hecht's department store, only to be caught in the act. That was the fifth bust in our mutual career. He was always stealing things. Like most of my juvenile clients, he stole not to buy food, not to pay heat or rent, but so he could *have* something, so he could *be* somebody—and because he seemed to think that's what was expected of him. It was only thanks to bureaucratic bungling that he was still on the street. His files were constantly being bounced back and forth between the judge supervising his probation and Judge McCord, who'd be sentencing him on this latest case; and at a few critical junctures the files were misplaced altogether, so that nothing at all could be done and he remained free.

Judge McCord was a diminutive man with judicial gray hair, some of which fell over his eyes when he flew into a rage, which he did every morning, first thing. This propensity for fury spoke well for him. He did not regard himself as the king, by divine right, of his court, as did too many of his judicial colleagues, once they donned the mystical black robes with which they were "invested" upon becoming judges. He considered himself a public servant with a job to do, and he was enraged when his efforts were frustrated, as they were every day.

This day he was angry because he saw that he was slated to handle the impossible total of sixty-five cases, and he got angrier when he saw that probation officer Delores Stone, despite his order to her to prepare an in-depth report on Leon Lincoln, had submitted, minutes before he took the bench, a hastily typed rehash of her previous reports.

Delores Stone did not mean, but be. She did nothing, and her awesome inertia made the idea of ever getting her to do anything, even go away, an impossible dream.

"There doesn't seem to be any mention at all in your report of any suggestions from Mr. Kunen. Didn't he communicate with you?"

"Your Honor," I interjected, "*before* I committed my ideas for a sentencing program to writing, I called up Ms. Stone and told her the ideas, and asked her for any criticism, any feedback, any suggestion, any input, asked her if there was anything I might do to assist her . . ." I could tell I was really rolling, by the ease with which the redundancies tripped off my tongue. Redundancies give a speech momentum, and lend a certain *legal* flavor to otherwise bland palaver.

"And what did Ms. Stone say?" the judge asked me while Ms. Stone sat, as she always sat, idly by.

"I would characterize her response as 'noncommittal,' Your Honor," I said. In fact, she was, as always, hostile, and had refused to discuss the matter, but I thought the dignified and understated "noncommittal" would get across the idea of her uncooperativeness without revealing that I couldn't stand her, which would only raise clouds of suspicion over everything I said.

Ms. Stone's only recommendation was that Leon be locked up at the Children's Center. "I don't have any illusions about the Children's Center," she said, "but we've run out of options. You can't sit down with him and say, 'You have to behave. There are better ways to deal with your problems than committing crimes.' It's not going to work."

"Your Honor, I completely agree with Ms. Stone," I said. "Just warning Leon isn't going to help."

I looked at Leon, a bantamweight boxer who once broke his girlfriend's nose, and I saw what a punk he really was, thought of his unending protestations of innocence to me, his taking me for a fool. I was fed up with him, past fed up.

"For the last four years Leon's been leading his life as a first-class jerk. Somebody offers him a stolen ring—he takes it. Somebody says, 'You want to go for a ride?'—he knows the car is stolen, but he doesn't say no. He's a jerk. We all know the type."

Judge McCord was nodding affirmation. All I heard in the courtroom was my own voice. "He goes into Hecht's, he wants a shirt, he's not going to pay for it like other people—no—he'll break the tag off and steal it. He's a jerk. He's a wise guy." Leon was gaping at me as though he had just realized his lawyer was a monster from outer space.

"But what do we do with wise guys?" I continued. "We have a choice with Leon: we can lock him up for two years, but he'll come out again, and I don't have to tell the court that he won't be the same when he comes out as when he went in. Or we can take advantage of the community counseling and training programs which are represented by the people who've come to court with us today, and try to make him a productive member of the community." I had assembled no less than three social workers from three different organizations, each ready to oversee some aspect of Leon's reconstruction.

Leon's father and two brothers were also in the courtroom. "You're lucky to have a loving family, who care enough about you to come down to court," Judge McCord said. "Why can't you be like them?" What the judge didn't know was that they had to be in court anyway, as witnesses in one of Leon's brother's criminal cases.

Because he'd been presented with "no real alternative," because Leon had such a concerned family, and because his crimes had been against property, not people, Judge McCord agreed to postpone sentencing while we tried my program for forty-five days; then if it wasn't working, he'd lock him up.

When we came back in January, Judge McCord found that Leon had not done anything he was supposed to do. But he had by that time turned eighteen, old enough to be treated as an adult if he were arrested again, and too old to benefit from the Children's Center, in Judge McCord's opinion. The judge, declaring that the juvenile justice system had failed in the matter of Leon Lincoln, closed the case.

Looking back on it, I realized that I had stumbled upon a principle in my "He's a Jerk" speech: don't argue for your client, argue for the community. If you take your client's part, the judge will see you, at best, as an advocate speaking from the biased perspective of one side, or, at worst, as the mouthpiece of a criminal. Far better to be an enlightened citizen helping the judge to do his job. What ends do we have in view when we impose sentence? *Deterrence,* of the defendant, specifically, and of others, generally, from committing crimes in the future; and *retribution,* to restore the moral order of society—both achieved through *punishment;* the *incapacitation* of a dangerous individual; and his *rehabilitation,* so that he will not be dangerous anymore. But all of these ends are only means to one transcendent end—the *protection of the community.*

If we avoid sending the miscreant to a character-warping school for crime, but, instead, control his time and mold his experience at home, we can best ensure the safety of the community. *That* is something a judge is *for.* "Giving him a chance," trying to "understand him," or otherwise being soft on crime is something a judge is *against.* So I decided I would always be against it, too.

But I figured the real key to the success of the "He's a Jerk" speech was that I truly believed it. I resolved to work toward the day when I'd be able to sound as though I believed what I was saying when I didn't; or to believe something at will, so that I could speak from conviction. To attain this skill would be to reach the height of the lawyer's art.

§4-06

One character plays a pivotal role in case after case: *the stupid policeman.*

My client Terry White was rousted from his bed at 6:30 A.M. one day in June and arrested on a warrant alleging that he had sold *one gram* of marijuana on a stairway in Anacostia High School in February to an undercover police officer posing as a student. It was after Thanksgiving when we went to trial.

Fortunately, the undercover man, Officer Green, shot himself in the foot, as it were. He had written on the arrest warrant that the Terry White in question was five foot seven. My Terry White was a very lanky six foot three. For good measure, he testified that after the sale, he had arranged to have Terry White lured to the principal's office on some pretext, where he looked at him through a keyhole to make sure he was the person from whom he had bought the drug. He said this occurred on April 16. Terry White, an alert kid, leaned over and whispered to me that he had been locked up in Maryland on April 16.

"Maybe we should give Officer Green the benefit of the doubt," I argued. "Maybe he was confused about the height. Maybe he was confused about the date. But we don't give the benefit of the doubt to the government. The government has to prove beyond a reasonable doubt that Terry White was the five-foot-seven person on the staircase."

The judge delivered his verdict in the pyramid style all judges use— least important things first, keep 'em hanging. Judges love your courtroom drama, too.

"I have no problem with the report of the laboratory chemist. I am convinced that the substance was marijuana." He went on, "I take note of the discrepancy of the description, which says five foot seven, when Terry White is at least six feet."

I'm starting to *pray.* But I say to myself, "I'm not going to pray about this." So I don't pray. But my inclination is to pray. I was desperate to hear the judge say "not guilty," not for Terry White, but for *me.* I was thinking, "I've *got* to win this case," because I had to feel, for the future, that winning was a possibility. If I didn't win this one, my third, where there were so many things wrong with the government's case, I was going to start to feel that I was just going through the motions, knowing I wouldn't win—like the Washington Senators charging out of the dugout, the organist's crescendo failing to still the mournful song within: "God, here we go again."

The judge continued, "I find the government has not discharged its burden of proof beyond a reasonable doubt, and I find the respondent not guilty.

"Young man," he said, "this does not mean that I don't have my suspicions, but I'm allowed to rule only on the evidence before me."

As we strode out of the courtroom, Terry turned to me and said, *"Me? Sell marijuana?"*

§4-07

Once a month I was assigned "duty day."

Duty day was one of P.D.S.'s more onerous tasks, yet, like all hard work, it could occasionally prove rewarding. Whoever was on duty, having failed to trade his day for some other attorney's safely distant future day, had to stay by his desk and answer any and all queries from that bizarre collection of souls known as the general public, whether presented by phone, or, worse, in person. Pensioners called about overdue checks. Federal penitents called from places as distant as dreams, impossible places like "Leavenworth, Kansas," and "La Tuna, Texas," complaining of miscalculated parole dates and unanswered appeals, devastating mistakes that kept them out of the living world, even their voices but briefly free, to be instantly yanked back behind the walls at the click of my phone. Victims of every sort of foul play—by CIA agents, slumlords, uninsured motorists—called seeking redress. And, because the good name (and public funding) of our agency was at stake, and because that's the sort of guys we were, no one was turned away without at least the phone number of someone more appropriate to call.

"I did a stupid thing," one caller told me. "I phoned in a bomb threat to the Iranian Embassy, and the police called me up, and I admitted it to them. And now I really can't afford to be convicted, because I have a top secret, highest priority security clearance. I'd lose my job."

"Even though you've admitted it to the sergeant on the phone," I told him, "don't say anything more to anyone, because what you have said might be thrown out as evidence, because, maybe, technically the sergeant didn't do everything he was supposed to."

"He didn't tell me about my rights or anything," the man said, definitely perking up at the idea of getting off on a "technicality," despite being, in all likelihood, someone who would rail against "criminals" getting off on technicalities. There was new hope in his voice.

It was gratifying for me to have a right-wing hooligan turn in his hour of need to the Public Defender Service. It's probably similar to the feeling a cop has when a public defender calls for help when his house is burglarized.

§4-08

Roberto Lewis's assigned attorney finally withdrew from the camera-murder case, and the judge assigned it to P.D.S. Since I had never handled a jury trial, let alone a murder, my boss put Ken Lloyd, who had five years' experience, on the case with me.

Lloyd, like most of the attorneys who entered P.D.S. in the mid-seventies, and like me, was a product of the late sixties' college "generation." This group tended to enjoy aligning themselves against the state, as defense attorneys do. Outwardly, Lloyd had preserved the trappings of "the Movement"—a beard, longish hair, and laborer's clothing; and inwardly, he had cultivated the bemused, ironic detachment characteristic of those who know they are going to lose most of their battles.

Lloyd and I found Roberto in the lockup behind Judge Davis's courtroom on the day of his arraignment.* When I walked up to the bars Roberto sprang toward me like a puppy in the pound who picks up some scent of possible adoption. I thrust my hand through the bars. Like all of my clients, he did not bend my arm around a bar to the point of breaking it and demand freedom in exchange for letting go, but simply laid his hand limply in mine, like a small dead offering. I shook it and let it drop.

We explained Roberto's situation to him, emphasizing that he would remain locked up for several months pending a trial. A marshal came

---

* The arraignment is the proceeding at which the defendant is formally notified of the charges against him and enters his plea.

through the door from the courtroom with a big brass key in his hand. The key was so big that it was not just a key: it also *meant* "key." It was a symbol, of the marshal's power and the prisoner's plight.

"Lewis," the marshal said. Lloyd and I stood aside, our backs against the wall. You don't get between the marshal and his prisoner.

Roberto was ushered into the courtroom, where he spotted his girlfriend and smiled. Judge Davis, looking almost comically Puritanical with her gray hair pulled back into a lacquered bun, a white bow at her throat accentuating the severity of her black robes, advised Roberto of his rights in her teeny-weeny nasal voice and asked how he pled.

"Mr. Lewis pleads not guilty to all counts, Your Honor, and requests a jury trial," Lloyd said.

Judge Davis daintily blew her nose, glanced at the handkerchief, and put it aside. "Twenty days for motions," she said. "Status date?"

It was agreed that we would return in a month to review the status of the case, and that the trial would be in three months. The marshal took Roberto back through the door.

Several weeks passed before we could arrange a discovery conference with the prosecutor. Discovery conferences were always held in the prosecutor's office, at the prosecutor's convenience. Though required by law to turn over certain information, the prosecutors always acted as though they were doing the defense a favor by doing so, and many of them treated defense attorneys as a king might treat bothersome supplicants, who, likely as not, are going to track cow manure on the carpets. I spent many an hour sitting in a brown vinyl shovel-shaped seat amid the dusty plastic philodendrons in the reception area of the U.S. attorney's office, like a stranded traveler waiting for a plane that's still on the ground in Chicago, wondering why it was that prosecutors never came to see *us* for the discovery conferences. The reason, I concluded, was that all the systemic momentum was on their side. A charge went in one side of the machine, and the ponderous gears would clank, and the pulleys groan, and the conveyor belts clatter until a conviction came out the other end. That was the normal operation of the machine, so the prosecutors wanted to do nothing but let it run. We wanted an abnormal result, so we had to *do* things: stand in the way, distract the operators, grab anything we could find and thrust it into the cogs.

Finally a certain astrological moment obtained, and I found myself with Lloyd in the office of Assistant U.S. Attorney Bruce Penley.

A skinny bald man with narrow stooped shoulders and pallid, sunken cheeks, Penley had the look of an undertaker. His face seemed painfully pinched, his small mouth squeezed below his beaklike nose, his narrow eyes huddled above it.

Lloyd introduced me to Penley. I extended my hand and found it viciously crushed in his pincerlike grip. What was he trying to prove? Before he let go of my hand I had already decided that Penley enjoyed locking people up—and I don't mean seeing that justice triumphed. I mean justice aside, slam, clank, *rot* in there, sucker!

Penley sat behind his desk flipping through his Lewis file in a bored but careful manner, holding it away from us in order that we not read it upside down, something all defense attorneys get good at.

He began by noting that the dead man ("decedent," to us) had been a twenty-four-year-old street vendor, the first and last thing ever said about his life by anybody involved in the case. He was a stick figure, who did not engage our sympathies as did, say, the occasional Georgetown University decedent. It was only his death that interested us.

That death, the medical examiner reported, had been occasioned by massive bleeding resulting from the penetration of the aorta by a .38-caliber slug.

The weapon had not been recovered.

There were no eyewitnesses to the shooting itself, but the state did have "one or more" witnesses who could say that Roberto had been sitting on a porch when the victim walked by carrying a camera. Roberto said to a friend, "Do you want that camera?" and was then seen following the victim. He apparently forced the victim into a nearby wooded area, where the body was found. Witnesses said that he returned ten minutes later with the camera, a watch and seven dollars. He gave the camera to the friend, and the police now had it. Another witness, who gave Roberto a ride later in the day, said that Roberto showed him a handgun.

Two police detectives, starting out with no leads at all, had questioned dozens of people in the vicinity of the woods where the body was found. Somebody told them the nickname of a young man who had said that his cousin had robbed someone in that area. The detectives had only the nickname of the young man, and no name for the cousin; but they found the young man, and he named his cousin—Roberto Lewis. The police showed a photo of Roberto around the neighborhood until someone told them where to find him. They arrested him three days after the shooting. Except for its speed, it had been a fairly typical investigation: a boast, a snitch, and a lot of shoe leather.

Following his arrest, Roberto signed two written statements. Penley gave us copies. The first was a rambling, internally inconsistent alibi, which was at best useless, since Roberto said he was alone, drinking a quart of Old English malt liquor outside a 7-Eleven at the crucial time.

(An alibi is no good without alibi *witnesses.*) The second was a confession, begun at four A.M., the traditional hour for confessions, whether to one-self or to officers of the law. In it, Roberto said that he had pulled a gun on the man only to scare him, but had himself become scared when the man came at him with a karate kick, and had fired, lest the man wrest the gun from him and kill him. Unfortunately for the equities of the case, Roberto's terror immediately subsided, and, he said, he went through the dead man's pockets and removed his wallet and watch, not forgetting the camera.

This added up to first-degree murder,* armed robbery, and carrying a pistol without a license, the first charge carrying a mandatory minimum sentence of twenty years to life.

Penley sat there glinting like a gold tooth. His wire glasses shone, as did his college ring, turned inward on his bony finger, as did the steel expansion band of his watch, which he wore on the pulse side of his left wrist—he checked it frequently as he talked to us. Even the clip on the black Skilcraft–U.S. Government ballpoint shone like polished sterling. Oh, to beat this guy!

Walking back across the street with Lloyd, I told him that I loved this case because it was impossible, yet we would win it! I dreamed of winning the unwinnable case, because then, and only then, could I be sure that it was my work, rather than the evidence, that won it.

He agreed that was what defense attorneys strive for, and recalled how a colleague, one time, had spent fifteen minutes holding up the defendant's coal-black raincoat—the perpetrator had worn black—telling the jury it was blue.

"And he won?"

"No."

§4-09

I picked up cases on Christmas Day. When I had gone to bed on Christmas Eve, it was raining torrentially. When I got up Christmas morning, the sky was a brilliant blue; the sun shone horizontally, tinting everything gold. The streets were wet, clean, and empty. It was a beautiful morning, and I felt like a beautiful person, going to the aid of (alleged)

---

* Under D.C. law, any killing, even if accidental, committed in perpetrating or attempting to perpetrate a robbery is murder in the first degree (22 D.C. Code 2401).

thieves on this of all days. I hoped I might get some family violence— Christmas hysteria. I wasn't disappointed.

A thirty-five-year-old mechanic in a neatly pressed red flannel shirt sat in the lockup, pensively wringing his callused hands. He had never been arrested in all his life, until he shot and wounded his brother on Christmas Eve. I didn't ask why he'd done it, but I had my ideas. Ugly necktie? Turkey overdone again?

The judge let him out pending trial, on condition that he not live with his brother. "But it's *my* house," he said to me as we walked out of the courtroom. "My brother lives with me. I have to get out of *my own* house?"

I could see the injustice in that, and assured him he need stay away only until he got his brother to leave.

For the moment, he said, his brother was in intensive care in the hospital.

"Well, then, there's no problem, is there?" I said. I liked that. The problem had given birth to its own solution. It seemed almost miraculous.

§4-10

K-*pong*-cha, k-*pong*-cha, k-*pong*-cha . . .

Our bed shook us awake each morning as it bounced with the blows of the pile driver in the back yard. I had watched in helpless horror as a bulldozer murdered my tomato plants, clearing the way for "James Place," seventy-seven "distinguished residences" where our garden used to grow. The Federalist row house Jan and I rented would soon be walled in on three sides by mammoth condominiums, an innocent little house from the nineteenth century imprisoned in the twentieth. I was powerless to resist the iron will of the speculators, the banks, the *Republicans.* Such was life in Georgetown.

Daily I made my escape to Court World, where reality was malleable, and I could at least try to bend it to *my* will, make two and two equal five, on a good day.

Deception is not deceit. Lawyers and magicians practice deception. Dishonest people practice deceit.

I utilized two classic forms of deception in Norman Trumpet's trial—

saying something that wasn't true, and not saying something that was. They were both perfectly ethical. The learned hand is quicker than the eye.

My client Norman, and his co-respondent, Steve Thomas, were charged with receiving stolen property. The police happened upon Norman and Steve in an alley transferring a stereo and TV from a junked car into the back seat of a white Pontiac.

The case hinged on whether our clients knew (or should have known) that the property was stolen. It was in this connection that I learned the Lesson of the Keys, which, mnemonically enough, happens to be the key lesson there is to learn about the lawyer's art: forget what you know, argue the evidence.

When Norman borrowed his cousin's Pontiac, he had told us, he was given only the ignition key, not the trunk key. But when all the evidence was in, no mention had been made of that fact. At Steve Thomas's lawyer's suggestion, we made what was to me, at that time, a novel and shocking argument: *obviously* Steve and Norman had no idea that the property was stolen, else why would they have been loading it into the Pontiac's back seat, instead of concealing it in the trunk?

The judge let that alone when he delivered the verdict. He convicted them of receiving stolen property. He decided to lock Steve Thomas up pending sentencing because Steve had another case awaiting trial and so seemed to pose a threat of running or raising havoc. He then turned his attention to my client. I knew that Norman's D.C. record was just an expired probation for a robbery four years before, but that he was *currently* on probation in Maryland for *carrying a gun.* The judge asked, "And what is Mr. Trumpet's record?" I stood quietly for a long two seconds. "Just probation in 1976," the prosecutor said. I thought about correcting him. Then I thought I'd stay out of it.

"Okay, he can go," the judge said.

In the hallway, Norman, wide-eyed, asked, "How come you didn't tell him about my probation?"

"I figured he didn't ask me," I said.

"And if he did ask you, you would have had to tell him the truth?"

"That's right," I said.

Norman seemed very impressed, as much with my speculative honesty as with my actual silence—with my *integrity,* I guess.

Back in the office, Ken Lloyd said my silence was "a close call," but he'd have done the same thing. His officemate said it wasn't even close: "It's not your job to get up and say bad things about your client. How would you like it if your lawyer did that?"

I checked the *Code of Professional Responsibility* and learned that I *could not* tell the judge my client's record if I knew of it from my client's having told me, because that would be a breach of confidentiality. On the other hand, *if* the judge asked me directly and I knew of the record from some independent source—as I always would, from looking it up—I would have to answer truthfully.

Norman Trumpet failed to appear for his sentencing.

§4-11

I'd managed to get free from court for a couple of hours and was looking forward to clearing my desk of the dozen files strewn about it like wrecked ships on a reef. But first, I stopped in to commiserate with the lawyer across the hall. The woman he had hired to take care of his disabled mother had embezzled his mother's funds. (I understood. I was representing a nurse who had done exactly the same thing to her employer, a young woman afflicted with multiple sclerosis.) At my colleague's suggestion, I resisted the urge to do paperwork and, instead, went over to court to watch a little of "the Butcher-Knife Trial."

The Butcher-Knife Trial was acclaimed throughout the courthouse as "a great case." Mystery, intrigue, passion, and colorful characters were important, but the more gory a case was, the more likely it was to be considered "a great case." The Butcher-Knife Trial was a particularly great case because of the butcher knife: a woman walking down the street with a twelve-inch knife sticking in her neck and out her cheek! I found a seat in the packed courtroom beside one of the courthouse regulars, an aged derelict in a filthy green herringbone tweed jacket. He, like a number of other street people, sought shelter and diversion at trials every day, but today his unshaven face bore an especially satisfied look—he'd found a good one.

A handsome young police officer was testifying that he came upon this skewered woman as she stood in the street, naked except for a bloody blanket clutched around her, hailing a taxi. He stopped his scout car and helped her into a cab, and told the cab driver that he would lead him to the hospital. "As we started off, I heard a call on my radio for an 'officer-in-trouble' at Euclid Street. So I turned off in that direction. I parked outside and ran upstairs, and along the hall and on the apartment door I noticed a trail of blood. When I got inside, it turned out the police officer was not in trouble, he just needed assistance. He'd radioed for an ambulance. On the bed there was a man, naked from the waist up. He was in bad shape. He'd been stabbed repeatedly and his intestines were hanging out. He was in a kneeling position on the floor, bent forward over the bed. His hands and feet were tied ... It turned out that this was the apartment that the woman with the knife in her throat had come from." SNAP! The faint tippety-tap of the court reporter's steno-type machine, a comforting, barely audible sound like rain on a roof, stopped abruptly as her tape recorder popped open at the end of its reel.

"Just a minute, please," the court reporter said, and the lawyer and witness froze, unwilling to move or speak until she was ready. The first words spoken by a lawyer in every case are, *"For the record,* my name is ..." The reporter embodies the ritual of the law and lends special importance to words uttered in the courtroom: everything is written down, every word. Language flows through the reporter's fingers in shorthand form at up to 225 words per minute. It takes 2,400 classroom hours plus a year of on-the-job training, three years altogether, for stenographers to get certified as court reporters, and they are paid accordingly. In addition to their salaries, they get two to three dollars per page when a lawyer orders a transcript, so they're making more money than most public defenders or prosecutors.

"Okay," the reporter said.

The prosecutor, who'd been standing stock still and silent, was reanimated, and the witness continued his story. It seemed that the woman had simply been in the wrong place at the wrong time when some dissatisfied parties to a drug deal came to register their complaint with the man on the bed, who paid with his life. The woman, left for dead, survived. "I went back downstairs after about five or ten minutes," the cop continued, "and the cab with the woman in it was parked there. Because, of course, the cab driver thought I was leading him to the hospital, so he followed me there, and then he got blocked in by the other scout cars that arrived after me."

The officer related this without any twinge of embarrassment, apparently unaware that there was anything the least bit curious about, or any fault to be found with, his actions. He couldn't even stop for a second, or even not stop, just shout to the cabby, "Go on without me!" No, the instant he hears "officer-in-trouble," nothing else exists for him except the compulsion to fly to that scene: "That could be *me* someday, that's a brother officer." The woman with the knife through her throat can wait. *She* he'll never be.

Perhaps it is not so unusual that the police do so much more for one of their own than for an ordinary citizen. I speculated to Rhonda Harrell, a young working-class woman who worked as an aide to us at court, that maybe the cops figure everybody treats them like shit, so they might as well watch out for each other, and treat everyone else like shit.

"They just think they have a right to treat people like shit, so they do," she said.

As I sat watching the Butcher-Knife Trial, I heard distant shouting somewhere in the courthouse, and some sort of reverberations coming through the walls, like bass notes. I went out into the hall and found two pools of blood and some smaller spatters, bright red, and a swabbed-up track turning maroon, and a crumpled piece of gauze bandage soaking there. Had someone been knifed? Or smacked on the head by a marshal's lead smacker? There was no one around. Just the blood. I find blood nauseating. I think it's the stickiness of it.

I walked down the block to Antonio's Cuban-Italian Carry-out to get some lunch, and there, along the curb, was a six-foot swath of bloody slush, fresh enough so that it had not been washed away, but not so fresh that it was undiluted—mushed-up bloody slush. A lot of it. Noontime. Sun shining. No one taking notice. *Is there a meat-packing plant near here? A butcher?* I looked around, never having noticed one before. No. Just blood in the streets. I went on about my business.

§4-12

We had a lot of snow that winter.

A two-foot blanket of water in pure white crystalline form descending silently from the sky is one of those phenomena which never lose their quality of bizarreness, despite being entirely natural, or because they are entirely natural. Washington when covered with snow assumes an especially unreal quality. This city under any circumstances has an air of unreality, having been laid out according to plan, and being marked by that overwhelming *arbitrariness* which can be achieved only through planning.

Let's have a two-mile-long lawn here. We'll put the Capitol dome at one end and the Washington Monument in the middle.

One can only stand in awe of these fantastic *objets,* the male and female forces captured and celebrated, totems of the vital power of the nation.

Then at the other end of the Mall we'll put the Lincoln Memorial. And let's dig a 2,292-foot ditch in the lawn and fill it with water.

I cross-country skiied one night a mile from my house along the river's edge up to the Lincoln Memorial. Approached from the rear, or river, side, its back to the South, the Memorial is unadorned by the representational statue of Lincoln; it is just a block surrounded by pillars, like the similarly proportioned, but only seven-foot-long, marble block that is FDR's memorial—abstract, more than can be said. It looked that night as though it were made from the snow itself, its floodlit stone having the appearance of a translucent ice sculpture illuminated from within. Surrounding it were tractors, row on row, parked there by protesting farmers who had paraded into town on them before the snow fell. Now the odd insectlike vehicles sat half-buried in the drifting snow, blue-white under the moon, everything still and silent except the American Farm Movement pennants on their antennae, snapping stiffly in the wind. It was a scene entirely unlike any that had existed before or ever would exist again. All I could do was look.

§4-13

Howard Robbins had himself completely under control as I spoke to him in the lockup before his presentment.* He was a boyish-looking man in his late twenties. The only indications that he was a homicidal maniac were his raincoat and his eyes, and the fact that he was accused of committing a maniacal homicide. The government said he had shot the girl next door and her boyfriend on the girl's birthday. Howard had walked

---

* The Constitution requires that an arrested person, without unreasonable delay, be brought before a judge or magistrate, who informs the defendant of the charges against him, and of his right to the assistance of counsel, including appointed counsel if he is indigent, and to a trial, and to a trial by jury if he faces punishment of more than six months in jail. If the charge is a misdemeanor (offense punishable by a year or less in jail), this initial appearance is the defendant's *arraignment,* and he enters his plea. If the charge is a felony, and the defendant has not yet been indicted by the grand jury, the initial appearance is the defendant's *presentment;* he is not formally charged and does not plead, but is informed of his right to a preliminary hearing, for which the date is set. At the arraignment or presentment, the judge determines if and under what conditions the defendant may be released until his next appearance.

up to her as she stood in front of her house with her beau, shot each of them a couple of times, and then run off to buy some groceries for his mother. The girl survived. Her boyfriend didn't.

This was all very deep water for me, who had yet to try so much as a petit larceny before a jury. In fact, I assumed that my assignment to the case was at least a mistake and possibly illegal—weren't you required to have some experience before handling a homicide by yourself?*—but I wasn't letting on, and Howard wasn't letting on. We were two very controlled young men.

Howard's raincoat was stained right about where you'd expect drool to hit, and he was wearing it buttoned all the way up to his neck, despite the fetid heat of the lockup. As I explained that I was his lawyer, and that everything he said to me was a secret, and so on, and so forth, he listened attentively, his eyes fixed on mine. He was looking *at* my eyes, not into them, and I was looking at his. His brown eyes were almost completely surrounded by white, they were open so wide. They looked as if they were straining to contain some enormous pressure inside his skull which was on the verge of blowing them out like two gelatinous cannonballs.

He heard me out patiently, then informed me that he was sure to be released, as his arrest was obviously a mistake, which would be quickly cleared up. All he knew was that he had gone to the grocery store to buy some pickles for his mother, when some policemen came up and asked him if he was Howard Robbins. He said yes, and they arrested him.

"Did they search you?"

"Yes, they searched me."

"Did they find anything?"

"Just the pickles."

"In case the judge does decide to hold you," I said, "where would you rather go, the jail or St. Elizabeths [mental hospital]?"

"That's like asking me which color bars I want to stand behind," he said. He declined to choose.

I found Howard's mother and his older sister in the witness room adjacent to the courtroom. His sister sat quietly drunk. His mother, a stout, solid-looking woman of about sixty, with a handsome, intelligent face, was on the verge of crying, but did not cry. Everything she said to me she said apologetically, as though her troubles did not quite merit the attention of a man in a pinstriped suit.

She'd known something like this would happen, she said. Howard had been sick for a long time. He had been violent before; he'd roughed her

* No.

up. He had been taken to mental hospitals three times, but the doctors had always let him out. "But," she said, chiding herself with a shake of the head, "that's all in the past."

(Under D.C. law,[1] a person brought against his will to a mental hospital cannot be detained for more than forty-eight hours unless the hospital administrator within that time petitions the court for an order authorizing continued hospitalization for emergency observation and diagnosis, which itself can last only one week unless civil commitment proceedings are begun. To commit a person, a family member, guardian, law officer, or doctor must petition the Commission on Mental Health. The commission must promptly hold a hearing, at which the person is entitled to appear, with appointed counsel, to present and cross-examine witnesses. If the commission finds that the person is mentally ill *and* a danger to himself or others, it reports that finding to the superior court, which holds a hearing or, upon the demand of the person, conducts a jury trial. If that proceeding results in the determination that the person is ill and dangerous, he may be committed. By design, in order to protect the individual's rights, the process is complex and cumbersome, and Mrs. Robbins had not been able to get Howard through it.

(In other countries, the Soviet Union for example, it is much simpler to commit people. When it is simpler to commit people, many more people are committed. By committing fewer people, we no doubt marginally increase the number of offenses committed by the mentally ill. But we choose to pay that price because we traditionally place a high value on not locking people up unless they have committed a crime.)

My colleague Ken Lloyd, who had happened by, took me aside. "Here's something you're going to have to live with for the rest of your life," he said, and told me that because Howard wanted to get out, and he was my client, and I was his lawyer, it was my duty to try to persuade his mother to accept custody of Howard, no matter how dangerous he was, so that I could convince the judge to release him.

I asked Howard's mother if she would be willing to take him home. She said she feared he would kill her if she took him home, but if she didn't take him home, he'd get out sometime and kill her for sure, for leaving him in jail. So, she said, she'd take him.

Augusto Flores, a big-gun prosecutor, dressed in all three pieces of a charcoal pinstriped suit, wheeled into the courtroom, having put aside his administrative duties especially to handle this one case. I recognized him as the driver of the shiny black Datsun 240-Z with which I had had annoying encounters from time to time in the courthouse parking lot. Two-forty Z's, like Mazda RX-7's and Corvettes, are inexcusable. The owner has spent a fortune on a 130-mile-per-hour car, which he will either never drive over seventy, in which case he is guilty of the most extravagant Walter Mitty-ism; or habitually drive at speeds far in excess of the legal limit, in which case he is a peril to my life and yours, as well as a dangerous hypocrite if he happens to be a law enforcement professional. The car itself lacks all subtlety, hitting you over the head with its virtually anatomical phallicism. It is to cars what gold ingots on a chain are to jewelry. And all the heartbreakingly beautiful Dannon-bodied babes on M Street *go for it.*

Of course, the clerk called the case the moment Mr. Z cruised into the room. He stood at the prosecution table, and I at the defense, side by side, casually eyeing each other like two motorheads at a light. *Hrum-ba-dum-ba-dum-ba-dum-ba* ... Listen to that baby hum. The judge signaled, "Yes?" Boom! Mr. Z floored it: "The government is requesting twenty-five thousand dollars bail, Your Honor."

Why not make it twenty-five million?

"Excessive bail shall not be required, nor excessive fines imposed, nor cruel and unusual punishments inflicted," the Eighth Amendment provides.

The Supreme Court has confirmed that the sole purpose of bail is to ensure that the defendant will appear for trial; that the setting of reasonable bail is an absolute right in all cases involving offenses not punishable by death;* that what is reasonable is whatever amount is necessary to secure the appearance of the particular defendant, taking into consideration his circumstances, including his financial ability; and that bail set at a figure higher than an amount reasonably calculated to secure a defendant's appearance is "excessive," in violation of the Eighth Amendment. Emphasizing the "traditional right to freedom before conviction," the Court has noted, "Unless this right to bail before trial is preserved, the presumption of innocence ... would lose its meaning."[2]

When the Supreme Court says how things ought to be, that doesn't necessary make them be that way. By 1960, urban jails throughout the country were filled with people detained pretrial because of their inability to post bail. Aside from being unfair, such detentions are very expensive (thirty-five dollars a day in D.C., in 1981).[3] An experiment conducted by the Vera Foundation in New York City in 1960 showed that people released upon their personal promise to return showed up just as regularly as people released on bail. Based on that and other data, Congress in 1966

---

* D.C. has no death penalty.

passed the Bail Reform Act, prescribing release on personal recognizance (promise to return) as the preferred type of pretrial release in federal courts and the courts of the District of Columbia.

Now, over 70 percent of defendants are released without having to post bail, in Washington.[4] For defendants released on nonfinancial conditions—the most common conditions imposed being simply to promise to return, stay away from the complainant, and telephone the Pretrial Services Agency* regularly—the appearance rate was 94 percent in 1981; that is, of every one hundred scheduled appearances, only six led to the issuance of a warrant for failure to appear. Over half of these failures to appear turned out to be excusable, because, for instance, the defendant had been hospitalized or incarcerated.[5] The *best* appearance rates are for defendants charged with murder or rape. The worst are for those charged with petit larceny or soliciting for prostitution.[6]

The Constitution would not seem to permit the use of bail for the purpose of keeping people incarcerated for the protection of the public. Bail has always *been* used for that purpose, but judges and prosecutors always pretend that risk of nonappearance for trial is the reason for setting high bail. To keep Howard off the street, the government was relying on its traditional improper practice of asking high bail for an indigent person.

The prosecutor handed the judge and me copies of the police report of the incident, as he had to: a defendant cannot be held in custody without a prompt judicial determination that there is probable cause to believe he committed the crime. He augmented the report with his own vivid narrative of Howard shooting his next-door neighbor at point-blank range, then shooting her boyfriend as he heroically lunged for the gun, and shooting him again as he staggered from the first mortal wound, then firing repeatedly at the young woman as she thrashed about on the ground, screaming in terror and pain. Not a pretty picture.

I was horrified. My voice quavered as I argued that Howard should be released on his personal recognizance because he had no record, had lived at one address in D.C. all his life, had all of his family here, and did not have the financial resources to leave town. The judge imposed $3,000 bail, far more than Howard or his mother had.

(The bail could be made in cash or by posting a "surety bond," that is, paying a professional bondsman 10 percent of the bail amount, which he

* The Pretrial Services Agency, or "bail agency," interviews each defendant and, on the basis of objective criteria such as employment status, length of residence, and family ties, recommends to the judge whether the defendant should be released on personal recognizance. It also maintains contact with released defendants, reminding them of their court dates.

keeps, in return for his commitment to pay the full amount to the court should the defendant fail to appear, an eventuality that the bondsman is expected to try to prevent. Bondsmen prefer to do business with repeat offenders whom they know. Howard looked like a bad risk, and no bondsman would write a bond for him.)

At the request of the prosecutor, the judge ordered a "forensic screening" to determine whether Howard was competent to stand trial. A defendant is *incompetent* if he is unable to understand the proceedings against him or to assist in his own defense. The defendant's *competency* depends on his mental condition at the time of the court proceedings; his *sanity* depends on his mental condition at the time of the offense.

Howard leaned over and whispered urgently, "What does he mean, in detail, that I need a mental screening? I want to hear that in more detail."

"Howard, look," I said, "it was detailed enough for the judge. He ordered it. Don't say anything." He was getting agitated.

"Okay," he said as the marshals led him away, "but from now on, whenever anybody says anything like that, I want to hear it in *detail.*"

Four days later we were back in court for the report on Howard's forensic screening. The report simply stated the conclusion that Howard was competent.

Mr. Z asked Judge Sweeney to commit Howard for further mental observation to review his competency and to get an opinion on his sanity.

I objected, arguing that it's up to the defendant to raise the defense of insanity, which we had not yet done.

The judge ordered a thirty-day mental observation. "I can see what's before me," he said. "I can see there's something not quite right. Maybe it takes one to know one." Judge Sweeney was aware that with age and infirmity he had grown somewhat idiosyncratic in his own behavior. "I'm losing my mind," he once said in the middle of one of my juvenile trials.

I felt I was losing control of the case. Howard would be in the hands of psychiatrists who, though nominally working as neutral advisers to the court, were notoriously prosecutorial in outlook. My dismay was nothing compared to Howard's, however. He got very worked up, not bothering to whisper as he complained that it was Sheila, the female shootee, who was crazy, not he. Of course, by his loud protestations he was exhibiting the very essence of craziness—a poor sense of decorum.

"Maybe the defendant would like to address the court?" Judge Sweeney asked, his interest piqued.

I, taken aback, was just starting to say, "I've advised him not to," when Howard began shouting, "Why don't you ask Sheila? Sheila will tell you the truth!"

"Who's Sheila?" Judge Sweeney asked.

As Howard started answering, I grabbed the microphone and said loudly, "Your Honor, I really must insist that my client not be interrogated any further." I was trying to muck up the tape recording* so that Howard's admissions would not be in the transcript.

"All right, you're right," Judge Sweeney said, not hiding his disappointment.

We were back in court three days later for Howard's preliminary hearing. I went back and found Howard, still in his raincoat, in the lockup. I explained to him that the preliminary hearing would last only two or three minutes; that its only purpose was to enable the judge to decide, after listening to a police officer's testimony, whether there was "probable cause" to believe that he committed the crimes with which he was charged, or whether the complaint should be dismissed.

"The police can't just go arrest somebody and put him on trial," I said. "A judge has to review what the police did. But, as a matter of fact, ninety-five times out of a hundred, the judge will decide that there's enough evidence to have a trial.† Since he's going to decide that anyway, the real point of the hearing, as far as we're concerned, is that it gives us a chance to hear what the cops have to say, so we're a little bit less in the dark. So you'll notice that I don't go out there and be Perry Mason and say, 'But you don't know what you're talking about, do you?' and 'Aren't you full of shit?' and try to knock holes in the cop's story, because the time for that is later, when it counts, at the trial. Right now I just want to lay back and let it flow, let him talk and talk and talk. And none of what happens today comes before the jury at trial. At trial we start fresh."

"And I won't say anything, because that was a mistake the last time, when I started to talk," Howard said.

"That's right," I said, "and you won't get excited, because you know that nothing that's said can hurt you. You'll just sit there calmly, because you know none of it matters."

And he did sit there, quiet and calm.

The same couldn't be said for Judge Sweeney. He wanted to cut off my cross-examination because the cop had testified that the woman victim had said she was shot by "Howard Robbins," and that was probable cause right there. I was trying to discover (and "lock in" the arresting officer's testimony about) the circumstances surrounding Howard's arrest: Was he near the crime scene? Did he seem to be trying to flee? Did he match a description, or have incriminating evidence on him? From the prosecutor's point of view, these questions were all impermissible attempts at discovery, irrelevant to the issue of probable cause. A portion of the transcript of my cross-examination shows that, while the prosecutor is supposed to be my adversary, the fiercest competition often comes from the police officer and the nominally neutral judge:

BY MR. KUNEN:
Q. In which direction did the victim say the perpetrator was heading?
A. Headed east on V Street.
THE COURT: Sustained. [There had been no objection.]
BY MR. KUNEN:
Q. Is that V as in Very?
A. V as in Victor.
Q. Now, when you first saw Mr. Robbins, where were you, Officer?
A. In the scout car.
Q. Where was the scout car?
A. Middle of the street.
Q. And where, on what street was the scout car?
MR. FLORES: Objection.
THE COURT: Sustained.
BY MR. KUNEN:
Q. At what distance was Mr. Robbins from you when you first saw Mr. Robbins?
THE COURT: Sustained.
BY MR. KUNEN:
Q. Where was Mr. Robbins when you first saw him, Officer?
MR. FLORES: Objection, Your Honor.
THE COURT: Sustained.
BY MR. KUNEN:
Q. How would you describe the pace at which he was walking, making haste or walking at a normal pace?
MR. FLORES: Objection.
THE COURT: Sustained.
BY MR. KUNEN:
Q. Did the complainant give you any physical description of the person who shot her?
THE COURT: Sustained.
MR. KUNEN: I didn't hear any objection, Your Honor. It would seem to me, if my client is going to be accused of a crime and if the Court is going to find that there is probable cause—
THE COURT: I am going to find probable cause, unless you're going to attack the credibility of the victim. Now, if you're prepared to do that, let's go.

MR. KUNEN: I am doing that through my questioning. That's exactly what I'm doing.
THE COURT: All right.
MR. KUNEN:
Q. Was Mr. Robbins carrying anything when you stopped him?
MR. FLORES: Your Honor, at this point, I would like to state the basis of my objection.
THE COURT: What difference does it make? Sustained. Sustained.
MR. KUNEN: Well, Your Honor, if I am not going to be allowed to ask any more questions, then I won't ask any more questions.
THE COURT: The victim said, "Howard Robbins shot me." Are you going to break that down?'
MR. KUNEN: Not if I'm not allowed to.
THE COURT: Go ahead and ask the question, and that better be relevant when you get there, hear, and you better make an argument when you're through.
MR. KUNEN: I understand that.
THE COURT: All right.

The odd thing about Judge Sweeney was that when he was through yelling at you, he almost always allowed you to conduct your examination, whether it was proper or not. The only limit to your questioning was how much you could take of being yelled at by an old man sitting up above you in the front of the room while one hundred people you couldn't see, sitting behind you, looked on. For me, it was necessary to enlist the support of those one hundred, to get them on my side, and feel them there. It's a talent to be able to do that. It would probably be an even greater talent not to need to.

When the dust settled, we had learned that Sheila, though severely wounded, seemed to the police officer to be clear-headed when she said, "Howard Robbins shot us," and that the deceased man said, "Howard did it," just before he died.

(Students of the law will recognize the latter pronouncement as a classic "dying declaration," which, as an exception to the hearsay rule, is admissible at trial as the equivalent of testimony, on the ancient theory that no one would lie when he was about to meet his Maker.)

"See, we didn't know before that they were going to say that the man also named you," I told Howard afterward. "Now we're a little less in the dark."

"Yeah, I didn't know they were going to *say* that," Howard agreed, then passed quickly to his favorite topic: the imminent dismissal of the case.

He patiently explained the whole situation to me again. Sheila was angry at him because he had fathered a child, now thirteen, by her sister, and not by her. (The sister had since died of a heroin overdose.) And she was jealous because he had a new girlfriend, named Lois.

Now Sheila was putting a lie on him, to try to get him locked up. The cop at the hearing said that Sheila said she knew Howard from the neighborhood, and had gone to the same schools. Howard shook his head and laughed. This was preposterous! How could they have gone to the same schools, when he was six years older than she! This proved that 1) Sheila was trying to get Howard in trouble, and 2) Sheila needed psychiatric help, since "only a crazy person would tell a lie that could be so easily proved wrong."

Howard cocked his head expectantly, waiting for me to agree with him.

"I understand what you're saying," I said.

He speculated that what probably *really* happened on Sheila's birthday was that Sheila and her boyfriend had an argument and ended up shooting each other. Sheila, in her pain and anguish, called out Howard's name, out of love for him. Later, realizing the trouble she was in, she decided to frame Howard and thus protect herself.

He seemed pleased by the way his theory *accounted for everything*.

Howard maintained that I could easily verify everything he'd said, and get his case dismissed, merely by getting hold of his past complaints of harassment by Sheila. He said he had gone to the Citizen Complaint Board at the prosecutor's office five times.

I promised to subpoena their records.

He added that he had called the police about Sheila at least forty times.

"Did you call nine-one-one?" I asked. "They record those calls. Maybe I can get the tapes."

"No, I dialed the full phone number of the precinct," Howard said. "I think nine-one-one should be saved for real emergencies."

§4-14

Roberto Lewis, facing twenty years for the camera-robbery murder, wouldn't listen to my co-counsel Lloyd and me. As far as he was concerned, we were part of the conspiracy to lock him up.

"I know this isn't what you want to hear from your defense attorney," I told him during one of our many conversations at the jail. "You want to hear me say, 'Here's how we're going to beat this thing.' I wish I could say that, but I wouldn't be doing you a favor, because then we'd go to trial and lose, and you'd do twenty years. My job is to defend you, to protect you, to keep the damage as light as possible. And the way to do that is to plead guilty, because we can't beat this case."

That wasn't what he wanted to hear from his defense attorneys. We offered him no alternative, no way out. We were there to tell him that we were not getting him out—no one was getting him out—he should plead guilty to second-degree murder and *maybe* he'd be sentenced under the Federal Youth Corrections Act, which allowed indeterminate sentences for offenders under twenty-two years of age; then *maybe* he'd get out in eight or ten years. Otherwise, he'd go down on first-degree murder and get a mandatory twenty-to-life. He'd be thirty-seven when he got out, at the earliest.

(I wondered about the rationale for the mandatory minimum of twenty years. Wouldn't ten be time enough to take a look at him for possible parole? Ten years, like twenty years, was too horrible to imagine. Ten years, like twenty years, was a lifetime to a seventeen-year-old. The only logic I could see for the twenty years was that his testosterone level would be that much lower when he came out.

(As men age, their violent criminal activity rapidly diminishes. In 1980 in the District of Columbia, for example, among males aged fifteen to nineteen, there were 921 arrests for violent crimes; among twenty-five- to twenty-nine-year olds, 593; among thirty-five- to thirty-nine-year-olds, 182. The arrest rate for violent crimes by women, while uniformly much lower, declines more gradually with age. Among females aged fifteen to nineteen, there were 77 arrests for violent crimes in D.C. in 1980; among twenty-five- to twenty-nine-year-olds, 67; among thirty-five- to thirty-nine-year-olds, 31.)[1]

Roberto said he would not plead because he was not guilty. He denied knowing anything about the shooting. He said his confession was not what he told the police, but what the police told him. He just signed what they put in front of him, after they had choked him and threatened him, he said.

We moved to suppress the confession, of course, arguing, among other things, that the police did not effectively communicate Roberto's "*Miranda* rights" to him; that Roberto did not knowingly, intelligently, and voluntarily waive those rights; and that his statements had been coerced.

In *Miranda* v. *Arizona,* in 1966, the Supreme Court held that before questioning a suspect who is in custody or otherwise deprived of his freedom of action, law enforcement officers must warn him that he has a right to remain silent; that any statement he makes may be used against him in court; that he has the right to consult with a lawyer before answering questions, and to have the lawyer with him during the questioning; that he will be provided with a lawyer if he cannot afford one; and that he may assert any of these rights at any time, even if he has begun answering questions. The prosecutor has the burden of proving that the defendant was expressly informed of these rights, and that he made a knowing and voluntary waiver of them, before any statements made in response to custodial interrogation can be introduced in evidence.

I didn't doubt that Roberto's statements were coerced. It was much easier to imagine Roberto being threatened and frightened and roughed up than being overcome by a guilty conscience. If he had a conscience, he wouldn't have shot the guy in the first place. But I was also sure that we couldn't establish a *Miranda* violation, and that the confession would be admitted into evidence.

Police *love* the *Miranda* decision. They speed-read the suspect his rights and then tell him to fill in and sign a printed waiver form. He's frightened; he doesn't understand what was read to him; he's afraid he'll look guilty if he doesn't sign; he signs, and school's out. The signed waiver is almost impossible for the defense to overcome.

Printed at the top of each and every page of Roberto's written statements to the police was the following:

WAIVER OF RIGHTS AND STATEMENT

YOU ARE UNDER ARREST. BEFORE WE ASK YOU ANY QUESTIONS YOU MUST UNDERSTAND WHAT YOUR RIGHTS ARE.

YOU HAVE THE RIGHT TO REMAIN SILENT. YOU ARE NOT REQUIRED TO SAY ANYTHING TO US AT ANY TIME OR TO ANSWER ANY QUESTIONS. ANYTHING YOU SAY CAN BE USED AGAINST YOU IN COURT.

YOU HAVE THE RIGHT TO TALK TO A LAWYER FOR ADVICE BEFORE WE QUESTION YOU AND TO HAVE HIM WITH YOU DURING QUESTIONING.

IF YOU CANNOT AFFORD A LAWYER AND WANT ONE, A LAWYER WILL BE PROVIDED FOR YOU.

IF YOU WANT TO ANSWER QUESTIONS NOW WITHOUT A LAWYER PRESENT YOU WILL STILL HAVE THE RIGHT TO STOP ANSWERING AT ANY TIME. YOU ALSO HAVE THE RIGHT TO STOP ANSWERING AT ANY TIME UNTIL YOU TALK TO A LAWYER.

DO YOU UNDERSTAND THESE RIGHTS?_____

DO YOU WISH TO ANSWER ANY QUESTIONS?_____

ARE YOU WILLING TO ANSWER QUESTIONS WITHOUT HAVING AN AT-
TORNEY PRESENT?_____

The blanks were filled in, in Roberto's handwriting, YES, YES, YES.
And at the bottom of each page:

I HAVE READ THIS STATEMENT GIVEN BY ME OR HAVE HAD IT READ
TO ME. I FULLY UNDERSTAND IT AND CERTIFY THAT IT IS TRUE AND
CORRECT TO THE BEST OF MY KNOWLEDGE AND RECOLLECTION.

_____
SIGNATURE OF PERSON GIVING STATEMENT

with Roberto's signature.

In any event, as I explained to Roberto, with the witnesses the government had, they didn't even need his confession to convict him.

Our only alternative to a guilty plea was an insanity defense.

Unfortunately, my co-counsel Lloyd said, Roberto's was not a good
case for the insanity defense. It was the classic case of a robbery gone bad:
the victim "bucked," and Roberto shot him—simple as that.

"I still say it's *crazy* to shoot a guy for a camera," I said, "and if I have
to, I'll convince twelve people of that."

I made an appointment for Roberto with a psychiatrist. "You've got to
get the shrink up for it," Lloyd said, "get him excited and interested." So
I told the doctor about Roberto's "inappropriate smiling"; his two suicide
attempts at the Children's Center (the records there said they were
"manipulative," not real); his new-found interest, since his latest incarceration, in the Muslim religion (religiousness always raises a suspicion of insanity); and his claimed history of seizures—great potential
there: the lawyer for a white cop who shot a black child dead convinced a New York jury that his client was not responsible for the act
because he was suffering a one-time-only attack of an obscure form of
epilepsy.

When the psychiatrist called me up to report on his interview with Roberto, he *was* excited. "This is the first *bona fide* instance of Ganser's syndrome I've ever encountered!" he said. Ganser's syndrome, he explained,
is the name not of a condition but of a cluster of symptoms—the giving of
"approximate answers" being its prime characteristic. For example, when
the shrink pointed to his necktie and asked what it was, Roberto said, "A
shirt." Asked where he was, he said, "A warehouse," not a jail. He identified a newspaper as "trash."

Ganser's syndrome aside, Roberto also denied knowing his home address or his mother's name, and said he had seven brothers and sisters, when, in fact, he was the eighth of thirteen children. He insisted that he was not charged with murder, but with unauthorized use of a vehicle, explaining, "I stole a car because I wanted to commit suicide. I crashed it into a tree because he told me to do it." Roberto would not say who "he" was. When the shrink asked Roberto why "he" told him to crash the car, he said, "I never asked." He added, "Him and his boys come through and are making a parade, and I can't see it. When I'm asleep, he'll be squeezing my brain and I'll be trying to wake up."

The shrink concluded, "Without any doubt, Mr. Lewis is attempting a deception. I assume that he does know what his mother's name is, how many siblings he has, and what he's charged with."

("Why does the shrink assume that?" my student investigator, Bert Meyers, ever troublesome, asked later. "I don't know," I admitted. "I guess he can just tell.")

But, the doctor went on, crazy people can lie, too, and Roberto might be crazy as well as a liar. Ganser's syndrome is sometimes associated with hallucinations and delusions.

"But, Doctor," I asked, "isn't it possible that this 'syndrome' is just a system for lying?" (It's necessary to subject a defense expert's report to adversarial testing, but basically I was acting out an annoying personal trait which happens to be useful to a lawyer—the tendency to take the opposite view from whatever anyone else says.) "Mark Twain said," I said, " 'the nice thing about telling the truth is that you don't have to remember what you've said.' If you're going to lie, you need a system to keep your story consistent. Maybe Roberto thought, 'I'll always give the first answer that the true answer makes me think of.' Also, isn't it possible that if I had just killed someone, I might want to deny it, and to do so, might deny everything, deny reality? Mightn't a person in that situation try to shake loose, try to get some room to maneuver, *insist* that is not a tie, that is not a newspaper, this is not a jail, I am not guilty of murder?"

"You seem to have an intuitive grasp of Ganser's syndrome," the doctor said. (I was flattered, always liking to hear that I have an intuitive grasp of anything, although, upon reflection, I realized that my knack for Ganser's boiled down to knowing how to lie, which is easier and more common than knowing how to tell the truth.) He said that, as a matte) of fact, Ganser discovered the syndrome among institutional inmates, in prisons and hospitals, people facing the situation I had described.

"So," I asked, "as likely as not—no, more likely than not—this syndrome arose *after* the shooting, not from a 'mental disease or defect,' but as a reaction to incarceration?"

"That's right," the doctor said. He said he would explore further if we wished, but that he probably would not be able to testify in support of an insanity defense.

§4-15

As the date for the report on Howard Robbins's mental condition drew near, I went to talk to him at the D.C. jail, a modern building made of concrete mixed to look like a sort of pink granite. Some progressive architect had designed it to resemble a modern college dormitory, not that ambitious an undertaking, since modern college dormitories tend to look like jails. There are no bars on the windows, the windows themselves being made of something impenetrable, probably a spinoff from the space program. The jail is located adjacent to D.C. General Hospital, the poor people's hospital; everyone who has lost his freedom is dumped in one convenient location.

A long line of visitors waited outside the jail for their entry slips, and then formed another long line to be frisked and pass through a metal detector. Lawyers were exempt from the first line, but not the second. I watched as visitors removed from their pockets Bic lighters, which make terrific flamethrowers and are forbidden inside. Each would pick a spot that suited him on the ledge above the outside doors and stick his lighter there. It reminded me of people sticking little pieces of paper into particular, fateful cracks of the Wailing Wall in Jerusalem, except the people in Jerusalem were hoping for miracles; these folks just wanted their lighters back.

The woman officer whose job it was to receive money for prisoners' accounts sat chatting and laughing on the phone while a dozen people stood waiting for her to do her job. I imagined someone shooting her in a rage. But all they did was leave five dollars, two dollars, five dollars, and take their receipts. She was behind bulletproof glass, anyway.

The sergeant behind the glass divided his time between looking up prisoners' locations on a computer and feeding himself potato chips and root beer. He obviously didn't know the first thing about nutrition, or if he did, he didn't care. He certainly didn't care about locating prisoners.

He'd look one up, and then he'd take five with the soda and chips. Then he'd look up another, and reward himself again. Often, you'd be told your client was not in the jail—*what, did he step out?*—and then you'd talk to him later and find out he'd been there all along. Or you'd wait half an hour, and finally you'd be sent the wrong man. *What is the point of this man's life?* I asked myself as I watched the sergeant savoring his junk food. He's not in rehabilitation. He's not even in guarding. He just looks up names once in a while. Maybe he has a hobby.

A beautiful eight-year-old, all dressed up with bows in her hair to see her father, took off her coat, without being told, handed it to a guard, and stepped through the metal detector. The guard greeted her warmly. They knew each other.

Upstairs, as I sat in a blue Fiberglas ass-cup waiting for Howard, I watched the visiting going on. One woman, lovely like a model, sat sidled up to the glass wall between her and her man. She was wearing the poor person's standard fake leather jacket, but she also had on a long, pleated flower-print skirt, incongruously elegant. The man talked to her via telephone through the soundproof, bulletproof glass. Those phones make you sound like you're a million miles away. He smiled at her. She smiled back. They took no notice of me, or the fifteen other prisoners in blue workshirts and blue pants seated along the inside of the glass, or all the women seated outside looking in, identically posed, phones to ears. *Reach out and touch someone.* On the countertop beside the beautiful woman an infant lay, calmly drinking its bottle—a good baby. The woman pressed her hand to the glass; the man pressed his hand against the glass. Perhaps some warmth gets through. I've never tried it.

A guard in the control room motioned me into a glass booth. I sat down inside, thinking of *The $64,000 Question.* Lawyers were allowed "contact visits," since the danger of passing drugs or weapons was considered small, although not so small as to exempt the defendant from a strip search after each conference with his lawyer.

Howard shuffled in. I stood up and shook his hand. I always did that. I didn't always feel like standing up, but I did. Respect, respect, respect.

Somehow I had never gotten around to asking Howard if he had an alibi, so I did that now.

As a matter of fact, he had. The shooting was at 8:15, according to the police. He was watching the news from 5:30 to 7:30, then *The Waltons.* During the news, the phone rang. Howard went downstairs and asked his mother who was on the phone. She said the phone had not rung.

"During *The Waltons,* Sheila called me—but keep that quiet. She told me that David [her boyfriend] was drunk. And she said she heard that

Lois and I were getting married. She was upset about it. In fact, she called me about it several times that week. I hung up on her several times."

"Did anybody see you while you were watching TV?"

"Yes, my mother's friend Johnny was there. He was joking with me, telling me to put down the window."

I didn't understand the joke, but decided to let it go.

"Howard, the prosecutor tells me that a friend of yours—he didn't say who—heard you say, on the night of the shooting, 'I'm in big trouble. I just shot two people.' "

"He'd have to be insane to say that," Howard said. "He already apologized to my mother for saying that."

That was taken care of. Howard wasn't worried about it. He wasn't worried about anything, except the fact that his mother had not raised the money to bail him out, which made him very angry.

"While you're in for mental observation, you can't be bailed out anyway," I reminded him. He, not his mother, was my client, to whom all my loyalty was due, but I had fallen into the bad habit of looking out for her interests, trying to protect her from his wrath.

He told me again that if I'd get hold of his complaints against Sheila to the Civilian Complaint Board, the case would be dropped. I told him that I had subpoenaed them, but the U.S. attorney's office couldn't find any.

"Talk to Sheila's mother," Howard said. "She knows that there's *another* Howard Robbins who went around Sheila's house sometimes. And I got a neighbor who can testify that I *liked* Sheila and David, and that I'd never hurt them. He knows how bizarre this is." He gave me the names of five other people who could say the same thing.

I told him I'd have all of them interviewed, which I did. I did everything he asked me to, to try to win his confidence, so that he would believe me when I told him that he had lost his mind.

He pulled some tightly folded sheets of paper from his pocket.

"What are those?" I asked.

"Just some work I been doing on my case," he said.

The notes were block-printed in a large, childish hand on pink-lined steno paper:

> The reverse situation is easy to understand: a sick insane *man* testifies and lies repeatedly. . . . Sheila could be protecting someone. It could be anyone. A drug pusher or criminal. And herself. . . . I will file suit against Sheila if set free. Or when. Sheila should be put away behind bars. Or in St. E's. Sheila once got very angry about her daughter and I playing and talking together. She said she was afraid and that we would make love together when she got older or as a woman. Me making love to mother and daughter.

§4-16

Dum-di-dumdum.

"Come on in, Bert."

I knew it was Bert Meyers at my door. Bert, the scrawny guitarist who was interning as my investigator, always announced himself by rapping out the portentous rhythm of the *Dragnet* theme.

"Hey, boss, here's the Howard Robbins report from the shrink," he said, tossing an envelope on my desk. "Something else might interest you: did you hear about Howard and windows?"

"He said something to me at the jail about somebody joking with him about putting a window down, but I didn't understand it."

"Way-ell," Bert said, his eyes twinkling through his thick glasses, "everyone made fun of Howard because he got very anxious if every window in the house wasn't shut tight. Even the slightest crack upset him, even in the dead of summer."

"The dead of summer *in Washington?*" I said. "Now *that's* crazy! That's the sort of thing we're looking for. You tell a jury about a senseless murder, they're going to think, 'Hell, *I* could do that, I've thought of it many times.' But shutting the windows in summer—that's *insane.* Now we're getting somewhere."

The report from our retained psychiatrist began by reviewing Howard's hospital records. (Howard, being adamantly opposed to raising an insanity defense, refused to sign the releases that were required before the hospitals could legally turn his records over to me, but they handed them right over anyway.)

Howard had not displayed any mental problems as a small child. When he was in junior high school, however, people noticed he was spending an inordinate amount of time staring off into space. He began suffering nervousness, depression, insomnia, and nightmares. Howard became dependent on drugs, especially heroin and Bam (phenmetrazine), which he used so frequently that he had ulcerated sores on top of both feet, where he shot up. When, two years before he became my client, his brother died, Howard's condition deteriorated. He began imitating his brother's behavior and calling himself by his brother's name.

At that time, his brother-in-law, a lawyer, took him to a hospital, where he was initially diagnosed as a paranoid schizophrenic, who was "danger-ous to himself and others." After a couple of weeks, he went AWOL from the hospital to try to score some methadone; because he'd been admitted as a voluntary ("non-protesting") patient, he was automatically dis-charged after eight hours' unauthorized absence, and was refused re-admission to the hospital when he returned later that same day.

A year later, Howard's sister brought him to a hospital emergency room. He'd been complaining that bees were bothering him. The psy-chiatrist on duty observed him repeatedly licking his fingers and dragging them across the floor, muttering, "I caught Sam when he crawled out of my body, and I have to stay here to capture him." That doctor's initial diagnosis was paranoid schizophrenia. He described Howard as "quiet and cooperative," and concluded, "Potential to harm himself and others is negligible." Howard walked out before any treatment could be begun.

Six months before the shooting of Sheila and David, Howard was brought to St. Elizabeths psychiatric hospital by his brother-in-law and the police, after he had punched his mother.

"He feels that no one wants to be friends with him, that someone is trying to kill him," the admitting psychiatrist noted. "Also speaks of a former girlfriend who died several years ago in a manner which implies she is still alive and they are married. He says the police picked him up for no reason. Denied any history of being assaultive. Claims his mother and a girl are trying to hurt him. Says his prior hospitalization was result of his girlfriend hitting him in the head with a shoe. . . . According to the mother, he sleeps with a large cross, and once burned candles all around his bed. He often spoke of hearing a female friend speak to him, although she was not present. He reads the Bible frequently." He was diagnosed paranoid schizophrenic, "potentially dangerous." Howard signed himself out of the hospital "a.m.a."—against medical advice.

"Mr. Robbins does admit to a degree of depression, which relates to his brother's death," our defense psychiatrist reported.

He admitted to frequent spells of crying, though he very carefully denied having any suicidal thoughts. On the other hand, he claims that he stopped going to work after his brother's death because of a fear that he "wouldn't be careful" and, as a result, "cut my arm off" in one of the machines at work.

Mr. Robbins was also adamant that the female victim of the shooting was in fact the person who was probably responsible for the shooting. She is seen by him as a love-starved child, who had grown desperate in her attempt to gain his affection.

The major abnormality of this examination, which is suggestive of incomplete remission from a psychotic state, was blanket and overwhelming denial, not only of his involvement in the offense, but also regarding any suggestion that he is mentally ill.

As a result of my examination, it is my contention that at this time Mr. Robbins is not fully competent to stand trial.

Our shrink was not yet ready to venture an opinion as to whether Howard had been insane at the time of the offense, but suggested that there was "a good possibility that an insanity defense might be appropriately raised," since Howard appeared to be suffering a manic-depressive psychosis aggravated by the use of Bam, which can itself produce "a toxic state that is psychotic in nature."

The obstacle to a successful insanity defense was that, as our doctor told me, "with a manic, the crimes aren't crazy; it's his judgment that's distorted." It was not *how* he killed, but *that* he killed that was crazy. Howard didn't paint his victims red or cut them into little pieces, nor did he shoot down complete strangers from a rooftop. He shot the girl next door and her lover, as many a jealous man had done before; and—the D.A. had told me—he bought gloves to wear, to leave no prints on the gun; and he ran away afterward, and got rid of the gun—all very "rational" and indicative of a recognition of the wrongfulness of his conduct. It could be a tall order, convincing a jury of laymen that he was nuts at the time of the shooting.

In fact, I was having enough trouble getting the court psychiatrist to see how screwed up Howard was. The problem was, as our psychiatrist told me, "Mr. Robbins has an unfortunate tendency to present himself as sane, and he has good cognitive understanding, so he fools people." At the conclusion of his "thirty-day mental observation" (which actually consisted of two brief interviews in the jail infirmary), the court psychiatrist reported that Howard was competent to stand trial, and that he was not insane at the time of the shooting.

When I telephoned the court psychiatrist and asked him what the basis for his conclusion about competency was, he said that Howard was able to explain what it meant to plead guilty, and his account of the offense was "consistent"—he continued to deny it. His mental status was "good": he was "oriented times three" (knew who he was, where he was, and what time it was); he was able to interpret a parable; and his "serial seven" was "very impressive" (he was able to count backwards from one hundred by sevens).

It was in Howard's best interest to be found *incompetent*. When a defendant is found incompetent, he can be held for a period of time reasonably necessary to determine if he is likely to become competent in the foreseeable future. If it appears the defendant will remain incompetent, the government must either institute civil commitment proceedings or release him.

Civil commitment is preferable to commitment following a verdict of not guilty by reason of insanity, in that the defendant may be held in a somewhat less restrictive facility and may be released sooner. Even if the government puts him on trial when he finally does become competent, his chances at that point of being found not guilty by reason of insanity are greatly enhanced by his track record of having been found nuts enough to be civilly committed.

Howard was pleased to be found competent, but I asserted his right to a full hearing on the matter anyway, which was set down to be held in a month. He was returned to the jail.

Meanwhile, I told the court psychiatrist that *our* doctor, who was well regarded among Washington's community of 1,000 psychiatrists,* had found that Howard was *in*competent. The court psychiatrist suggested that I ask the court to order him to evaluate Howard again, so that before the hearing he might file a report agreeing with our doctor, and that way "a court battle could be avoided." (Read: "I won't have to come to court and sit around all day.")

§4-17

While I was dealing with the Robbins and Lewis murders, I had forty other cases—forty-two people I was responsible for. I wouldn't compare it to bolting bumpers on Chevettes, but for me it was hard work.

I remember one day I was in a groove. I needed to talk to a prosecutor, and I bumped into him in a hallway; I went to look for a file in the clerk's office, and it was there; I walked into a courtroom, and my case was called, and the same thing happened in the next courtroom, and the next. There is in reality such a thing as being in a groove; the improbable will happen every so often. But typically I had the opposite sort of day: I called only people who didn't answer; I went to see only people who had just left; I looked only for things that couldn't be found.

The client for whom I'd been putting in the most work was a man

---

* The Washington metropolitan area, with approximately 1,000 practicing psychiatrists, ranked third in the nation for psychiatrists per capita, behind New York and San Francisco (private conversation with Dr. Harold Eist, President, Washington Psychiatric Society, May 21, 1982).

named Shirley Browning, who had been arrested for carrying a pistol without a license, conviction for which would trigger revocation of his parole from an earlier sentence and put him back in prison for several years. I'm sure it wasn't easy being named Shirley, but that's as far as my sympathy went. I really disliked the guy—he was a complainer, for one thing—but that didn't stop me from trying to sculpt the facts and law into some stunningly innovative work of art that would win the suppression of the gun as the fruit of an illegal search by the off-duty police officer/fellow patron who arrested him in a topless dance bar. However, the more that Bert Meyers investigated, the clearer it became that the search was legal* and, incidentally, that Shirley was a vicious and dangerous man, who beat up his girlfriend and forced her to turn tricks as a prostitute for him. The latter information was not my concern, and I honestly based my recommendation that Mr. Browning plead guilty on my professional judgment that he would be found guilty if he went to trial.

You're not always rooting for your client. The trick is, and your ethical duty is, not to let your feelings interfere with your efforts on his behalf. I knew one woman lawyer who went so far as to get a male colleague to co-counsel a brutal rape case with her because she was afraid she might not try hard enough to get the guy off. When he was ultimately convicted, she was glad, and she was able to be glad because she knew she had done her best for him.

I received a letter from Shirley Browning accusing me of being "a cheap dishonest lawyer trying to sell me out and trick me to plead," and "threatening" to replace me with another lawyer (how could I *stand* it?). I didn't view it with the amused detachment I would have expected from myself. It angered me.

"I've got to start looking for jobs," Ken Lloyd said when I told him about it. "I can't take much more of these assholes."

Lloyd, the residually countercultural fellow who was my co-counsel on the Roberto Lewis murder case, had been at P.D.S. for five years, and would be there only six months more, as it turned out. Few lawyers stayed more than five years; many left sooner.

You get tired of the exertions of the practice, having to be in court— several courts—every single day. And you get tired of the pressure —someone's freedom always riding on you. And you get tired of what the exertion and the pressure are all about: you're defending the Constitution, you're defending *everybody's* rights, but you're also, more often than not—*much* more often than not—defending a criminal. That needs to be

---

* Because it began as a frisk based on an articulable suspicion that Shirley was armed, and, therefore, it was not an unreasonable search or seizure in violation of the Fourth Amendment.

done, but it doesn't need to be done *by you,* not all your life. After a while, it's somebody else's turn.

The job takes a toll on your emotions. Of course, you feel sympathy for the victims ("complainants," we called them—just "c/w" [complaining witness] in our memos), but you suppress it. It gets in the way. Nor can you afford to feel a lot of sympathy for the clients ("Δ" [defendant] in our notes). Some of them earn the courthouse epithet "dirtball," but most of them are likable enough when you're trying to help them, and you'd have to be a moral moron not to see that they are victims, too. It's just that too much sympathy for the clients gets in the way of doing your job. You have to sell them on the advantages of doing five years instead of ten. You have to watch the iron doors closing behind them all the time. Even now, I know exactly where some of my clients are, and I will continue to know, exactly, to within a couple of hundred feet, where they are every minute of every day for the next ten, twelve, fifteen years. I hardly ever think about it. You don't get worn out from all the pain and sadness. You get worn out from *not feeling* the pain and sadness. You get tired of not feeling.

And you leave because you want to make some money. Most public defenders, and prosecutors, go into private practice eventually, where their litigation experience can be quite valuable.

The day I got the annoying letter from Shirley Browning, Todd Winfield's juvenile trial for assault with a dangerous weapon (pipe) was set, as was the preliminary hearing of John Fisher, a hapless middle-aged deinstitutionalized mental patient who somehow had managed to stab his girlfriend, another halfway house resident, through the neck without killing her. At 9:30 I told the juvenile court that I had to be upstairs at adult court, which was true. At 10:00 I told the adult court I had to be downstairs in juvenile court, which was also true. I could have gone on like that all day, although a few hours was usually sufficient to get a matter "kicked over" to some future date. It wasn't my fault that the Superior Court of the District of Columbia couldn't organize itself half as well as any mom-and-pop bakery—"take a number"—and I didn't see why I should run out of my way to make sure that the ax fell efficiently on my clients.

I really was supposed to be a lot of different places at the same time. Most of the criminal lawyer's job involves running around to various places in order to *be* there, nothing less and nothing more, so as to ensure that the defendant's every right is honored. It is this requirement of presence that forms the hard pit of boredom at the core of the lawyer's profession. Were you not there—at lineups, at arraignments, at status hearings—all sorts of exciting things might happen: bogus identifications, pressured pleas, forced confessions, anything the mind could conjure up to inflict upon a reviled and powerless man, which is anything at all. But because you were there, absolutely nothing would happen, save a few more clanks of the gears. If I was there, I needn't have been there. I always thought there should be a way out of this conundrum, but the solution must await further advances in robotics. I pin my hopes on Japan, where they have very few lawyers, incidentally.

Justice delayed is justice as usual. As time passes, to paraphrase a famous jurist—*I could provide the exact citation in a memorandum if I could have a few days, Your Honor*—witnesses disappear and memories fade. Also, passions cool, and the defendant gets the opportunity to compile a long record of good citizenship (no arrests) against the day he faces sentencing, should that day ever come. All of this is good for the defendant if he is out of jail. If he is in jail, delay is helpful to the prosecution, since with every passing month, the defendant is likely to become more amenable to pleading guilty. (If he is ultimately acquitted, the defendant doesn't even get an apology for the time he spent in pretrial detention; but if he is convicted, the time he has served is deducted from his sentence. If the length of his detention approaches the likely length of his sentence, he might as well plead. In any case, by pleading he can escape the cramped confines of the jail, where there are no recreation programs, contact visits, or diversions of any kind, and move on to the relative freedom of prison. Life is much harder for those behind bars who are presumed innocent than for those who have been proven guilty.)

Since every defendant is either in or out of jail, delay is good for at least one side. And it is always good for the judges, who have more cases than it would be humanly possible for them to try, even if they worked more than six hours a day. The majority of my continuances were attributable to the lack of an available judge. The only party who has no interest in delay is the victim, and he doesn't even have a lawyer.

I'd managed to get the elderly woman-stabber Mr. Fisher out on bail, and he hadn't appeared for his hearing. Why not delay and give him every opportunity to wander in before a bench warrant was issued for his arrest? What would you want your lawyer to do? And why not get pipe-swinging Todd Winfield's assault trial continued for a fifth time, and maybe wear out the complainant? What would you want your lawyer to do? But that day, because I was annoyed by Shirley Browning's letter, I was not in the mood for rule-stretching delaying tactics. I figured, Mr. Fisher is not going to show up; I might as well get his case called, and go do Todd's trial.

* * *

"A feral child" who literally lived in the streets, Todd Winfield virtually cried out for intervention by the state. He was so unsocialized that he had not thought to wash either his clothes or himself "since the memory of man runneth not to the contrary," to borrow a phrase from the common law. I had been trained always to sit close to my client, to put my arm around him and whisper in his ear, in order to forge an association between him and my likable self in the mind of the trier-of-fact. In this case, that was quite impossible.

Todd was a nice enough fifteen-year-old, albeit a somewhat wary and taciturn one. He needed counseling, parenting, teaching, shrinking, job training, discipline, good food, and a clean bed. He needed everything except to be put in a penal institution, which was the one thing the government intended to do with him.

Todd was accused of breaking the arm of a Korean grocer with one whack of a lead pipe, during an altercation that arose when the grocer accused him of having burglarized his store—a charge for which he was to stand trial separately.

As is often the case when one gets down to the most concrete aspects of reality, such as lead and bone, there was no question about what ultimately had happened; Todd had swung the pipe and broken the arm. The slack in the causal chain was encountered when one backed up a few links: what had caused Todd to swing the pipe? Self-defense, we said.

The altercation had taken place in and around a candy store, the proprietor of which, a Mr. Jesse, was our star witness.

The big thing in our favor was that the complainant scarcely spoke English, but, as luck would have it, Mr. Jesse was blind, so we came out of the gate about even.

Mr. Jesse was maybe sixty-five—it's hard to tell with people life's been cruel to. He spoke middle-class standard English with a firm dignity. He wore dark glasses and was conservatively, simply, cheaply dressed in black slacks and a black cardigan sweater. He was led everywhere by a shambling bum named Teddy Mulberry, but you got the feeling that it was Mr. Jesse who took care of Teddy Mulberry, mostly, and not the other way around.

I led Mr. Jesse down the aisle to the witness stand as he tapped his long white cane ahead of him. He testified that Mr. Park, the grocer, came into his candy store and started arguing with Mr. Jesse when the latter denied that he was Todd's father. "A lot of the boys from school nearby are like kids to me," Mr. Jesse testified, "but I'm certainly not his father in reality." Then Todd happened in, and Mr. Jesse heard Park shout at him,

JAMES S. KUNEN · 146

and grab him by the neck, and choke him, and throw him against the soda machine. He heard Todd fall to the floor, and heard Mr. Park stand over him, shouting. Then Park and Todd went outside. Asked what Todd's reputation for peacefulness was in the community, Mr. Jesse replied, "About average for a boy his age in the ghetto."

Things went swimmingly with Mr. Jesse, but the prosecutor got him to admit that he hadn't *seen* anything, and the judge, exhibiting our culture's bias for the visual over the aural, seemed skeptical. I resolved that in the future, when I have a blind witness, I will first ask him a lot of questions about the exact layout of the crime scene, *and of the courtroom,* in order to demonstrate his reliability, so that the factfinder isn't asked to take on faith that he knows what he's talking about. The extreme example makes the general principle clear: lay a foundation for your witness's credibility.

As so often happens when one finds oneself in a rocking boat, I stood up and made matters worse, in this case by calling Teddy Mulberry to pick up the story with what had happened outside the store. This was a terrible lapse on my part, ascribable to panic born of inexperience, for I had learned and forgotten many times over that Mr. Mulberry had no idea what happened outside the store that day, or anywhere else at any other time, for that matter. In fact, I had subpoenaed him only to provide an escort for Mr. Jesse and to enrich their commonweal by an extra thirty dollars' witness fee—an eminently just appropriation of public funds, in my view. But, finding my case dangling in the higher pan of justice's scales, I reached for the weight nearest at hand, and it was he, and I listened in horror as he described what sounded like an unprovoked assault by Todd, insofar as any sense could be made of his ramblings.

At the luncheon recess, I crossed the street to the Courthouse Carry Out (*"Come In.* It's KOOL inside"). One of the lovely Korean women behind the counter looked at me and said, "The usual?" I nodded. "The usual," she said to the woman at the sandwich board. This was one thing about being a lawyer that turned out just as I had pictured it: being known, being a regular at a courthouse joint, being recognized. It made me feel like a real lawyer. I was grateful to the Korean ladies for that. And their sandwiches were cheap.

Little brown bag in hand, I continued on to the office. In the distance, I could hear the quiet "poof-poof-poof" of a twenty-one-gun salute for the currently visiting head of state—the King of Morocco or somebody. I paused to gaze, as always, at the statute of Diana and the Fawn which stands in the middle of the walkway. "Erected by His Friends with the

Sanction of Congress in Memory of Joseph James Darlington—Counsellor, Teacher, Lover of Mankind, 1849–1920"—*let's see, that means he was seventy-one*—C. P. Jennewein's 1922 sculpture portrays a noble-countenanced, nubile Diana, soft and strong, her left hand poised protectively over the little fawn's shoulder, her long, delicate right index finger raised, her lips slightly parted, about to speak. *"Listen, fawn, there's one thing you should know . . ."*

The fountain on which the statue stands doesn't run anymore. It fills up with rainwater and other stuff, and smells like a sewer. Diana's gold finish was half-covered with brown crud, or so I thought, until Jan and I tried to polish her up one Saturday and found that she was not gold covered by brown dirt, but brown base metal covered by gold leaf, half of which had worn away. Score one for the pessimists.

I went on in to the weekly lunchtime staff meeting, which was devoted for the most part to comparing notes on judges and prosecutors so we could have the benefit of one another's experience, rather than to planning concerted action, such as "Let's all refuse to plead anybody guilty until the U.S. attorney's office has to improve its plea offers or face a complete breakdown of the system." We weren't a radical organization. Anyway, our first duty was to our individual clients. You can't force one client into a road accident of a trial in order to win better plea offers for other clients in the future.

I interrupted the meeting toward the end by excusing myself with the announcement, "I have to leave now. I am *going to win* a case with my final argument." I was trying to paint myself into a corner, after the manner of Dr. Norman Vincent Peale, deservedly the most influential clergyman of our century—influential on me, anyway. I had decided that there was too much complaining in our office about the judges' being biased toward the prosecution. *Of course* they're biased toward the prosecution. That's like a baseball player complaining that first base is ninety feet away. *Just get on! Little bingle!*

In summation I argued that Mr. Park's English, like that of the interpreter provided by the prosecution, was incomprehensible; that Mr. Jesse was blind; that Mr. Mulberry's testimony was a shambles; and that, unfortunately, it was therefore impossible to know with any degree of certainty *what* had happened on that fateful day, ergo there could not but be a reasonable doubt, ergo the only possible verdict was not guilty.

The judge agreed. Todd walked out a free man, and a free man he remained, for two weeks, until he was convicted in his other case, of burglarizing Mr. Park's store, as the prosecutor gloatingly informed me.

§4-18

Roberto Lewis's camera-robbery murder trial was one week away.

Our shrink reported that Roberto "claimed that he had ultimate freedom in the jail and could come and go as he pleased. As evidence, he offered that he had yesterday visited his mother's home." Roberto also described hearing voices "just laughing at me." Nonetheless, the psychiatrist concluded that Roberto was "not suffering from a substantial mental illness, at least in the customary interpretation," and advised us to forget about an insanity defense. He emphasized Roberto's "hostility and capacity for harm . . . [Roberto] warned that if anyone tried to make him plead guilty, he would 'punch him in the mouth.' Obviously, he should be approached with caution."

Roberto was his same old laconic self as he shuffled into the jail interview room and gave me his hand. I had nothing to fear from him. We grew up in court together.

"If we go to trial on Monday, you're going to be found guilty of first-degree murder," I said, "and you're going to get twenty to life. The judge isn't even going to have a choice. How old are you?"

"Seventeen."

"Twenty years is even longer than your whole life. Do you follow basketball?"

"No."

"Well, anyway, picture this." I wasn't prepared to switch metaphors. "A young kid, just out of college, a hot prospect, joins a pro team. He's a rookie, and no one's sure if he'll make it. But he's great, all season long, all eighty games. And he comes back the next season, and he's great again. And the year after that. Year after year. He becomes the backbone of the team, the main man. He gets older. He slows down. They have to rest him a lot. But he's the grand old man of the team. Finally, after ten years, he quits because he can't run anymore, and they have a celebration for him, and they retire his uniform, they put it in a museum, because he *is* the team, people don't know how the team is going to get along without him. But the team is lucky because they've found a great college player, and they sign him. He's a rookie. He does great all season long, and the next one, and the next. He carries the team, he's Mr. Basketball, for ten years, until he's too old, and they put *his* jersey in a museum.

"You take those two careers, those two whole *lives* in basketball, that's twenty years."

Roberto didn't say anything.

"Let me put it to you this way," I said. "It's forever."

Roberto just kept looking at me.

"And the worst thing about being locked up isn't that if you walk twenty feet in any direction you hit a wall; the worst thing is that you don't have any control over your own life, isn't it? You're like a crate in a warehouse. If you plead guilty, the judge could give you the Youth Act, and you could work toward getting paroled. That means you'd have some control over your life. You're a Muslim, right? In the Muslim religion, there's a lot of importance put on learning, isn't there?"

"Uh-huh."

"Do you have a high school diploma?"

"I'm workin' on that now."

"You could work on that, then you could start taking college credits. And if you were studying and doing well and behaving yourself, they could take account of that, and they could release you. In maybe five years, seven years, ten years, you could get out. It's a long time. But, the point is, *what you do* could affect your life. If you don't plead guilty, you *are* going to do twenty years. You could invent a cure for cancer, and you'd just stay in prison and read about it in the newspapers. *Nothing* you could do could affect your life."

Roberto smiled and lowered his eyes.

"If you want to think it over, we can ask for a mental observation to determine if you're competent. That would put the trial off sixty days."

"What's 'competent'?" he asked. I'd explained it to him before, but he hadn't been interested.

"First of all, it means you understand what's going on in court. Like, do you understand the judge is like a referee between two lawyers—one for the government trying to convict you, one for you trying to get you off. You understand that?"

"Yeah."

"But some people don't. They're not competent. Like they think the judge is Rockefeller and the defense attorney is somebody from the CIA."

Roberto threw his head back and laughed. I always liked to tell him little jokes.

"I think you're competent. We just need the sixty days for you to think. One thing for sure, you don't want to plead guilty and then feel you were rushed into it."

"Well, I think I want to plead guilty," Roberto said, "but would you call my mother and tell her about it? And I want the sixty days to think."

"Okay. But if you do plead guilty, and the judge sentences you to twenty to life anyway," I hastened to add, lest he think I was *promising* him anything, "we're not going to go, '*Oh, my God!* Why did we plead guilty?' because that's only the same thing you would have gotten anyway."

Remembering his Muslim religion, I said, "I hope I'm not offending you, using God's name in vain."

"It's all right," he said.

As I was driving away, it occurred to me that it was a little bit ironic, my saying, "I hope I haven't offended your sensibilities, taking the Lord's name in vain," to someone who shot somebody for a camera. What it is—I put myself in my client's position, entirely. I don't think about the victim very much, nor should I.

"You forget that this is just a kid," Ken Lloyd told me when I related Roberto's request that I talk to his mother. "What his mother thinks is very important. Try to get her on board for a plea."

Roberto obviously had denied to his mother that he'd shot the guy. And the biggest obstacle to pleading guilty, all along, had been that if he pled guilty, he'd be admitting *to his mother* that he'd killed someone, *and* that he'd lied to her when he said he didn't.

When I called Roberto's mother to make an appointment to see her the day after next, she said that she'd lined up a ride to go shopping that day, and asked if it could wait. I accommodated her.

("You wonder why he kills people?" Lloyd said.)

A few days later I took Pennsylvania Avenue a mile and a half southeast from the White House, across the John Philip Sousa Bridge, over the Anacostia River, to Anacostia. The beauty of that sequestered fourth of Washington would surprise the nine out of ten white Washingtonians who, having no reason to go there, and being afraid to go there, have never been there. (When Air Florida Flight 90 crashed into the Fourteenth Street Bridge on January 13, 1982, Ted Koppel, the Washington-based ABC News anchorman, said that the rescue helicopter had taken off from "Anacostia, Maryland.")

Pennsylvania Avenue rose steeply from its river crossing, past stately fieldstone mansions into the woods of Fort Davis Park, where Alabama Avenue veered north, along the forested border of Fort DuPont Park, site of summer public jazz concerts which I was never sure it was "all right" for me to go to. As Alabama descended, the big houses of the hill's crest gave way to neatly kept working-class cottages, and those, in turn, to *the projects* in the scrubby hollows along Benning Road.

The projects, depending upon their vintage, were different from one another, but they were more different from everything else. One type, with a tall brick smokestack at the end of each two-story, four-entry apartment block, looked like ancient mills in need of a stream. Another type, squat, rectangular buildings with cracked concrete steps leading to green iron doors, looked like so many cell blocks. A third type, product of a more recent and liberal time, was distinguished by façades that stepped in and out, and gabled roofs—a reasonable facsimile of lower-middle-class "garden apartments," except that there were no bulbs in the fixtures over the torn screen doors; the rot of the window frames, which had not seen paint in ages, had been accelerated by cascading water from the rusted-out roof gutters; and erosion had transformed the lawns into backyard badlands of six-inch buttes and canyons. All of the projects were clearly *projects,* designed to communicate the same reassuring message to the subsidizing taxpayer: *you wouldn't want to live here.*

Mrs. Lewis lived in one of these "garden apartments." She invited me to sit down on the gray plush sofa in her living room, which was decorated with faded color graduation and communion photos, in Woolworth's gold frames, of some of her thirteen children, and a dozen high school football trophies won by one of Roberto's brothers. Behind the sofa, a single row of gold-flecked mirror tiles crossed the middle of the wall as far as the exposed water pipes in the corner. A K-Mart stereo radio pumped rock and roll from the windowsill across the room.

Mrs. Lewis was an enormous freckle-faced black woman of about forty-five. The great weight of her body matched the great weight of her life. (Besides Roberto, she had one other kid in trouble—a son doing time for armed robbery—and he had enemies in prison, and she feared he might be killed any day.) With an effort she lowered herself into one of the matching gray chairs facing the sofa.

Speaking loudly over the stereo, which only I seemed to hear, I explained to her, not for the first time, her son's limited options. She nodded expressionlessly and said, "Um-hum, um-hum, um-hum," at regular intervals. I said that I thought Roberto was reluctant to plead because he didn't want to admit his guilt to her.

"Okay, then," she said when I had finished. "I'll tell him to go ahead and plead guilty." She looked weary.

I thanked her and drove back over the bridge to my world.

§4-19

That Saturday I got home from the office at 8:00 P.M.

"Hi, I'm home!" I called brightly as I came through the door. Silence. "I'm home!" I shouted again.

From downstairs, quietly, "Hello." Amazing how much the intonation of one neutral word can convey. I went downstairs and was not surprised when Jan turned her back to me, her skinny little body a fortress, rays of anger shimmering off her golden-brown hair. That's when I noticed the champagne, fresh fish, and strawberries she'd bought. I'd promised to be home for dinner by seven, and she'd taken off time from her own work as a graphic artist to put together this meal.

You see, I had chosen to wait for the bus rather than pay for a cab. I should have known that was a mistake when I saw three buses leave, bumper to bumper, just as I ran up to the bus stop. But I was hoping against hope that there would be a straggler. I was made optimistic by the first foggy warm spring air of March, by distant lightning flickering silently behind the white Capitol dome, by the world-historic, here-I-am-in-Imperial-Rome presence of the Archives of the United States of America across the street from the bus stop. I let twelve cabs go by. Then I said, forget it, I'll take a cab. Then there weren't any more cabs.

As I was waiting, alone except for some dauntless nineteenth-century hero (and his horse), I was thinking, it's frigging *Saturday night* and I've just spent five solid hours writing a motion for someone who wants to withdraw his guilty pleas (to possession of drugs and a pistol) and go to trial. He pled guilty basically because he was guilty, and if he goes to trial, he'll be *found* guilty. But I'm his lawyer now, and I know that a good motion to withdraw guilty pleas before sentence will succeed. It might accomplish nothing in the long run, but the point is he wants his guilty pleas withdrawn, and a good lawyer will prevail at that. The precedents are on his side.

I'm thinking, what a way to spend my energy, my substance, my life—this is my life, this is it—on this deadbeat who's guilty anyway, and who's going to be found guilty anyway, all for some principle, that he should be getting the ultimate of my ability in service to him. That would be fine if I were fighting for welfare rights, or tenants' rights, or any important cause that you could apply your legal talents to; but for some deadbeat—what the hell is the point of that?

That's what was creeping up on me at the bus stop: if I'm going to work till 8:00 P.M. Saturday, I should either be setting a precedent benefiting all poor people, or making a lot of money.

"You have to remember that 'frontiers of freedom' stuff," Jan said. "If *he* can withdraw *his* plea, *you* can withdraw *your* plea. It's important."

If I had it to do over again, I'd take the first taxi I saw.

§4-20

Any crazy lead Howard Robbins gave me, I investigated, to fulfill my duty to investigate,* to convince him I was on his side, and to turn up evidence of his insanity. To convince a jury that a defendant is insane, what you want is lay witnesses, people like the jurors, who can testify to crazy things they have seen him do. Just because Howard was mad as a hatter, that by no means meant that a jury would find him not guilty by reason of insanity. My supervisor had a case in which a parade of psychiatrists retained by the defense, as well as the usually prosecutorial shrinks on the court payroll, testified that the defendant's act was the product of a mental disease, and the prosecution couldn't put on a single psychiatrist to disagree. The jury convicted him.

Exactly what insanity *is* has always been subject to debate, but the debate has heated up considerably since a federal court jury found presidential assailant John Hinckley, Jr., not guilty by reason of insanity. Critics called the Hinckley verdict an unprecedented case of coddling the criminal, a verdict symptomatic of the degeneration of our courts, culture, and *cojones*. But the verdict was not unprecedented. In 1835, one Richard Lawrence was tried—in what was to become the P.D.S. office building— for attempting to assassinate President Andrew Jackson. Lawrence said that he was heir to the British crown, and that he had to get Jackson out of the way to strengthen his claim to the throne. He was "proven of unsound mind," acquitted, and committed to a lunatic asylum.[1]

* An attorney is obligated to investigate every case. "The duty to investigate exists regardless of the accused's admissions or statements to the lawyer of facts constituting guilt or his stated desire to plead guilty" (American Bar Association, *Standards Relating to the Defense Function* [approved draft, 1971], Sect. 4.1).

Letters to the editor expressed outrage that Hinckley had been "let off" and would "go free." In fact, like anyone found not guilty by reason of insanity (N.G.I.) in Washington, he was automatically committed to the John Howard Pavilion of St. Elizabeths Hospital, a facility sufficiently secure* and unpleasant to satisfy the most vengeful of penologists; and he will stay there until he can prove to a judge that he is no longer a danger to himself or others. Getting a psychiatrist to testify in support of that proposition is harder than ever, now that there are precedents for holding psychiatrists liable for damages when their released patients hurt someone. It's a safe bet that Hinckley will be incarcerated as long as or longer than if he had been convicted and sent to prison.[†]

All the controversy surrounding the Hinckley case has created the impression that insanity is a very wide loophole through which criminals commonly escape. In fact, of the 934 felony cases handled by the Public Defender Service in fiscal 1980, *one* ended with a verdict of not guilty by reason of insanity after a trial. (Five N.G.I. pleas were not contested by the government.)[2]

After the Hinckley verdict, more than forty bills were introduced in Congress to modify or abolish the insanity defense in federal courts, and many state legislatures are considering changes.

Insanity is a legal concept, not a medical one. In the federal courts, those of half the states, and in the local courts of the District of Columbia,[‡] a person is "not responsible for criminal conduct if at the time of

---

* The John Howard Pavilion was built in 1959, and there had been only two escapes by 1983 (private conversation, Philip Baridon, Ph.D., Chief, Evaluation Branch, Forensic Division, St. Elizabeths Hospital, May 6, 1983).
† A St. Elizabeths study found that a sample of patients committed following verdicts of not guilty by reason of insanity (N.G.I.) on a variety of charges spent an average of thirty-nine months locked up before they were even allowed to walk the grounds of the hospital. The average incarceration of a similar sample of prisoners in the D.C. correctional system was thirty-two months.
Among N.G.I. patients released from St. E's between 1974 and 1982, 23 percent of those who'd been charged with murder or rape had been in the hospital for more than ten years, as had 21 percent of those who had been charged merely with "public order" offenses such as disorderly conduct:[3] In the latter cases, the patients suffered deprivation of liberty for more than forty times as long as the ninety-day maximum sentence that could be imposed on a person convicted of the offense. The Supreme Court decided in the summer of 1983 that such commitments in excess of the maximum sentence are legal, in *Jones* v. *United States*. Michael Jones was accused of shoplifting a coat in 1974. He had been in St. Elizabeths ever since.[4]
Once St. Elizabeths N.G.I. patients are released, their recidivism rate is lower than that of ordinary prisoners. Of 227 N.G.I. patients released into the community under ongoing supervision between April 1977 and March 1978, only 29 (12.8 percent) had gotten into any trouble by the end of 1978. That is considered an adequate follow-up period, because released prisoners who run afoul of the law tend to do so quickly. The comparable recidivism rate for federal prisoners is 25 percent.[5]
‡ Like the District of Columbia itself, the D.C. court system is a hybrid with local and federal aspects. Although its judges are appointed by the President of the United

such conduct as a result of a mental disease or defect he lacked substantial capacity either to recognize the wrongfulness of his conduct or to conform his conduct to the requirements of the law."[6]* A "mental disease or defect" includes "any abnormal condition of the mind which substantially affects mental or emotional processes and substantially impairs behavior controls."[7]

By this standard, if, when the defendant was slashing his victim's throat, he thought he was slicing a cucumber, he's not guilty by reason of insanity. If the defendant thought that he was Abraham Lincoln and that his victim was John Wilkes Booth, he could be found guilty anyway, because you can't go around killing people just because they're out to get you—unless, of course, he thought John Wilkes Booth was at that moment pulling a gun on him, and that he was acting in self-defense. If the defendant killed his girlfriend because she left him for another man, and he knew that's what he was doing, and knew it was wrong, but was no more able to stop the action than a moviegoer at a movie or a dreamer in a dream, he's not guilty by reason of insanity. If he thought he was obeying the command of his neighbor's dog, he's guilty—you can't do everything a dog tells you to—unless he thought the dog was God and obeying his commands could never be wrongful, in which case he's not guilty.

Noting that the insanity test "asks the jury to wrestle with such unfamiliar, if not incomprehensible, concepts," former Chief Judge Bazelon of the United States Court of Appeals, District of Columbia Circuit, wrote, "The best hope for our . . . test is that jurors will regularly conclude that no one—including the experts—can provide a meaningful answer to the questions posed by the . . . test. And in their search for some semblance of an intelligible standard, they may be forced to consider whether it would be just to hold the defendant responsible for his action."[8]

No matter what definition a judge reads to them, what juries always ultimately decide *is* whether the defendant ought to be held responsible. "Not guilty by reason of insanity" means "not held responsible for his act," nothing more or less than that. One can argue about criteria which have led juries to make that decision, or which should lead juries to make that decision, but it is that decision itself which defines "insanity." You are insane if you are not responsible; you are not responsible if the jury decides not to hold you responsible; if the jury decides not to hold you responsible, you are insane.

States and its criminal cases are prosecuted by the United States attorney's office, the D.C. court system has had, since the Court Reform Act of 1971, its own case law and its own rules.
* There are some variations in wording from jurisdiction to jurisdiction.

That's the real basis on which lawyers usually argue insanity cases. I listened to the closing arguments at the insanity murder trial of a man who garroted a prostitute, and I didn't hear much talk about "emotional processes" or "behavior controls." The defense counsel insisted that his client was "bats," "batty," "sick as a bedbug." "You have to rely on your common sense," he told the jury. "He was sick, he was out of control, he couldn't help what he did."

The prosecutor retorted, "He's perverted. He's not normal. He's sick. But he's not crazy. . . . He's accountable."

Insanity, like, for instance, self-defense or duress, is an "affirmative defense." That means the defendant is *presumed* to have been sane, not to have acted in self-defense, and not to have been forced by another to commit the crime, so that the prosecution ordinarily doesn't have to introduce evidence on those points to prove its case. Rather, the defendant has the burden of introducing some evidence of insanity, self-defense, or duress in order to raise the issue.

Once the defendant has raised the issue of insanity, in the federal courts and those of half the states, the burden shifts to the *prosecution* to prove *beyond a reasonable doubt* that the defendant was *sane.* In the local courts of the District of Columbia and half the states, the burden remains on the *defendant* to prove insanity "by the preponderance of the evidence," that is, to prove that, *more likely than not,* he was *insane* at the time of the offense.

This distinction in the burden of proof may have influenced the outcome of the Hinckley trial. The jurors *weren't positive* that Hinckley was *sane,* so, following the instructions of the federal court judge, they returned a verdict of not guilty by reason of insanity. Had they been listening to instructions across the street in D.C. superior court, if the jurors were not convinced that Hinckley was, more likely than not, *insane,* they might have convicted him.

A widely proposed post-Hinckley reform would put the burden of proof of insanity on the defendant in jurisdictions where this is not already so. The suggestion has a certain appeal, because the elusive presence of "sanity" is peculiarly difficult for the government to prove beyond a reasonable doubt. On the other hand, even in jurisdictions where the defendant has the burden of proving insanity, juries are always instructed that the defendant does not have to prove he is not guilty; the government still has to prove that he is guilty beyond a reasonable doubt—which *means* that he was sane at the time of the offense, beyond a reasonable doubt.

It's to be expected that a certain amount of confusion surrounds the issue of insanity. There's no general agreement about what mental illness is, or what constitutes responsibility, so it should surprise no one that we are unable to state with precision how these two vague concepts interact. No matter how the line is drawn between sanity and insanity, there will always be close cases that could teeter-totter on either side of it.

A more pernicious "reform" being tried out in several states is the replacement of the N.G.I. verdict with a verdict of "guilty but insane" or "guilty but mentally ill," under which the convicted person would be sentenced as an ordinary criminal, but would get psychiatric treatment while serving his time. As defined in one bill before Congress, "a defendant is guilty but mentally ill if his actions constitute all necessary elements of the offense charged other than the requisite state of mind, and he lacked the requisite state of mind as a result of mental disease or defect."[9]

Such legislation represents a radical departure from Anglo-American legal tradition, which for centuries has required that to convict someone of a crime, the prosecution must prove not only that he did a particular act—such as pulling a trigger—but that he did it with a particular state of mind. As Supreme Court Justice Felix Frankfurter wrote, "a muscular contraction resulting in a homicide does not constitute murder."[10] For a killing to be murder, it must be done with "malice," that is, a vicious and wicked state of mind. This mental state is as much an element of the crime of murder as the physical killing itself.

"Guilty but mentally ill" is an irrelevancy if the defendant, despite mental problems, was sane. It is a semantic attempt to hide a logical contradiction if the defendant was insane: "Guilty but insane" is a contradiction in terms, because insane means not capable of forming a criminal intent, not responsible, and, therefore, not guilty. Lawmakers would do well to remember that the verdict of not guilty by reason of insanity doesn't "let off" guilty people; it provides a means of locking up dangerous people who are not guilty of a crime.

It is impossible to devise a system which will result in *all* the innocent going free and *all* the guilty being punished. To ensure that *most* of the innocent go free, you have to let a certain number of the guilty go free. To punish *all* the guilty, you'd have to punish a certain number of the innocent. That is the choice. You'll never hit it on the nose. And if you revise the system to deal with the rare case, you throw the whole thing out of whack.

The "guilty but insane" law would start to tilt the entire system against the defendant. Considering the rarity of insanity cases, one wonders whether that isn't exactly what the "reformers" want. They don't want *any* "guilty" people "getting off." They don't recall, or they choose to forget, what John Adams said.

Do you remember what John Adams said? If not, please turn to page vii.

Most of the tiny number of people who are found not guilty by reason of insanity under present laws never go before a jury at all. They are so clearly *nuts*—a word forensic psychiatrists use interchangeably with "insane"—that the prosecution doesn't contest the N.G.I. plea. If you find yourself in front of a jury with an N.G.I. case, you're in trouble.

If the crime appears "rational" and comprehensible—like a love-triangle murder—a jury will doubt that the defendant was crazy. If the crime appears utterly deranged—like the torture-murder of a stranger—a jury will be disinclined to accept an insanity defense because they are afraid the defendant will get back on the street. Your best shot at a successful insanity defense should be with a crime that's weird enough to be crazy, but not so bizarre as to be horrifying. The ax-man of the drive-in movies is not going to be found not guilty by reason of *anything*.

We had to build a strong case to show that Howard Robbins really was nuts, not only to convince a jury but to convince *him*. I needed his permission to present a defense of insanity, and he was dead-set against it. (A judge *can* interpose a defense of insanity for an unwilling defendant, but rarely does.)

Howard had told me that his "girlfriend," named Lois, could testify that Sheila was tremendously jealous about their impending marriage (and therefore likely to try to do him dirt by this "frameup"), so I asked a student investigator, Amy Strader, to talk to Lois, a neighbor of Howard's.

"He used to be all right until a couple of years ago, when he broke up with his girlfriend Sheila," Lois, a slender twenty-one-year-old waitress at a fast-food shop, told Amy. "After that, he really went off. Somewhere around that time he came to my front door at four in the morning and asked my mother to let him out the back door. Let him in the front door so he can go out the back door!

"He told folks we was going to get maried, but there was nothing between us," Lois continued. "You know, I'd be sitting there on the porch. I'd have male company, and Howard would come up the steps and just stand there, staring. I'd say, 'What you want, boy?' and he'd say 'You!' then laugh and smile. I'd be real rude and just say, 'Get the hell off my porch! Get out of here, boy!' But he was always just coming back. Howard was real gentle. He didn't seem like what he is.

"That boy needs help," Lois concluded. "He should be locked up for good. St. E's or something maybe could help. But I was never afraid of him. I don't know why. I guess 'cause he just seemed normal."

"I had Lois interviewed, like you asked me to," I told Howard at the jail. He looked at me with just the hint of a smile on his face. "She says you were never going to get married. She says she was never even your girlfriend."

Howard's expression did not change. "Well, it's easy to figure out why she'd say that," he said. "She must be afraid of what Sheila would do to her if she admitted we was getting married, especially after she already shot David. That's obvious.

"Me and Sheila were 'brutal'—that means even closer than getting married," he went on, assuming a for-background-only tone. "We were engaged once, but Sheila decided not to get married. But we were both too hip to let that bother us. We even saw the Parliament Funkadelic at the Capital Centre together. There is no way the police can avoid it in their own mind that Sheila shot David, and herself. It's real easy for two people to get shot by the same gun."

"Yeah, I can see that," I said. "But the problem is, Howard, Lois is not going to testify that Sheila had any reason to put a false charge on you."

"Well, you see, that don't make no difference," Howard said, turning his palms up, "because there's no way this case is ever going to make it to court. It'll be dropped way before that. Because it just don't make sense. How can the D.A. say I shot Sheila for 'no reason'?" he demanded, leaning forward into his argument. "Anyone would shoot someone if they was being harassed. And if it *was* for 'no reason,' how can he turn around and say it's first-degree murder 'cause I planned it ahead? How can you *plan* something without a reason?" He arched his eyebrows quizzically. "That's crazy. That makes all of God's creation a cartoon. The D.A. can't have it both ways, but that's what he said. The stenographer got it down. It's cold turkey for him." Howard settled back in his chair.

"It may not make any sense, Howard, but that doesn't mean you're not going to be tried and convicted and sent to Lorton for twenty years if you don't let me put on an insanity defense."

He dismissed my argument with a wave of the hand. "I'm not worried about these charges. Can you show me any difference between a parking ticket and a murder charge? The police, they'll shoot you dead over a parking ticket if you ain't done nothing, if you don't do exactly what they want. And I'd rather spend the rest of my life at Lorton than spend one day in St. Elizabeths."

After humoring him, listening, listening, listening, nodding, agreeing, I decided to say, and said, "Listen to me, Howard. I'll look you in the eye and say this, and if you want to fire me for it, go ahead: If you would rather spend the rest of your life in Lorton prison than one day at St. Elizabeths, you're nuts."

"I'll tell you three things," Howard retorted. "I don't want to go to Lorton, I don't want to go to St. Elizabeths, and I'm not nuts."

§4-21

"I hope I didn't keep you waiting," Howard Robbins's mother said, with a bashful smile, as she walked into my office the day before his arraignment.

"Not at all," I said. "No problem."

She settled into one of the two banged-up wooden chairs facing my desk. She could just fit into it. I'd never thought of her as fat—she was a handsome woman. I was thinking she must have been lovely when she was young. She left her coat on, and lay her briefcase-sized pocketbook on her lap.

I poured my fifth cup of black instant coffee of the afternoon, returned one last phone call, and switched my phone so it would ring at a remote, probably unattended, secretarial outpost.

I had asked her to come in because she might be a better witness than any psychiatrist to Howard's present incompetence, as well as his insanity at the time of the shooting.

"How has Howard been acting lately?" I asked. She'd visited him at least twice a week for the two months he'd been in jail.

"When I visit, he talks about last year when we had the police take him to St. Elizabeths after he punched me. He talks about it every time. I've had only one pleasant visit." She smiled ruefully. "That was last week. He talked about other things. He talked about war. He sounded almost sensible.

"He talks about that time he went to St. Elizabeths like it was yesterday. He says, 'Who called the police on me?' He's accusing me. It makes me *very* uncomfortable. It upsets me now, just talking about it." She was afraid of her son, and she loved him, and she was mystified.

"Before he went to jail, he used to knock on my bedroom door at twelve or one at night, rubbing his head, asking me, 'Was it you, Mama? Did you call the police on me?' It'd look like he was sort of in a daze.

Then he'd go back to his room. It was frightening. I put a lock on my bedroom door. . . . We have locks on every door in the house," she added quietly, telling herself for the thousandth time what her life had become.

"He insists he's in jail for only one reason—that I sent him to the hospital back then, and they think he's crazy." She shook her head. "Sounds like thunder," she said as the skies collided outside. It began to rain, hard. The leaves would be fully out in a few days.

I relayed a psychiatrist's advice about convincing a jury that Howard was ill, not evil. If it responds to medication, it must be an illness. If it runs in the family, it sounds like an illness. "Has anyone else in the family had problems like Howard's?"

Mrs. Robbins told me that she had one daughter who "took sick when she was thirteen. She had whooping cough and contracted pneumonia. She suffered brain damage and spent from age thirteen to forty in St. Elizabeths. Now she's in a foster home.

"Then, of course, Howard's sister Aileen is an alcoholic. If she drinks, she'll do awful things, then ask the next morning, 'What did I do last night?' Howard's the same way, except that he won't believe you when you tell him what he did.

"When he first started hearing and seeing bees and giant flies—that was twelve years ago. We took him to St. Elizabeths, but they let him come home." Her eyes drifted back to the past, to the point where Howard's help and hope were lost, and hers. Finally her sorrow spilled out in tears. She sobbed for just a moment, then collected herself. "He really did see giant insects," she said. "He should have been committed. Then he started hearing Sheila's voice about five years ago. He'd known her all his life. First he knew her sister. Her sister had his child."

"Is it really his child?" I asked.

"Oh, yes. He looks just like Howard. Howard loves that little boy.

"Two years ago, when he said Sheila hit him in the head with a shoe and broke a bottle over his leg—there were no marks on him—the voices got much worse. He'd say to me, 'You don't hear them? Don't tell me I'm crazy! She tells me to have sex with my sister, tells me to have sex with my grandmother, and all these dirty things. She sees me all the time, even when I'm trying to take a bath.' Finally I'd tell him, 'Yes, Howard, yes, I hear them,' because he'd get so upset. One time he was crying, and I was holding his hand. He said, 'All the girls think I'm a freak. When I try to have sex, Sheila gets between us, and I can't function.' "

"Did he say she'd get *physically* between them?"

"Physically. She'd push them apart. He said it was more than three years since he had sex.

"All last summer, people would laugh at him because he'd dress so strangely. When he'd go to the playground to play basketball by himself, kids would throw stones at him and call him 'crazy Howard.' He asked me, 'Should I get them, Mama, or should I see who their mother is, and talk to their mother? Because I don't want to hurt them.'

"Howard says he doesn't want to go to St. Elizabeths, because he wants people to respect him, not call him crazy. He says if he goes anywhere, he'd rather go to Lorton. He says he could get a job, get married, and have children when he gets out of Lorton. But if he comes from St. E's, he'll always be labeled crazy. And you can't disagree or he'll get up and leave."

"This is exactly the sort of stuff we need," I said.

"Do you think there's any way it would be possible for you to let me know what happens at Howard's arraignment tomorrow?" she asked, extremely hesitant to ask anything.

"No problem," I said.

At Howard's arraignment, we pled not guilty to first-degree murder, assault with intent to kill while armed, and carrying a pistol without a license. It was reported that the court psychiatrist, after seeing Howard again, had come to the conclusion that the defense psychiatrist was right—Howard was incompetent. At Howard's insistence, I demanded a hearing at which to contest the finding of incompetency. Then I approached the bench and told the judge that I really thought Howard *was* incompetent, and I moved for the appointment of an *amicus curiae* ("friend of the court"—independent counsel) to present Howard's argument for a finding of competency when the time for a hearing came, as I felt I could not in good conscience argue for something I thought was against Howard's best interest.

There is often a conflict between what the lawyer considers his client's best interest, and what the client wants, a conflict that the lawyer is ordinarily bound by his ethics to resolve in favor of the client's wishes: an attorney is the client's advocate, not his guardian. The ethical question is always troublesome when the client appears to be a poor judge of his interests—as with juveniles—and becomes a real dilemma when the client appears to be, but has not been legally declared, incompetent.

Judge Milmoe said perhaps an *amicus* should argue for *in*competency—what my client didn't want—but I should argue for competency—what my client did want—else I would destroy our lawyer-client relationship. But I didn't want some deadbeat grabbed from the courthouse corridor arguing for incompetency, and I for competency, because I figured I would out-argue him and win, which I didn't want to do.

The government moved for a further thirty-day inpatient examination for competency and sanity at St. Elizabeths Hospital, hoping that close scrutiny would reveal that Howard was faking incompetency, or, if he wasn't, that psychotropic medication would straighten him out enough to stand trial. I opposed the government's motion.

Judge Milmoe, as judges will, decided not to decide anything. He said he'd make his rulings at a status hearing in a few weeks. Meanwhile, he sent Howard back to the jail.

§4-22

Three weeks later I went to see Howard at the jail, to explain what was happening and to try once more to get him to go along with an insanity plea.

I had by then received an investigator's report of an interview with a Washington *Star* paperboy who had been out collecting on his route when two men and a woman came walking down the street toward him, arguing. Moments after they'd passed him, he heard two shots and turned to see one of the men on the ground and the other pointing a pistol at the woman, who was screaming. The man shot the woman once, as the paperboy recalled, and ran away. The boy recognized the man with the gun as Howard, whom he knew from the neighborhood.

Howard's mother's friend Johnny, the man who teased Howard about putting the windows down on the night of the murder, had also been interviewed. Johnny described Howard as having been "spaced out" that night, "not himself." "He was here, but he wasn't here, if you know what I mean. He could have been in heaven or hell, or somewhere in between, but he wasn't here."

Howard greeted me by saying that he didn't want me to be his lawyer anymore. "The way things are going, it's not too heavy a case. You've done a real good job," he said with an appreciative nod, "but instead of having investigators go out, I think it would be better to just let the government go ahead and get itself in trouble. I've talked to a few lawyers in here, and they say the less I talk to you, the better."

I told him that with the information we'd developed, we had an excellent chance for a successful insanity defense, and no alternative.

"I'm not crazy," he insisted. "My mother wouldn't have given me money to go shopping if I was crazy. Johnny wouldn't ask me to put the window down if I was crazy."

"That's one thing I didn't understand, Howard," I said. "What is the joke about putting the window down? I don't get it."

Howard stood up abruptly. "I think we better end this right here. As far as I'm concerned, we haven't talked."

"As you know," I said soothingly, "I'm fighting the government's motion to send you to St. Elizabeths."

"Well, you can stop fighting," Howard said. "They can't hold me just because I don't want a lawyer. If they do that, they might as well hold me"—he looked toward the floor for a second—"because I got shoes on, or something."

§4-23

"I'm feeling kind of lousy," I said to my colleague Ken Lloyd on the eve of the hearing on my motion to suppress the pistol found on Shirley Browning, the annoying client who'd accused me of lying to him about his chances at trial. "I have a horrible cold, but I don't suppose that's a good reason to ask for a continuance. After all, Carl Yastrzemski plays with pain."

"Carl Yastrzemski gets paid six hundred thousand dollars a year," Lloyd said.

He had a point. But I felt somehow the time had come. I'd been working on the case for months. Now I had to *do it*.

Against all the odds, I won. I did it by presenting evidence suggesting that the arresting officer had been sexually involved with a woman whom Browning had lived with (and beaten up), and that his frisk of Browning had not *in fact* been based on an "articulable suspicion" that he was armed, whether or not it *could* have been, but on a personal animus. In other words, as they say on the street, the cop "had a hard-on for" Browning—he was out to get him.

I didn't know whether it was true that the officer had been sleeping with Browning's woman, but it was true that there were facts, provided me by my investigator, out of which to construct that implication; and it was certainly true that the cop was stupid. That was a fact, that was reality, that was the truth—and the truth will out. In fact, he wasn't on the police force anymore, having been dropped in his rookie year after three times failing to pass a written test.

("That's sad," Lloyd said with a frown. "Imagine—too dumb to be a cop!")

The ex-officer testified that he had never been to Browning's girl-friend's house, then told me, two questions later, on which floor of her apartment building she lived. The judge decided that the cop had been caught in a lie, and one lie threw all of his testimony into doubt. There-fore, the government could not prove that finding the gun resulted from a permissible frisk, rather than an unreasonable search or seizure barred by the Fourth Amendment. The "exclusionary rule" requires that illegally obtained evidence be suppressed. Without the gun in evidence, the gov-ernment would not be able to prove at trial that Browning was carrying a gun.

This was one of only two motions to suppress physical evidence I ever won, although, like any competent defense attorney, I moved to suppress in virtually every case involving physical evidence. Search and seizure issues are explained to the police by prosecutors, so police always try to testify that searches took place in such a way as to make them legal, and it comes down to their word against the defendant's, usually. Judges, for their part, bend over backward not to suppress evidence, since they know that to do so will result in the dismissal of charges.

The occasional suppression of evidence and consequent dismissal of charges against an apparently guilty defendant upsets a lot of people. There are increasing demands for the elimination of the exclusionary rule as it pertains to physical evidence seized in violation of the Fourth Amendment. (The exclusion of *statements* obtained in violation of the Fifth and Sixth Amendments is less widely criticized, because viola-tions by police of the right not to be questioned without an attorney are less arguably "accidental" than their violations of privacy rights; exactly what constitutes an unreasonable search or seizure is extremely unclear.)

The Fourth Amendment bans unreasonable searches and seizures, but it doesn't say anything about what should be done with illegally obtained evidence. The exclusionary rule is a judicially declared rule of evidence which the Supreme Court has said is "implied" in the Fourth Amend-ment—that is, the Fourth Amendment doesn't make any sense without it. Recently the Supreme Court has been retreating from that position.

If it's true that the exclusionary rule costs society more in unpunished guilt than it benefits society in protected rights—a premise that has not been established*—then perhaps it *should* be eliminated. (Of course, Justice Holmes insisted, "It is a lesser evil that some criminals should escape than that the government should play an ignoble part,"[1] but leave that aside.)

Whenever you change one part of the system, though, shock waves are felt through the rest of the system, often in unforeseen ways. A common suggestion is to eliminate the exclusionary rule, allow the introduction of illegally obtained evidence, and deter violation of the Fourth Amendment simply by fining or otherwise punishing police officers who are found to have violated it. At present, there are no sanctions against officers who seize evidence illegally.

One consequence of this change would be that guilty people wouldn't go free as the result of the suppression of illegally obtained evidence. Another consequence would be that there would no longer be hearings on motions to suppress such evidence. Without such hearings, the defense would lose its most important means of discovering the government's case, and its only opportunity to question government witnesses under oath before the trial. That change could tip the scales of justice violently.

Beyond that, without hearings on suppression motions, society would lose ongoing judicial scrutiny of the rules limiting police activity. Granted, rules are made to be broken. If they are not broken, they are not experienced as rules, and they have no circumscribing effect. But if there is no one arguing that they *have* (or have not) been broken, their position is never fixed, and they are not rules at all. If the only issue is whether a cop should be fined, we are not going to have our best lawyers arguing about it all the way to the Supreme Court, as we do now.

Of course it's terrible for guilty people to go free. *That's the price we pay* for not having cops crawling in and out of our houses. Everybody wants something for nothing.

All the charges against Shirley Browning were dismissed. A broad smile spread over his tobacco-stained teeth. No word of thanks. He just instructed me to get back his gym bag, which had been seized along with the gun.

"What a job you did for that guy!" Lloyd said. "You have to admit it makes you feel good."

---

* In fact, the evidence is to the contrary. A National Institute of Justice study of 520,-993 felony cases presented from 1976 to 1979 to prosecutors in California found that only 4,130, or 0.78 percent, were rejected for prosecution because of search-and-seizure problems. (Nearly three fourths of those were drug-related cases, rather than violent crimes.) Of felony cases that were presented in court, only four tenths of one percent were dismissed because of search-and-seizure issues. (Tom Wicker, "Exploding a Myth," New York *Times,* May 10, 1983, p. A-25.)

"Not as much as it would if it were a widow or an orphan," I said.

"Well, that's pretty hard to come by," Lloyd said.

Thanks to my efforts, plus some good fortune—another pending case against him was dismissed because the government couldn't get a tourist/armed robbery victim to come down from New York to testify— Browning was a free man, for a while, anyway. A couple of months later I was walking from the jail after visiting another client when I heard a voice calling to me from somewhere high in the building. "Mr. Kunen! Mr. Kunen! It's me! Shirley Browning!"

"Write me a letter!" I shouted, and kept walking.

§4-24

Roberto Lewis gave the court psychiatrists a run for their money. The first two reports filed during his sixty-day mental observation stated flatly that he was competent, but a different doctor wrote in a third report, "In response to questions about the court process such as: Before which judge have you appeared? He responded, 'There is only one judge, God. I don't know any other.' His affect is generally flat and he appears to have difficulty answering simple questions." The doctor called Roberto's competency "doubtful."

Roberto remained mute during a fourth examination. However, as he was being led back to his cell, the doctor observed him stop and chat with some women inmates who had just arrived in the jail's medical unit. The court psychiatrists concluded that Roberto was competent. Roberto agreed that it was futile to contest that finding, since our own shrink had come to the same conclusion.

Four and a half months after his arrest, Roberto came into court to plead guilty to second-degree murder while armed, and robbery, lesser offenses than the first-degree murder, armed robbery, and carrying a pistol without a license charges on which he had been indicted. This got him out from under the mandatory twenty-to-life provision of the first-degree murder statute.

I had given him my standard pep talk on guilty plea comportment. "You stand up straight, and you look the judge in the eye. And you don't say 'yeah' or 'no'; you say 'Yes, Your Honor' or 'No, Your Honor,' because she's a judge, and you think that's *great,* and you respect the hell out of her."

I warned him that the judge might ask him whether the prosecutor's version of the crime was true. "I'll say it's none of her business," he said, but he was just teasing me. I told him to admit his guilt and express deep regret about his past and profound hope for his future.

The judge asked him only what grade he had completed in school, to ensure that the record would show that he understood what he was doing when he entered a plea.

"Eighth, Your Honor," he said, "but I'm studying for a high school diploma. But the man don't come to the jail regular. It's not as regular an education as I need, Your Honor." He was a good student.

He answered all of the judge's questions correctly: No, no one had threatened him; no, no one had promised him anything; no, he was not under the influence of drugs or alcohol; yes, he had had enough time to consult with his lawyers, and yes, he was satisfied with their services; yes, he was pleading guilty because he was guilty and for no other reason. The judge accepted his plea and sent him to a federal youth facility (prison) for a pre-sentence study.

§4-25

Fifty-one percent of the felony cases handled by the Public Defender Service in fiscal 1980 were disposed of by guilty pleas. Only 8 percent went to trial. The remainder were dismissed, often as part of bargains for guilty pleas in other cases. Of the felony cases in which the Public Defender Service did go to trial in fiscal 1980, 44 percent ended in guilty verdicts. Thirty-six percent ended in not guilty verdicts. Fifteen percent were mistrials because of hung juries. Five percent were mistrials for other reasons.[1]

It is impossible to describe any complex human activity accurately with numbers alone. For example, in baseball—which has been subjected to far closer statistical scrutiny than the courts ever will be—you can look at a player's batting average, slugging average, on-base percentage, total bases, homers, runs batted in, runs produced, runs produced per at-bat, average with men in scoring position, even game-winning r.b.i.'s, and still not be sure whether he's a bum in clutch situations who jacks up his stats in 13–1 May romps over the Mariners.

Court statistics don't even come close to quantifying reality. Defendants are not cases, and cases are not counts. A defendant is one person (or corporation, which is a "legal person"). A count is a single violation of a single law. A case is a charge, or a group of charges that are triable together, against one defendant. One trial of three co-defendants is three cases. If a defendant is tried on four counts, and the jury finds him not guilty of murder, not guilty of rape, not guilty of kidnapping, and guilty of possession of a hypodermic needle, his case is counted as a guilty verdict. Many cases that are dismissed before trial are begun again under new docket numbers, so the same underlying case may be counted as a dismissal and as a verdict or plea.

Statistics indicating that "only 8 percent of felony cases go to trial" and "41 percent are dismissed" are misleading, and are often used by "law-and-order" politicians to mislead. But it is true that the vast majority of cases are pled to or dismissed. Trials are the exception.

There isn't time to try everybody, and there isn't room to lock everybody up. (On any given day, there are more than half a million people under lock and key—awaiting trial or already sentenced—in America's criminal justice system, the world's third highest per capita incarceration rate, after the Soviet Union and South Africa.[2]) So the prosecution wants to bargain. The defense wants to bargain to make the best of a bad situation. If it's likely to lose at trial, it will surrender, if, in return, the prosecution will reduce the charges. There is also the hope that the judge will go easy at sentencing. (In Washington you can bargain for the prosecutor to support, or at least not oppose, a particular sentence, but ultimately you roll the dice not knowing what the judge will impose. In New York City the judge makes a promise about sentencing before the defendant has to decide whether to plead.) "He pled, Your Honor" means "He played ball, Your Honor." It suggests not so much that the defendant is repentant, on the road to rehabilitation, as that he has saved the court a lot of work.

Some critics have suggested that since people who are convicted after trial usually get heavier sentences than those who plead guilty, a penalty is being imposed for the exercise of the constitutional right to a trial.

The Supreme Court doesn't see it that way. "We cannot hold that it is unconstitutional for the state to extend a benefit to a defendant who in turn extends a substantial benefit to the state and who demonstrates by his plea that he is ready and willing to admit his crime and to enter the correctional system in a frame of mind which affords hope for success in rehabilitation over a shorter period of time than might otherwise be necessary," Justice White wrote in an opinion[3] typifying the Court's lofty perspective on, and consequent hazy view of, the criminal justice system.

As a practical matter, my clients generally benefited from plea bargaining. Aside from affirming your human dignity, giving you a civics lesson, and making you the center of attention for once in your life, a trial doesn't do that much for you when you're caught with your hand in the cookie jar. Thanks to overcrowded dockets, a guilty pleader could at least get some charges dismissed, even if the legal maximum sentences of the remaining counts did leave the judge sufficient discretion to hit him over the wall.

Everyone in the system knows roughly what a given case is "worth." By balancing the seriousness of the crime and the defendant's record (how much time the prosecutor wants the defendant to do), against the strength of the evidence and the skill of the defense attorney (how likely the prosecutor is to get a conviction), a specific deal is arrived at. Only when a deal cannot be agreed upon is it necessary to go to arbitration (a trial). Although prosecutors' plea offers theoretically conformed to specific guidelines, in practice some prosecutors routinely dropped charges that could easily be proved, while others refused to give an inch, even trying to get the defendant to "eat the whole beef" (plead to all the original charges) by claiming to have all sorts of evidence—"positive" identifications, for instance—that didn't exist. It was generally acknowledged that better offers were extended to defendants with P.D.S. attorneys than to those with most private attorneys, because of P.D.S.'s reputation for winning trials, or at least making them arduous. The particular plea bargain struck for a particular defendant, then, depended to a large extent on who his lawyer happened to be and who the prosecutor happened to be. In that respect, it was similar to the outcome of a trial.

A primary function of the defense attorney is to advise his client whether the bargain offered is a fair deal, just as a personal injury lawyer tells his client with considerable exactness how much a particular injury is worth. The weaker the government's case, the better the plea offer will be—so that an *innocent* person will likely be offered the greatest inducement to plead guilty. Conversely, a person caught dead to rights, of whose conviction the prosecution feels confident, will be offered very little and may have little to lose by going to trial.

No decent defense attorney would ever urge an innocent person to plead guilty. Most innocent people simply will not plead guilty, anyway. The same is true of many guilty people. Since I couldn't be sure with which category of person I was dealing, I would in every case ultimately give the same advice: "It's your ass."

§5-01

It was my second summer as a public defender.

I could hear the Baltimore City Jail from a block away—a cacophony of blaring radios and shouting men. As I approached, I saw a few young women on the sidewalk, leaning up against the fence, bantering suggestively with the captive audience inside. The men were invisible from the street, but they could see me. "Hey, Slim! Slim!" someone yelled through a slit in the sooty stone wall. "Back up! Are you an attorney?"

I was the attorney for Billy Pepperidge. He had been on parole from a Maryland auto theft sentence when he was arrested in D.C. for stealing another car, and had been shipped back to Baltimore to await a parole revocation hearing.

A handsome young black man in an absurdly large gray shirt and gray pajama pants, prison garb intended to preclude his blending in with the populace in case of escape, was ushered into the jail's interview area and sat facing me through an iron screen. He was wearing a tight white cap. The baggy clothes and tight cap made him look like an elf or forest creature.

I thought my visit would be brief. Somehow I'd gotten the impression that he wanted to plead guilty in his D.C. case. Any reasonable person would have. Plead guilty to unauthorized use of a vehicle (five years), the government will drop grand larceny/receiving stolen property (ten years) and drop destruction of property (ten years). The evidence against him was overwhelming. The cops said he was driving a gray Scirocco in a "suspicious manner." (He didn't fit the young-and-white-in-Georgetown Volkswagen profile, I supposed.) They looked on their "hot sheet," a printout of all the license numbers of cars reported stolen in the metropolitan area. The license was on the list. They radioed in to headquarters and asked whether the car was still unrecovered, a question quickly answered in the affirmative. They put their flashing lights on. The Scirocco sped off. High-speed chase. Crash. Three males got out and ran. The police caught only Billy. They found personal papers bearing his name in the car, which had been stolen seven days earlier.

(A typical car parked on a street is worth $4,000 retail, twice that if cut up and sold for parts. A lucrative proposition, in some towns car theft is big business. You've got to figure the guy who does the stealing must get at least $1,000, be on easy street for a couple of weeks. In Boston, where the business is organized, there were 3,085 cars stolen per 100,000 population in 1978. In Washington there were only 472 cars stolen per 100,000 population in 1978.[1] My clients had no connections. They'd steal cars *and ride around in them* until they got caught.)

I explained the elements of unauthorized use of a vehicle: even if Pepperidge did not steal the car (grand larceny), if he "knew or should have known" that the car was being used without the owner's permission, he was guilty of U.U.V.

(All kinds of factors are relevant to the issue of whether a defendant "should have known" that a particular car was a stolen vehicle. One client of mine, a Black Muslim who had bought a two-year-old Camaro on a street corner for $2,000 from a blue-eyed blond man in a blue blazer, told me, "I didn't think the car was stolen because he was a white guy. If he was one of my people, or any minority type, I would have figured there was something wrong, but he was a white guy.")

Pepperidge had fled when the police approached—strong evidence that he knew the car was stolen.

"I was sitting in the back seat," he said. "I didn't know anything about the car."

"The best *Perry Mason* could get you is U.U.V.," I said, "so why not waltz in now and have U.U.V. *guaranteed, plus* the sentencing advantages of pleading?"

He looked me in the eye and said, "I'm not worried about the time." He said that he pled guilty once, and he wasn't going to make the same mistake again. He was promised certain charges would be dropped, and they weren't.

"Yeah, you're not going to make the same mistake, you're going to make a different mistake," I said. "Last time you pled when you shouldn't have; this time you won't plead when you should. You've got to make a new decision for a new situation."

He said he would not plead because he was not guilty, and because a conviction would lead to the revocation of his parole: he would have to serve out the remainder of his Maryland sentence before even beginning to do his D.C. time.

The air-conditioning was making me cold. I wanted to leave. "Okay," I said, "it's your ass. So, what happened?"

He said that he wanted to buy drugs, but not on the street. So he told the drug dealer he'd make the buy in the dealer's car. He got in the back seat. The dealer and another man, neither of whom he knew, were in the front. They drove around. A police car put its lights on. The driver sped off. He figured the driver was fleeing because he had drugs. When they crashed, he jumped out and ran.

It was a good story. I thought it might be true. I should have listened to it before I urged him to plead.

I told Pepperidge he had a chance, we'd give it a shot, and I'd give him a good trial. I didn't tell him that I had never tried a case in front of a jury.

§5-02

I was sitting across the table from Roberto Lewis in the interview area upstairs at the D.C. jail. To prepare for his sentencing. I was trying to get some character references, which were, understandably, hard to come by.

"There's Mrs. Wayne. She was the general manager of the Sixty-fifth Street Apartments, but we had to move three years ago. Aunt Jean—she used to be a nurse—she's knowed me all my life. My brother is in Lorton. He's down there for accessory to a murder. I worked for PRIDE, Inc. My supervisor lived on Southern Avenue. My brother down at Lorton used to go with my supervisor's sister. There's Barbara Valley, my friend's mother. She's knowed me since I'm small."

"She's nuts, isn't she?"

"People think she's crazy because she goes to church all the time." Roberto got up, walked to the window, and shouted to some girls hanging around outside, "I'm in for twenty years! I choked the President! Hold up! Hold up! I'll be out in a few minutes. I get out today." He came back and sat down. "Her minister knows me. I went to that church."

§5-03

At about 7 P.M. on July 14, 1980, two young black men boarded a Metrobus at Fourteenth Street, N.W., heading east on U. They were arguing about something. As they sat down in the rear of the bus, one said to the other, "I'm going to shoot you, nigger!" and did, with a .38, in the face. He jumped off the bus at Thirteenth Street opposite Ben's Chili Bowl and ran away. The police arrived within minutes, talked to witnesses from the bus, and broadcast the following description of the gunman:

"Black male, five foot seven, slim, twenty-one to twenty-two years old, white T-shirt, black Levi's."*

At about 6:50 P.M., William Buie, a quiet twenty-two-year-old tree trimmer, had gotten off a Metrobus headed *west* on U Street, at Eleventh Street, right by Eaton's Modern Barber Shop. He walked three blocks north to his home, washed up, and was walking toward his girlfriend's house, *toward* the scene of the shooting, when, at 7:20 P.M., a policeman pulled up beside him and told him to stop.

Buie was wearing black jeans and a white T-shirt bearing the words "Kansas, You Are the Sunshine of My Life," a green four-leaf clover, and a brown and yellow sunflower. The officer radioed back to the scene, "Was there a design on the T-shirt?" He was answered, "Negative. Just a plain white T-shirt. But bring him back anyway."

Buie was put in the back seat of the police car and driven to the scene of the shooting. Two passengers from the bus were waiting with the police there. One was asked to close his eyes while the other looked at Buie, still seated in the police car. She nodded affirmatively. Then Buie was taken out of the police car and was walked a few paces away. The second witness then opened his eyes and affirmed that Buie was the perpetrator. A third witness, a little girl in the crowd which had gathered at the scene, also told an officer that she recognized Buie. He was placed under arrest. Two other black males brought to the scene because they were wearing black pants and white T-shirts were not identified, and were released.

The victim arrived at the Washington Hospital Center MEDSTAR unit at 7:25, "with a history of gunshot wound to the leftside face," according to the hospital records, "with cardiac arrest en route." A .38-caliber slug was lodged in his brain. "After vigorous resuscitation, cardiac massage, with pharmacologic support, cardiac activity resumed. No spontaneous respiration. Neuro consult: brain dead at 9:09 P.M. Patient declared officially dead. Resuscitation stopped. At 9:13, spontaneous return of cardiac activity. Family consented to organ donation. Patient went into asystole [his heart stopped] before Harvest Team ready to receive him."

The next morning, Buie was herded into the lockup at superior court with four dozen other men arrested the previous day. He was sweaty and

---

* Police radio transmissions are taped and can be subpoenaed by the defense.

bleary-eyed after a sleepless night and wasn't entirely sure that he wasn't dreaming. Nothing made any sense, and everything was unfamiliar. Even the clothes he was wearing were strange and didn't fit. They'd been given to him by the police when they took his shirt and pants for evidence.

Finally a young white man on the other side of the iron screen called out Buie's name. Buie rushed over. The man said his name was Kunen, and he'd been assigned to be Buie's lawyer. It wasn't clear exactly who this Kunen was or who had "assigned" him. Nevertheless, he was Buie's best hope, and, in a torrent of words, Buie desperately tried to explain that a ghastly mistake had been made. The white guy seemed unimpressed, laconically observing that Buie's innocence wasn't "the issue" that day. He was more interested in a lot of biographical information which Buie had already given to the police the night before, and to somebody from the bail agency that morning. At last the white guy let Buie tell him his alibi. He said it was very good that Buie was able to remember everything he'd done, everywhere he'd been, everyone he'd seen the previous day. He said it was "unfortunate" that Buie had waived his *Miranda* rights and given all this information to the police in a signed statement.

Five dirty, hot, tired, hungry hours later, Buie was passed in front of a judge for ninety seconds. Because he was a lifelong resident of D.C. with no criminal record, because he was employed full-time, because he lived with his mother, he was allowed to leave on "personal recognizance."

"Don't worry, you have a good lawyer," Kunen said.

"I'm still worried," Buie said.

"What a *dream* case!" Kunen thought. "Innocent (?) man takes a bus ride to destiny."

§5-04

I walked through the simmering sun of early Washington summer to the National Bank of Washington, being careful to give a wide berth to the side door in case some progressive elements had deposited a bomb at the office of the Argentinian naval attaché, which for reasons known only to the Argentines shares that obscure little branch bank's building. Once safely inside the bank, I got eighty dollars out of the money vending machine, as pocket cash for a weekend trip to Virginia Beach.

As I walked back to my office , I was dismayed to see Johnny Angell swinging toward me on crutches. Johnny Angell was a somewhat unsavory character, as was often true of my clients who had committed only trivial crimes, or, as in Mr. Angell's case, no crime at all. An elderly man had told a police officer that someone had hit him in the head *from behind* and stolen a paper bag containing *jewels*. The policeman had driven the complainant around the neighborhood, and the complainant had pointed out Mr. Angell. Although Mr. Angell had no jewels and no bag, he was arrested.

Mr. Angell had lived in doorways, shelters, and mental hospitals for most of his forty years, occasionally joining the work force as a dishwasher during periods of lucidity or self-discipline. He received workmen's compensation checks, which, rather remarkably, he deposited in a savings account against a truly torrential day.

I cited his history of employment and frugality as "indicia of reliability" at his arraignment, arguing vehemently that Mr. Angell should be on the street (literally, in his case) while awaiting trial. Judge McCord, one of the more earnest fellows on the bench, asked me if I weren't concerned that Mr. Angell, who was both ranting and raving even as we spoke, might harm himself, were he at liberty. I suffered one of those inexplicable lapses into guilelessness which beset me from time to time, and replied that it was not my job to worry about that; my job was to get what my client wanted, and my client wanted out. (After all, no one would question my arguing for the release of an accused murderer, and if a possible murderer, why not a possible suicide? It's a distinction without a difference.)

The little judge flew into one of his daily earnest rages, upbraiding me for being an "idealist" with abstract notions of legal duty and no contact with reality, adding that I typified everything that was wrong with the Public Defender Service. I was pleased to hear all that, because I did not believe in the doctrinaire statement I had just made, and I shared the judge's preference for doing what you think is right, as opposed to what you are supposed to do—although I know such thinking causes horrendous traffic jams, among other things.

The judge ordered Mr. Angell held at the jail until such time as he posted his two hundred dollars' life savings for bail. As he was being led away, Mr. Angell, to express his displeasure with the court and its functionaries (me), ripped his forearms with his fingernails. This earned him a "thirty-day inpatient mental observation." The judge pointed out to the entire courtroom that Mr. Angell's self-destructive behavior had proved just how wrong Mr. Kunen had been. Of course, the judge had his causal chain hopelessly snarled—Mr. Angell had mangled himself *because* the judge detained him. I let it go. It was just one of those days.

There was nothing wrong with Mr. Angell that a little Thorazine couldn't control, and after a mere five weeks of incarceration, he was allowed to bail himself out.

And here he was hobbling toward me outside the bank.

"What happened to your foot?" I asked, glancing at the filthy cast on his ankle. He mumbled something about a bus.

"Could you lend me some money, Mr. Kunen?" he whined.

"I can't do that, Mr. Angell. Do you know how many clients I have? If I give it to you, I'd have to give it to everybody."

"Please, Mr. Kunen. I only have two dollars, and I can't go to my cousin in New York because I have to stay in town until the trial."

Like all conversations with unwashed, urine-soaked people in the hot sun, this one had gone on too long.

"What am I supposed to do, Mr. Kunen?"

"How do I know? Do what you always do—be poor," I thought. "Okay," I sighed, and reached for my wallet. I was damned if I was going to give him a five. I gave him three singles.

He looked at the bills with undisguised disappointment, but he thanked me. He was nothing if not polite.

"Take care of yourself," I said.

The case against Mr. Angell was dropped a month later. The U.S. attorney's office makes a practice of not revealing *why* a case is dropped. In Mr. Angell's case, it is likely that the complainant could not be found by the government. I know *we* couldn't find him. Mr. Angell was not in a position to recover damages from the government because he would have been unable to show that the police had acted in "bad faith."

§5-05

Jan and I were lying on a broad yellow beach by the dark-blue sea of Block Island. The sun was so bright and the air so clear that everything, even distant objects, took on that hyperclarity, that surreal sharpness that renders all beach scenes dreamlike and inseparable one from another. Roberto Lewis was at that time being "studied" in a federal prison, to be sentenced right after my vacation, and we were talking about him.

"Roberto says, 'Oh my God, this guy's gonna take this gun away from me and kill me,' " I said. "And he falls back, and there's an explosion.

And the guy's lying dead. What can Roberto do to make that moment not exist? Does he really have to spend the next twenty years locked up because of that quarter of a second? The court's saying, 'Don't do that!' But he already did it. What effect will twenty years have that ten years wouldn't have?"

"Deters his friends," Jan said.

"Then 'justice' is 'screw somebody over to affect somebody *else's* behavior'?"

"What about the 'villain' who happened to be walking down the street with the camera?" Jan demanded.

"What does it have to do with him?" I asked.

"You're talking about justice," Jan said.

"What does it accomplish? Twenty years does nothing for the victim. As far as deterring others, it's not fair to use Roberto for that."

"Roberto crossed the line when he went out there with a gun," Jan said—the archetypical "reasonable person," she had just invented the felony-murder law.

Judge Davis sat impassively and Roberto stood still, two poles between which my co-counsel Lloyd and I vibrated as we argued for an indeterminate sentence under the Youth Act.

Touching the highlights of our previously submitted sentencing memorandum, I reminded the already decided judge that Roberto's record of prior offenses was "not indicative of a hardened heart," and that "the instant offense" had not involved an *intent* to murder; rather, Mr. Lewis had set in motion a chain of events that ended in tragedy. According to his "uncontroverted confession," he fired in a moment of panic. He had expressed remorse on more than one occasion.

The judge's eyebrows slowly rose, then her chin elevated and her face tipped back, as though her whole head were hydraulically controlled by the brows. She looked through the bottoms of the big square glasses balanced on her tiny nose, and carefully blinked. Blinking was her broadest gesture. She would vary the speed and the height to which she lifted her eyelids, and might blink anywhere from one to three times, depending upon how emphatic she wanted to be. This was merely a "Continue, Counselor" blink.

I pointed out that Roberto's problems had not begun with himself. The eighth of thirteen children of an alcoholic father, Roberto was himself an alcoholic; he read at the third-grade level; and he had, according to the pre-sentence study, a "feeling of inadequacy which creates anxiety feelings and causes him to withdraw into emotional apathy."

I concluded by quoting a D.C. jail guard: " 'Roberto's not a bad guy, really. He has a mental problem. If you pay attention to him, he'll respond.' "

The judge blinked "thank you" and turned to Ken Lloyd.

Lloyd, having delegated the emotional appeal to me, got down to facts: we were asking that Roberto be given an indeterminate sentence under the Youth Act and be sent to a federal prison facility,* where he would come under the authority of the Federal Parole Commission. According to the federal commission's "salient factors" formula, which weighs factors such as the defendant's age, the severity of the offense, the number of his prior convictions, and his history of narcotic dependence, there was no way Roberto could get out in less than eight years; so the judge could give him the indeterminate sentence we sought, without fear that he'd be right back on the street.

Lloyd then addressed himself briefly to a troublesome new problem: while in jail awaiting sentence, Roberto had been involved in a brawl among inmates, one of whom sustained a skull fracture and died. Roberto was charged with *another* first-degree murder. He had yet to be tried, and was "presumed innocent," but the judge was free to take the new charge into consideration when she decided on Roberto's sentence.

Lloyd stressed that Roberto was charged with criminal responsibility for the jail death as an "aider and abettor."† No one claimed that Roberto, personally, had fractured the dead man's skull. Anyway, there was strong evidence that the decedent was done in not by the head injury, but by malpractice at D.C. General Hospital. And Roberto's involvement "could best be characterized as stupid and impulsive, not calculated or cruel."

It was Roberto's turn to speak.

Sentencing is no time to start being honest. It would not do for the defendant to say, "I don't like the consequences for me of what I did, so I won't do anything like that again." Renunciation and transformation are what's called for.

The big favorite with judges is "I thought a lot about it, and I realize *I*

---

* About 30 percent of men convicted of felonies in D.C. are sent to federal prisons rather than D.C.'s Lorton Correctional Facility, either because they have enemies at Lorton or because the judge or the defendant himself wants the defendant in a program available only at a federal facility.

† "A person aids and abets another in the commission of a crime if he knowingly associates himself in some way with the criminal venture with the intent to commit the crime, participates in it as something he wishes to bring about, and seeks by some action of his to make it succeed" (Instruction No. 4.02, *Criminal Jury Instructions, District of Columbia,* Third Edition, Young Lawyers Section, The Bar Association of the District of Columbia [Washington, D.C.: 1978]).

wouldn't want somebody to do it to me." Personally, I always find it hard
to believe that the defendant *just* discovered the Golden Rule. Nor can I
believe that, after long familiarity with the Golden Rule, he suddenly
understood it. *I* don't understand it.

What is the logic of the Golden Rule? Is it utilitarian: if each of us does
no harm, then harm will be done to none of us? Or does it rest on a belief
in a just world: if I do no harm, then I won't *merit* being harmed, so I
won't be? Or is it something about harmony/unity/integrity (Walk it like
you talk it) as an end in itself? Or is it just God's law: I won't do this because God doesn't want me to? (That's a reason?) I try to observe the rule,
but I don't claim to understand it.

Judges love it, anyway. And lawyers know that, so they tell their clients
to say it. The clients say it, and the judges figure, "Of course he doesn't
mean it, but at least he was willing to recite his catechism, he's tractable,"
and they don't feel annoyed, and they don't spontaneously add a couple
of years to what they've already decided on.

Standing beside me in his blue jail clothes, Roberto looked like all the
other prisoners in their blue jail clothes, just as Lloyd and I in our pinstriped suits looked like all the other lawyers in their pinstriped suits, uniform interchangeable parts in the criminal justice system. Roberto's one
touch of individuality was his belt buckle, which read "DIOR."

Roberto told the judge that he'd been doing some thinking, and he
wouldn't want someone to make his mother cry the way he'd made someone else's mother cry, and he was sorry, and he wanted to improve himself and make something of his life. I thought he did very well, although
he might have spoken with more feeling.

Judge Davis, with one emphatic blink, "hit him over the wall." Her
bright-red lipsticked mouth barely moved as she stated in an emotionless,
seemingly prerecorded voice, that Roberto had committed this crime
while an escapee from incarceration for an earlier crime, so that he had
demonstrated that he was not a good candidate for rehabilitation. Therefore, she would not sentence him under the Youth Act. She sentenced
him to a minimum of fifteen years, a maximum of life, in prison.

I had to hand it to her. She didn't discount the value of the victim's life
just because he was a person of no account. Roberto got exactly what
he'd have gotten for murdering, say, a white lawyer.

As was generally true at sentencings, there was no hint of moral con-
demnation, because judges know that society is unjust and the defendants
started the race way behind the line; or because they are steeped in a psy-
chologically deterministic outlook and feel that no man creates himself;
or because they are racist and feel that the defendants are less than

human and thus do not inhabit the same moral universe as they; or because they expect the world to be nuked out of existence, so what does it matter? Still, like engineers aboard the *Titanic,* the judges do their jobs, because they have to be done to keep the ship moving, for as long as it can move.

I followed Roberto back to the lockup. "Now that's behind you," I said after the door was closed. "You can get on with your life. You're seventeen now. When you get out, you'll be thirty-two. That happens to be exactly how old Mr. Lloyd and I are—not that old." I shook his hand through the bars and told him I'd call his mother. That was the one thing he was concerned about—call his mother. He didn't seem to "get" what had just happened to him, or care, if he did.

On the escalator down from the courtroom, Lloyd commented on what a good speech Roberto had made to the judge. "He's a much improved individual," he said, "a very likable young man."

I told Lloyd I was worried about what was going to happen to me in the next courtroom, as, concentrating on Roberto, I had not prepared for the guilty plea I had to do there. I said I was sure I was going to catch shit from Judge Morrison.

"You have to get used to that," Lloyd said. "To a large extent, that's what lawyers are for. That's what you do for your clients."

"Act as a buffer?"

"That's right. Be a shit buffer."

§5-06

I held my shoulders back and my head high as I walked across the street to begin Billy Pepperidge's jury trial—my first. "Here's Bernie Carbo," I thought, "striding to the plate in the sixth game of the '75 Series, two on, two out, down by three runs . . ." Bernie hit one out, as everybody knows. *Just keep your eye on the ball, Jim.*

The prosecutor looked at home in the courtroom. He was handsome in a smooth, regular way. All the men in the U.S. attorney's office, like the television sportscasters whom they generally resembled, seemed to use electric shavers, leaving an even shadow instead of discernible stubble—a polished look which I have never been able to bring to my own face. This uniformity of visage, no doubt, resulted from the same hiring system that prevails in all organizations at all times, namely, the selection of hirees who remind the hirors of themselves; so that this electric look was no longer consciously sought, but simply borne forward by the prosecutors' culture from some long-forgotten primordial Norelco.

In their uniforms of charcoal gray, the prosecutors appeared dignified and orderly. We defense attorneys wore easier clothes day-to-day, slacks and jackets, and those donned grudgingly, scarcely concealing the denim souls within. We were individuals, we were free. We worked for freedom, not justice, not freedom when merited, not freedom for the innocent—for freedom itself, for being loose, for staying outside.

When actually in trial, we'd suit up, of course, suit up for the jury, with a nod to the judge. Then it was haircut time and shoeshine time, because we were dignified and sincere and above all professional; the jurors dressed up when they came to court, so it was only fair to dress for them. Myself, it was the vibrant colors I put my stock in, and the only place for that was the necktie. I wore bright, happy ties—a flowered number on this particular day. The jurors would keep their eyes on a splash of pink and yellow in the beige courtroom. And what they'd see, I hoped, was that no one wearing such a necktie could possibly have a guilty client.

There was a rattling at the door behind the bench.

"All rise!" barked the clerk as he put down his newspaper. "The court is now in session, the Honorable May Wexler presiding. God save this honorable court!" Judge Wexler swept through her private doorway to the bench. "Please be seated," she said with the quiet authority of a grammar school teacher. Everybody sat down.

The case was called: *United States of America* versus *Billy Pepperidge.* Some match-up! (But wait! Who's his lawyer?)

The first order of business was jury selection. Billy and I stood respectfully as fifty prospective jurors filed into the courtroom, filling the spectator seats one row at a time, left to right, front to back, as they were instructed. They all had white plastic tags clipped to their chests with a red superior court seal in the center and the word JUROR in large black letters at the bottom—as close as many of them would ever come to having "credentials."

"Good morning, ladies and gentlemen," Judge Wexler said, folding her hands on her desk.

"Good morning, Your Honor," fifty-seven* voices sing-songed in unison.

---

* Like the jurors, the two lawyers, defendant, clerk, bailiff, marshal, and court reporter spoke when spoken to.

We're all in our places, with bright shiny faces . . .

For the next two minutes, as the judge explained the procedure for *voir dire**—examination of the prospective jurors—I frantically flipped through the list I had just been handed, which gave the name, date of birth, job title, and home address of all the jurors. I was trying to pick out those who were old (bad), young (good), rich (bad), poor (good), residents of white neighborhoods (bad), petty bureaucrats (bad), people who lived near the complainant (very bad). At the same time, I was exchanging a few friendly words with my client—*I like this guy*; glancing appreciatively at the jurors—*we're* all in this together; and attempting to project a look of quiet confidence mixed with just a hint of boredom—this is no contest at all.

I was given a chance to pose questions to the jurors *en masse,* supposedly for the purpose of ferreting out prejudice. Since no one in his right mind is going to explicitly avow opinions that are only tacitly acceptable—"I think every black defendant is guilty"—I had been trained to ask questions that *tell* the jurors things: "Do any of you know Mr. Pepperidge's mother Rose, who's active in the First Baptist Church ladies' auxiliary? His little sister Grace, the Cardozo High School cheerleader? You wouldn't give extra weight to the testimony of a police officer just because he is a police officer, would you?"

There were a few useful questions people could be expected to answer truthfully: "Are any of you employed by the police, FBI, or other law enforcement agency?" Enemies you don't need. "Are any of you lawyers or law students?" You don't want anybody with legal knowledge on the jury, not because they'd see through your arguments—it's just as likely that their training would help them understand your arguments—but because they might control the jury. There's only one person in the room you want to control the jury.

Each side was given unlimited challenges to jurors "for cause"—that is, because they had disclosed information suggesting that they would be influenced by anything other than the evidence. I tried to get rid of a lady whose own car had recently been stolen. The judge denied my request. Each side also got ten "peremptory strikes"—bumping jurors because you don't like their looks. Each judge had a different procedure for striking, all designed to keep the jurors from knowing who had objected to them. Judge Wexler used an arcane system, which I won't even attempt to explain, some combination of musical chairs and "hangman" involving marching the jurors through the jury box while the lawyers passed

---

* From Old French, "to speak the truth." The same term is used to denote a hearing during the trial, out of the presence of the jury, during which the judge determines whether, as a matter of law, certain evidence may be presented to the jury.

little scraps of paper to the clerk. I did not then—nor in any subsequent trial—have as clear an idea of what was going on during jury selection as I might have wished. I cling to the belief that it didn't much matter. Street dudes see through your client's scam and convict. Right-wingers lean over backward to acquit. And vice versa.

"Raise your right hand," the bailiff told the middle-aged white woman who owned the stolen car. "Do-you-swear-the-testimony-you-are-about-to-give-will-be-the-truth-the-whole-truth-and-nothing-but-the-truth-so-help-you-God," he said—it sounded less like a question than a ritual incantation.*

"I do."*

The woman testified that she had left her car in a parking lot and had next seen it seven days later, all crunched up. I dripped sympathy for her—terrible thing *somebody* did.

Sergeant Fox and Sergeant Doan, the arresting officers, testified next. They had found personal papers bearing Billy Pepperidge's name in the car. The D.A. introduced these in evidence.

Each cop said that he had clearly seen my client *driving* the car, even though they were chasing it down a midtown street at 60 m.p.h.

"You must have been looking back and forth to avoid pedestrians, weren't you?" I asked Sergeant Fox, who had driven.

"No. I just keep my eyes on the suspect vehicle at all times," he said. "We're trained to do that. If he hits his brake, I hit my brake."

"Suppose a lady with a baby steps into the street just as the stolen car goes by? You're counting on the *thief* to lead you around her?"

Ahh. What a wave went through the jury. The working-class blacks who are the majority of D.C. jurors tend to be churchgoing people with a firm belief in law, order, and morality. Unbefuddled by "liberal guilt," they are eager to rid the community of hoodlums, particularly the drug dealers who poison their young people. However, as black citizens until recently ruled by whites via a white police force, they have a realistic and not unduly respectful attitude toward cops. And these two, white guys in polyester western wear, were real beauties.

Sergeant Fox maintained that he was absolutely positive Pepperidge was the driver.

---

* In the common law, the original rationale for the oath was to invoke the belief in divine retribution for false swearing. At first the witness had to avow a belief that God would strike him down on the spot if he lied, otherwise he was not allowed to testify. Later a belief in punishment in the afterlife was sufficient. Only in the past quarter century has judicial opposition to testimony by atheists dissipated.

"How long have you been on the police force?"

"Twelve years."

"How many identifications have you made?"

"Thousands."

"Have you ever made a mistaken identification?"

"Never."

Never! Another wave crashed through the jury box.

Sergeant Doan said the same magic word: "Never."

Our case was to begin with Billy Pepperidge's younger brother, a clean-cut high school student, who would supply an alibi for Billy for the whole day the car was stolen, rebutting at least the grand larceny charge. They'd watched a lot of TV together, listened to a certain amount of radio, and then seen *Up in Smoke, Invasion of the Body Snatchers, Deathforce,* and *Silver Streak* at an all-night movie theater. "We were crackin' jokes and havin' fun. There was nothin' else to do," the brother had told me.

Ten minutes before he was to take the stand, the younger brother informed me that he was not going to tesify.

"Are you serious? Why not?"

"I'm afraid they'll recognize me."

"Who'll recognize you? From where?"

There was a long silence. "The police. From the car. I was in the car with Billy."

Oh, my God. It was bad enough that I'd just lost my alibi witness, but what about the defendant? Pepperidge was going to testify that he didn't know the other two people in the car. "Think on your feet, not with them," I always say, but this time I made an exception. I ran to the first respected attorney I could find. "How can I put on testimony that I really *know* isn't true?" I asked him.

"You don't know it isn't true," he said. "All you know is that your client told you one thing, and another person told you something else."

I sent Billy's brother home. He wasn't going to do us any good.

Billy Pepperidge took the stand. After he forthrightly and contritely confessed to having two prior convictions, one for receiving stolen property and one for interstate transport of a stolen vehicle, we moved directly to the day of the crash, since nothing could be worse than giving an alibi for the day of the theft and then not putting on an alibi witness.

On the day of the crash, Billy had gone to the unemployment office. As a matter of fact, one of the papers recovered from the car by the police was a certificate, stamped and dated, entitling anyone who would hire him to a tax break. He identified, one by one, the other papers the police had recovered: a diploma from a course in cardiopulmonary resuscitation; a certificate for seventy hours' study of blueprint drawing; certificates for advanced graphic design, offset duplication, bookbinding, and photography—all of them earned while he was in prison. Then there were the "help wanted, cook" ad and his last pay stub as a hotel janitor before he was laid off.

Here was a young man who really wanted to make good. He looked good, too. He should have. He was wearing my clothes. A secondary benefit of this sartorial strategy was that when I looked at my client, I saw myself. I believed in him. He deserved some credit for that. Some people are good at being clients. They know how to get the most out of their lawyers. Most defendants know enough to be polite to their attorneys—murder is easy to forgive, but rudeness I will not abide—and praise their expertise, and never treat them like friends, replicating as nearly as possible that paradigm of professional relationships, to which all lawyers aspire, that of doctor and patient. But the really smart clients know that the key is to act as though they *trust* their lawyer. That triggers a feeling of responsibility in him. Billy Pepperidge had from the beginning shown a lot of faith in me. Accordingly, in addition to my usual reason for wanting to win—which was *to win*—I also wanted to vindicate his trust.

Billy confessed to the jury his terrible drug problem and admitted that he got into that stranger's car to buy Bam. Yes, the keys were in the car; there was nothing to suggest it was stolen. No, he had never been in it before.

In summation, the prosecutor stressed the cops' positive identification of Billy as the driver.

I got up and suggested to the jury that a trial is very much like a radio—a similarity which had never struck me before. "You've got to tune it in. Don't listen to the static. Listen to the music." Just about everything the government had put on was *static*. The *music* was that "the Perfect Sergeant Fox and the Infallible Sergeant Doan" had made a mistake. Simple as that. They thought Billy was the driver, but somebody else was the driver—a case of mistaken identification. I gave an off-the-shelf defense example: "Haven't you ever walked down the street, and you see somebody you know, and you're about to call out to him, when you realize that you almost made a fool of yourself—it isn't who you thought it was? That happens to everybody, except the Perfect Sergeant Fox and the Infallible Sergeant Doan."

We closed on a Friday afternoon. The jury was excused, to begin deliberating Monday morning. I spotted a lesson there: never close on a Friday night. The effect of the closing argument would be dissipated over the weekend.

The jury deliberated for less than an hour, Monday morning. When they filed in to deliver the verdict, not one of them would look at us, and they weren't smiling.

The young woman foreperson got up and said, "To receiving stolen property—not guilty. To grand larceny—not guilty."

Clearly, it would be a compromise verdict: guilty of U.U.V. and destruction of property.

"As to the unauthorized use of a vehicle—not guilty."

We had won!

"As to destruction of property—not guilty."

I looked at Pepperidge. His face, rigid with tension, collapsed with relief. We smiled and shook hands. He said "Thank you." The jury smiled, too. Why had they put on that poker face?

The D.A. looked abashed. I turned away from him, because my impulse was to wink and shrug my shoulders.

(Months later, at a party, the D.A. told me that he had learned a lesson from that trial: always subpoena *all* your witnesses, no matter how inconvenient for them. He'd had a third witness, a passer-by, who was ready to testify that he'd seen Pepperidge at the wheel of the car, but the D.A. figured he didn't need him—he had the two cops.)

After receiving the verdict, I went back to my office for a meeting with a new client. When he'd told me his story, he asked, "Do you believe me?"

"Let me have one of your Kools," I said. I lit up and inhaled thoughtfully. "It doesn't matter," I said in a cloud of smoke. "All I'm interested in is the evidence." I didn't want to say I didn't believe him, because then it would seem I wasn't on his side. But I didn't want to say I did believe him, because then he'd think I was a fool. He was telling me that the eyewitness who saw him loading a stereo into his car's trunk outside a burglarized apartment was mistaken. He had stalled there, and he was putting away his jumper cables, not a stereo. He kept pressing, "Do you believe me? Do you believe me?" So finally I said, "You're my client. You want me to believe you? I believe you."

The A.B.A.'s *Code of Professional Responsibility* (Disciplinary Rule 7-102 [A] [4]) states that a lawyer shall not "knowingly use perjured testimony or false evidence," but leaves unclear what "knowingly" means. The A.B.A. *Standards Relating to the Defense Function*, Section 7.7, suggests that the defense attorney should refuse to question a client who plans to lie, and not refer to the client's testimony in summation—just let him sit up there and tell his story, and otherwise ignore him. But a federal court has held that for a defense attorney to refuse to argue his client's case to a jury because he believes the client is guilty violates the defendant's constitutional right of due process.[1] An academic debate goes on about what lawyers *should* do about perjury by their clients. There is little question about what they *do* do. Eighty-five percent of attorneys in the District of Columbia responding to a survey said that they would question a perjurious client in normal fashion.[2] To do anything else amounts to telling the judge and jury that the defendant is guilty, which hardly seems an appropriate thing for a defense attorney to do.

The defense attorney does his part to discourage perjury by pointing out to his client that if he testifies and is convicted, although he'll almost certainly not be charged with perjury (court dockets are too crowded), the judge will likely give him a longer sentence than if he did not testify. The client decides whether to take the risk.

To expect witnesses not to lie is like expecting soldiers to fight according to the rules of chivalry. A trial is not a game. It is *like* a game—a contest given shape by certain rules, with a beginning and an end, played out in a specially designated arena by competitors who will emerge as winner and loser depending upon their measure of skill and luck—but the consequences of the trial extend beyond the trial itself; that's where it differs from games.

Defendants are *expected* to lie. The judge instructs the jury, "The defendant has a right to become a witness in his own behalf. His testimony should not be disbelieved merely because he is the defendant. In weighing his testimony, however, you may consider the fact that the defendant has a vital interest in the outcome of this trial. You should give his testimony such weight as in your judgment it is fairly entitled to receive."[3]*

Police, perhaps originally to avoid the suppression of illegally seized evidence, now seemingly as a matter of principle, almost always lie. *Everybody* lies. Jury panelists, desperate to get out of the waiting room and onto a case, uniformly swear that their heads contain not brains but virgin snow, unmarked by the imprint of any experience. Complainants

---

* Until relatively recently, criminal defendants were not allowed to give sworn testimony at all, but were permitted at most to make "a statement" to the jury. "The competency of accused persons [to testify] was first declared in Maine, in 1864 ... It came later, in general, in the Southern States, and there it was sometimes accompanied by the proviso that the accused should testify, if at all, first in order of the witnesses on his own side. ... Until as recently as 1962, a criminal defendant in Georgia was not permitted to testify under oath" (John Henry Wigmore, *Evidence in Trials at Common Law,* vol. 2, revised by James H. Chadbourn [Boston: Little, Brown, 1979], p. 826).

lie, recalling five-second events from a year ago with a clarity and precision that make stop-action videotape look like a fading daguerreotype. Judges *require* the defendant to lie when pleading guilty: asked "Are you pleading guilty because you are guilty, and for no other reason?" the defendant must answer "Yes," though everyone in the courtroom knows he's pleading in exchange for a break.

It has been said that truth, like basketball, is a team sport.

I did my duty in the Pepperidge trial. It was not for me to decide whether my client was guilty. It was my job to defend him. It was the prosecutor's job to prove him guilty beyond a reasonable doubt, and he failed to do so. I was delighted that he did. Failure for him meant success for me, and for Billy Pepperidge.

"An advocate, in the discharge of his duty, knows but one person in all the world, and that person is his client. To save that client by all means and expedients, and at all hazards and costs to other persons, and, amongst them, to himself, is his first and only duty; and in performing this duty he must not regard the alarm, the torments, the destruction which he may bring upon others."[4]

When Lord Brougham, in this oft-quoted statement of the defense attorney's duty, says that the lawyer "knows but one person," he means that the lawyer is to take account only of the interest of his client. But, as a matter of fact, the client is also *literally* the only person in the case that the defense attorney *knows*. You spend a lot of time with your client. You grow to care about him. The people on the other side are just names.

I've heard laymen complain that the reasonable doubt standard enables some criminals to go free. It's supposed to. You remember what John Adams said (page vii). A couple of former public defenders who started their own firm printed on their business cards, "A Reasonable Doubt at a Reasonable Price." But just how much credit to give the reasonable doubt standard for the bias built into the system is problematical, because no one knows exactly what "reasonable doubt" means. Judges in D.C. read juries the following instruction:

> Reasonable doubt, as the name implies, is a doubt based on reason, a doubt for which you can give a reason. [Nowhere but in this instruction will you ever hear the word "reasonable" used to mean "for which you can give a reason." Can you think of a doubt for which you could *not* give a reason?] It is such a doubt as would cause a juror, after careful and candid and impartial consideration of all the evidence, to be so undecided that he cannot say that he has an abiding conviction of the defendant's guilt. It is such a doubt as

would cause a reasonable person to hesitate or pause in the graver or more important transactions of life. However, it is not a fanciful doubt nor a whimsical doubt, nor a doubt based on conjecture. It is a doubt which is based on reason. The government is not required to establish guilt beyond all doubt, or to a mathematical certainty or a scientific certainty. Its burden is to establish guilt beyond a reasonable doubt.[5]

Got that?

Like any other instruction, it means whatever the jury decides it means. I assume jurors figure that they're supposed to be really, really sure before they convict someone—as well they should be.

It is my job to argue that there is a reasonable doubt. I can't create that doubt; it has to be there, in the evidence. I do my job with pride, believing that the advocacy system is not only the fairest method of determining guilt but also the most reliable—reliable *because* it is fair: each side has the opportunity to negate the distortions of the other. It is not 100 percent reliable, however.

The foregoing rationale is fine, as far as it goes, but it sounds like bullshit to me. After all, though it may not have been my job to decide whether Pepperidge was guilty, I couldn't help but reach certain conclusions, and I *did* decide that he was guilty, when his brother told me that he had been in the car. And though it was indisputably my job as defense attorney to try to win an acquittal anyway, that doesn't explain why *I* should want to undertake that job, or how I could perform it with such enthusiasm.

It occurs to me that maybe I *like* putting criminals on the street; that, far from being an unfortunate side effect of the noble enterprise of defending the rights of the individual, maybe putting criminals on the street is the *main point;* that, possibly, I am motivated by the sheer joy of thwarting the will of authority. Maybe I became a defense attorney so I could *be bad,* and still be good. I don't know. How would I know?

I stopped leaning so hard on people to plead, after the Pepperidge trial. I would still try to tell clients when their cases were sure losers, but I had learned that sure losers were not so easy to spot. You never knew when you might win. And I had learned that I liked winning very, very much.

A few months later I saw Billy Pepperidge back in court, and asked him if he was in trouble again. He said yes. I didn't ask him what sort of trouble. I didn't want to know.

§5-07

Don Winn, an endearing, happy-go-lucky fellow from Panana, was accused of possession of marijuana. He had been in the process of selling some sort of greenish herbal substance to a couple of men when something about them, perhaps the simultaneous chewing of gum and smoking of cigarettes, tipped him off, and he threw the herb into the air and ran away, spontaneously declaring, "I was selling to get milk for my baby," which, like everything else he said—this was one of Don's endearing qualities—was true. After a bit of a struggle, the cops picked up him and the herb, which tested positive as marijuana. It was a locked case for the government, and, at my suggestion, Don, who had no record and therefore would not be locked up, agreed to plead, until the moment his name was called to stand up and do so. At that instant he decided to share with me his decision to go to trial.

I hastily informed the judge of our change of plans. The judge, who was not himself exactly beyond reproach—presiding over criminal cases while married to a prosecutor—had the audacity to upbraid me in open court for the "lack of professionalism" and "shoddy practice" evidenced by my failure to foresee this eventuality.

I beat a hasty retreat with Don to the hallway.

"Why don't you want to plead guilty?" I demanded with unconcealed chagrin.

"I don't *feel* guilty," he said. (He was confusing moral guilt with legal guilt.) "Some men drink too much. Some men gamble. Some men run around with women. I don't do none of that. I smoke a little herb. There's nothing wrong with that."

"Fine. Do you have any suggestion for a defense?"

"I didn't *possess* the herb. The herb was on the ground."

"Where you threw it. We're going to have to do better than that, Don ... I've got it! We'll say it wasn't marijuana."

The case was set down for trial in a month.

Now I had an idea how to proceed. First, I got myself up for the game, advertising it as "The Trial of the Century" to anyone who would listen. Then I took Amy Strader, an extremely innocent-looking young investigator, out to a sidewalk one night and had her play the role of Don Winn She took a nickel bag of oregano and threw it through the air as I took photos with an electronic flash. As I had hoped, the photos showed that falling vegetable matter flutters down over a wide area—"like stardust," Ms. Strader would testify. Ergo, it is impossible to pick up from the ground in a homogeneous clump, but must be scraped up, necessarily along with other substances, hopelessly compromising any lab test designed to detect marijuana. The photos would also show that the defense was a class operation.

At the trial—which, despite our genuine eagerness to get on with it, was postponed seven times, four for lack of a judge—a policeman testified that when Mr. Winn ran away, he tackled him, but Mr. Winn broke free and had to be grabbed again, but broke free again, until, on the third try, he was successfully wrestled to the ground.

"While you were struggling with him, you must have taken your eyes off the greenish herb on the sidewalk?" I asked, intending to argue that the cop had picked up the wrong greenish herb.

"No, I kept my eye on it at all times," he said. I shared a moment of head-shaking with the jury.

I questioned the lab chemist at length and in great technical detail, primarily to show the jury that I had worked hard and deserved to win, but incidentally to establish an element of our "argument." He proudly agreed that his tests were so sensitive that as little as two one-thousandths of an ounce of THC (or "tetrahydrocannabinol," as I impressively referred to it), marijuana's active ingredient, would trigger a positive reaction. Where in the District of Columbia can you scrape the sidewalk and *not* come up with two one-thousandths of an ounce of THC?

Mr. Winn did not testify. I told him he was an honest man, and this nifnaf charge wasn't worth lying about. Anyway, lying wouldn't work. I added that it was against the rules. He told me he'd never considered lying.

When Amy Strader took the stand, I walked up to her, flashed our eleven-by-fourteen glossies at the jury, and said, "Without showing them to the jury [they had not been admitted in evidence], I show you these pictures and ask if you recognize them." The prosecutor and the judge were on me like wildcats. They demanded to know just what the pictures depicted. I said they were a fair and accurate representation of a scientific test, but the judge didn't agree. He said it might have been windier on the night of the experiment than on the night of the arrest. I showed him the weather pages from the newspaper for each of the two nights. Wind was not a factor. "That's the wind at National Airport," he said. What a stickler! He said oregano might not fall the same way as marijuana. "What marijuana?" I said. There was no pleasing him. He wouldn't let Ms. Strader testify about the experiment, and he wouldn't let the jurors examine the pictures. (They were visibly disappointed.) He did let us introduce a picture of the sidewalk, which showed that its surface tended to collect dirt—and he wouldn't have let that in if he hadn't just kept out a lot of other pictures. Practitioners take note: you can never have too many photographs.

In summation, all the prosecutor had was a lot of facts. We had the high-handedness of government. "Mr. Winn's future depended on the outcome of that lab test," I said, "and the stuff they were testing had been *lying on the ground*. Suppose you have some disease that could ruin *your* whole future, and the doctors don't know what it is. So they call for a blood test. A lab technician is carrying the test tube with your blood in it, and, whoops! he drops it on the floor. And he says, 'That's cool. No problem. I'll just swab it up off the floor and test it anyway. Good enough for government work.' But is it good enough for *you*? Is it good enough for Mr. Winn? . . . As for the officer's testimony that he never took his eye off the substance on the ground: Wasn't that great police work? Wasn't that fantastic police work? Wasn't that *unbelievable* police work?"

"Not guilty," the jurors said. They were smiling.

The Winn decision was an example of "jury nullification." Although they are never so instructed, juries are in fact at liberty to nullify the law by refusing to convict despite the evidence. In this case, jurors told me that they were annoyed by the police officer's personal style—he wore gold chains and sunglasses—and by his gratuitous lie about keeping his eye on the grounded herb; and by the fact that the judge frequently asked witnesses prosecutorial questions, and made a point of reading and shuffling papers during the defense summation. They may also have thought the police should have better things to do than drag a man into court with one fourteenth of an ounce of "herb" in evidence (although convictions for the possession of small quantities of marijuana are common in D.C.). Once the jury decided to acquit, they had only to find something "to hang their hats on," that is, to find a *reason* for their verdict. They decided that they couldn't be sure the material scraped up from the sidewalk was the same material Mr. Winn threw down, or at least that they could say that.

Juries work in strange ways. A friend of mine who did jury duty reported that several jurors who had convicted a defendant said they would have acquitted him "if only he had shown some remorse."

§5-08

I won my third trial as well. The client who told me that he was putting jumper cables, not a stereo, into his trunk was telling God's honest truth. It turned out that the eyewitness, who was a dentist—that's what made me believe him, on paper—had seen more than one man at the crime scene, and he had gotten them confused.

Three-and-0! I was forming two opinions: that I was invincible, and that there is no way to tell whether someone is lying. I still hold the second opinion.

The crux of the state's evidence in my fourth trial was that a witness saw a blue car drive away with some stolen goods, and that the same witness saw my client in what he purportedly recognized as the same blue car, shortly afterward. I had recently seen a lawyer win a case in which he argued to the jury that if they convicted his client, they were convicting him for wearing a red sweater, and that was all. I told my jury, "If you convict this man, you are convicting him for driving a blue car, that's all," and that's exactly what they did. ("It only works with sweaters," my colleague told me.) As my client was led away, stern old Judge Hannon said to me, "Thanks for looking out for him, Mr. Kunen."

He understood.

§5-09

Lloyd and I drove the twenty-five miles down I-95 to Lorton, Virginia, to talk to Roberto Lewis about his pending trial for the murder of a fellow jail inmate. The Lorton Correctional Facility of the D.C. Department of Corrections holds 2,500 men convicted of felonies.* Located amid rolling

---

* Population in August 1982. Official capacity is 2,323. Women convicted of felonies in D.C. are sent to the federal correctional facility at Alderson, West Virginia. Misdemeanants serve their time at a facility in Occoquan, Virginia, or at the D.C. jail, which held 1,899 people in August 1982—544 over capacity. (Private conversation, Kirby Howlett, Esq., Public Defender Service, August 1982.)

pastures and wooded hills, the facility consists of a red-brick turreted fortress, "The Wall," for maximum-security prisoners; and, in the fields nearby, for the medium- and minimum-security prisoners and youthful offenders, a collection of barracklike "dormitories," which could be part of a particularly bleak and isolated state college but for the chain-link fences and concertina wire surrounding them. Time at Lorton is time lost. Life consists of exquisite boredom punctuated by frequent violence, and that is all. There is an auto mechanics course and a gourmet cooking course, but most inmates spend the day getting high on drugs smuggled in by visitors and, beyond question, by guards. When prisoners are transferred from Lorton to halfway houses for work release, they immediately undergo urinalysis for drugs. One half test positive.[1]

Roberto Lewis had been sentenced, at his own request, to a federal facility, where he hoped to get some job training and to avoid violence at the hands of enemies his older brother had made at Lorton, but he was being held at Lorton while awaiting trial for the jail murder.

Lloyd and I were escorted into the maximum-security facility, where convicts deemed to be dangerous, or to be in danger, may spend several years before being transferred to medium security—several years without ever being able to *see* beyond the thirty-foot Wall.*

We sat down with Roberto in a bare, fifteen-foot-square room, where maximum-security prisoners were allowed their "contact visits." Lloyd and I explained that we had a medical expert ready to testify that the cause of death of the young man who died ten days after a brawl with Roberto's crowd was not a blow to the head, but the continued administration of a certain drug long after a "textbook case of allergic reaction" had set in.

(Generally speaking, it is considered a foreseeable consequence of injuring someone that he is going to run into some incompetent doctors down the line; and the original bad actor who hurt the victim is held responsible for all the injuries that "result from" his blow, including those piled on by a little malpractice. But *gross* negligence can be deemed an "intervening cause," which cuts off the responsibility of the first bad guy. If, for instance, Roberto's victim had been accidentally dropped out a window at the hospital, at that point he would become the hospital's victim. That, we said, was *essentially* what had happened.)

We might be able to win a trial, so we had good leverage for a plea bargain. "We might be able to get you a plea which will add only a little to the time you'll be locked up," I said.

* Prisoners who are "disciplinary problems" or considered to be in extreme danger have it the worst, spending twenty-three and a half hours a day in small unairconditioned cells.

"I ain't locked up," Roberto said.

"Oh, you mean they can't lock up your soul?" I ventured. Roberto nodded.

"I know that," I said, "but the fact is there's a lot of things you can't do in here."

"Like what?" Roberto demanded.

"You can't take a walk in the woods."

"I don't do that."

"Well, you can't go out with girls."

Roberto nodded ruefully. But even granting that there might be some reason to care about the length of his imprisonment, he maintained his usual resistance to pleading—this time reinforced by a sincere belief that he could not *possibly* be guilty of killing someone he had not touched. Considering the rather marginal sentencing concession he had won by following our advice the first time—he got fifteen years instead of twenty, but he gave up his trial, and at a trial, you *never know*—we were not in the best position to lean on him now. He agreed to think about it.

On the way home, Lloyd and I decided that Roberto had been taken in by that ubiquitous Ben Shahn poster that says "You can lock a man up, but you can't imprison his ideas." They ought to lock Ben Shahn up, we decided. We'd tell him, "We have good news and bad news, Ben. The good news is, they can't imprison your ideas. The bad news is, they're locking your ass up for fifteen years."

As it turned out, the government didn't want the hassle of a long, complex, and expensive murder trial, so they made an offer even Roberto couldn't refuse. He pled to assault with a dangerous weapon and got just fifteen months tacked onto his sentence. One of the other defendants also got fifteen months, and the third had his charges dropped.

I suspected that they had all benefited from a domestic corollary of the "Mere Gook Rule." The Mere Gook Rule, as explained to me by Army lawyers in Vietnam, held that an American found responsible for the wrongful death of an "indigenous national" (Vietnamese) should receive light punishment, because the life lost was that of a "mere gook."

The Mere Gook Rule was, of course, unwritten, as it offended one of our fundamental values—all men are created equal. It was tacitly observed because it served another of our fundamental values—the punishment should fit the crime. So many people were killing so many Vietnamese that it seemed *out of proportion* to imprison somebody for a long time for doing what, regardless of nice distinctions based on motive or circumstance, came down to the same thing—killing Vietnamese.

It is, in any case, a well-recognized principle of jurisprudence that, although all men are created equal, for certain legal purposes they don't stay that way. Try running your car over one helpless old lady and one robust young Rockefeller, and compare your liabilities. All life is precious, but let's talk about potential earnings ... This sort of calculation has no place in the criminal law, but as a practical matter, sentencing judges take a particularly dim view of wasting prominent members of the community; for one thing, the disposition of such cases receives wide public attention. It almost amounts to a separate offense: Nth-Degree Murder—killing someone on the front page. By contrast, because the victim in Roberto's case was himself a lowly prisoner awaiting trial on a murder charge, it is possible that the judge and prosecutor, consciously or not, thought of him as a "mere gook."

§5-10

We—Gary Kohlman, head of the P.D.S. Trial Division, had stepped in to assist me on this high-stakes case—had learned from William Buie that one of the putative "eyewitnesses" who had "identified" him as the bus-murderer was a twelve-year-old neighbor of his who hadn't even seen the shooting, but had joined the crowd that formed afterward. She had said something to a police officer about recognizing Buie. This became a "positive identification" in the prosecutor's files.

The prosecutor confirmed that the little girl, whom he had never interviewed, was one of his witnesses. He would not tell us who the other two eyewitnesses were, and the judge denied our motion to order him to do so. The courts in D.C. put a higher value on the protection of witnesses than on the preparation of a defense, and the judge considered it an insufficient safeguard that we promised not to disclose the witnesses' identities to our client.

If two witnesses testified, "That's him," Buie would probably be eligible for parole in fifteen years. We had to get the prosecutor to drop the case, by *proving* that Buie did not commit the murder.

We had Buie take a lie detector test. The examiner found that Buie's physiological responses "were *not* indicative of deception" when he said he had not been on that bus, had not shot anyone, and had not asked anyone to lie for him. Our investigators established that Buie had never lived near, or gone to school with, or worked with the decedent. They showed

Buie's picture to the decedent's friends and family. No one recognized him. I personally interviewed the twelve-year-old "eyewitness" three times. In between long periods of vacantly sucking her thumb, she told me various stories that were inconsistent in every detail but one: she had not seen the shooting. In the presence of her mother, she signed a statement to that effect.

We took all our information to the prosecutor—the alibi, the polygraph, the recantation by his witness. We laid out our whole case. He refused to drop the charges. I couldn't really blame him. Our evidence strongly suggested that Buie was innocent, but his evidence suggested that Buie was guilty. It was proper for him to leave it to the jury to decide the fact of the matter. On the other hand, no one on the government's side seemed to care very much about investigating the case, once they had those "positive IDs" in hand, although, theoretically, the prosecutor's job is not to convict, but to see that justice is done.

("The United States wins its point whenever justice is done its citizens in the courts" is carved in the wall at the Department of Justice. "If you believe that," an ex-prosecutor once told me, "I have some Florida swampland that might interest you.")

"What's Buie's motive supposed to be?" I asked the prosecutor. "It couldn't be robbery. The decedent's money wasn't taken."

"We're working on that," he said. "We have an idea, a belief."

He wouldn't say anymore, but his "idea" probably had something to do with drugs. Our investigators had learned that the decedent had borrowed thirty dollars just before heading down to U Street, a heavy drug traffic area, and the prosecutor must have known that the dead man had needle tracks on his arms and a syringe in his pocket. The thing was, anybody would tell you Buie "wasn't about" drugs.

Just weeks before the trial, we learned that a certain defendant was trying to work a deal for himself by snitching on other people, and one person he was ready to inform on was a man who had bragged to him about shooting someone on a bus. This had not, of course, come to the attention of *our* prosecutor, because in criminal court, the thumb doesn't know what the index finger is doing. The snitch, unfortunately, was not going to give up his information to the government without a deal, and that would take time—too much time.

My colleague Kohlman, using an information network he had developed over the years, was able to come up with the name of the man who had bragged about shooting someone on a bus. It was a certain "B.J.," a former client of his.

Before we gave the name to the prosecutor, we at least had to make sure B.J. had been in town on the day of the killing. If we gave the prosecutor information that proved false, our credibility would be squandered. Kohlman thought it would be a good idea to go out and question B.J. He asked me if I'd like to come along.

This was something new. I had never before spoken to a murderer who was not my client. And this murderer, in particular, had interests adverse to mine. I was trying to get him *convicted* of a crime. He might murder *me*.

"Sure, I'd like to go," I said. I'd always been a glutton for experience. "I think it would be interesting. But I don't want to interfere. Maybe my curiosity isn't a relevant consideration."

"Well, the main point of all this is to amuse ourselves, after all," Kohlman said.

We made several forays to B.J.'s parents' home, a brick row house in the flat-as-a-pool-table area down by the Navy Yard in southeast Washington. B.J.'s parents held Kohlman in high regard because of his past services to their son, but when you see two white guys in neckties coming up your front steps, it can only mean trouble. Each time, we assured them that we just needed to talk to B.J. about another client's case. Each time, they told us that they didn't know where B.J. was.

"They're circling the wagons," Kohlman said.

Finally we ran into B.J. as he tinkered with a bicycle on the sidewalk in front of his parents' house. Kohlman told him straight out that we were representing a man accused of shooting someone on a bus in July, and asked him if he recognized the victim's name.

B.J. repeated the name thoughtfully as he studied the wrench in his hand. "No, can't say I do," he said, resuming his work on the bike.

Kohlman asked B.J. how he'd been and what he'd been up to, and established that B.J. had been in Washington around the time of the shooting. He didn't ask B.J. if he shot the guy.

I noticed that B.J. matched the description of the gunman, as did Buie, yet B.J. and Buie resembled each other only slightly. Buie was much darker, and had heavy-lidded, sleepy eyes. B.J.'s features were finer. He also seemed to have a harder, more aggressive look, but I may have imagined that.

Our investigators showed B.J.'s picture to the decedent's associates, and they *did* recognize him.

Kohlman, observing that legal ethics have to be "situational," resolved his tangle of ethical duties—to his former client B.J., to his sources of information about the snitch, to Buie—in favor of the "moral imperative" of averting the conviction of an innocent man: we took our information about B.J. to the prosecutor.

The prosecutor's relief was apparent. He obviously wasn't ready for trial, and was more than happy to join us in requesting a six-month continuance, which the court granted.

Buie, looking sharp in a blue parka and pants ensemble with gold racing stripes, came into my office to get the news. He was actually somewhat *annoyed* by the continuance. He'd been living with the murder charge for six months and craved *resolution.* His friends were ragging on him all the time—"Hey, killer, who'd you blow away *today?"*—that sort of thing, and he was sick of it. I apologized, adding, "But what's the hurry to be put on trial for murder? It's not that great an experience. It isn't our fault we found out about somebody else doing it only a week ago. We might never have found out. God loves you."

Just in case we had to go to trial, I asked Buie for a list of possible character witnesses. He had a long one, replete with employers, ministers, and schoolteachers.

"Fortunately, you've led a good life," I pontificated. I found myself doing that occasionally—it comes from sitting behind a desk in a chair that tips back. "This is why it pays to live a good life. You find yourself in trouble, you have all these good people ready to come forward and say, 'He's a good person.' If you hadn't lived right, you couldn't say, 'Hold it. I want to go back and do it right.' You have to do it right the first time."

"That's right," he agreed, smiling self-consciously.

"Character is fate," I said. "The truth will out." I felt, just for a moment, that in the scheme of things, I was a moral instrument, or that Buie and I together were, hammer and string.

§6-01

Mrs. Carolyn Ianini, sitting in her parked car 100 feet from the Bolling Air Force Base headquarters building, had just been thinking how quiet it was, when the shots rang out. Phil Rendle, standing atop the stone steps in front of the building, about to go in for his human relations seminar, ducked for cover. Sarah Joswick, waiting to pick up her husband at the curb at the foot of the steps, thought that he might be hurt and jumped out of her car to go look. Ron Janis, walking on the other side of the street, turned in time to see a man burst through the door, run down the stairs, and disappear through a hedge.

The fleeing man, they pretty much agreed, was white, five foot eight to five foot ten, medium build, about thirty years old, with medium-length brown hair, wearing a blue three-quarter-length jacket and khaki pants. He seemed to be tucking something into his right jacket pocket as he fled. Joswick thought she saw the outline of the barrel of a gun in the pocket.

Rendle and Joswick rushed into the building. They saw a young white man lying on his back on the floor in front of a desk in the employment office, a dozen feet from the building's entrance. Blood was gushing out of his nose and mouth, making a loud, gurgling sound. It was 2:55 P.M.

When the D.C. police arrived ten minutes later, the victim had already been rushed to the emergency room of a nearby hospital. Detective Miller from the Homicide Bureau, looking like a Princeton professor in his leather-elbowed tweed jacket, spoke to people at the scene, jotting down a few notes in his spiral pocket notebook. He spoke with Dave Johnson, a big, bearded man who resembled the Popeye cartoons' brutish Bluto. Johnson, a former airman, described himself as a close friend of the victim, an Air Force enlisted man named Irwin Sales. As he spoke to Miller, he was still clutching a Gino's bag containing two hamburgers, one for him, one for Sales. The hamburgers were getting cold.

Johnson told Detective Miller that Sales had told him three months earlier, "If anything happens to me, you'll know who did it: Peter Croft." Sales, an Air Force staff sergeant, had been having an affair with his fellow staff sergeant Croft's wife, and Croft knew it; and Croft had been following Sales around, Johnson said.

At 3:45 P.M., Sales was pronounced dead.

At 3:50 P.M, a D.C. Metropolitan Police Department crime scene search team arrived, roped off the employment office, and "processed the scene." One officer diagrammed the room on grid paper while another took photographs. There was a lake of blood three feet long. The ambulance men had walked through it, leaving a trail of crimson-brown ripple-soled footprints. There was a bullet hole in the wall behind Sales's desk, about one foot below the ceiling. A spent slug was found on the floor at the base of the wall on the opposite side of the room. A human canine tooth lay on the floor in front of the desk. The exact location of these items was marked by the search officer on his grid-paper map. Then he picked them up and put each in a four- by four-inch plastic bag, which he numbered, sealed, dated, and initialed.

The police called the Bureau of Motor Vehicles for a description of Croft's car and began searching for a green 1978 Datsun B-210. At 7:30 P.M. it was spotted, parked in front of the N.C.O. Club, not far from the scene of the shooting. A stakeout was established. At 8:00 P.M. a brown-haired man of medium height and build, dressed in a stylish gray three-piece suit, came out of the club and approached the car. Two Air Force security police plainclothesmen jumped out of the bushes, one leveling a sawed-off shotgun at him, the other holding a .38. The one with the .38 told him to lie face down on the street with his legs, arms, and fingers spread wide. He removed the wallet from the prostrate man's back pocket and looked at his driver's license. "Sergeant Croft, you are under arrest," he said.

He began searching Croft for weapons or evidence. "I haven't got anything on me, but there's a weapon in my trunk," Croft said. He handed his keys to the officer, who found a shotgun in the trunk. The officer cuffed Croft's hands behind his back and helped him to his feet. He was put in a car and taken to the local D.C. police precinct, where Detective Miller was waiting. Miller read him his *Miranda* rights from a Metropolitan Police Department rights card (form P.D. 47).

He then uncuffed Croft and had him answer in writing the Four Questions printed on the back of the card, which he did as follows:

1. Have you read or had read to you the warning as to your rights? *Yes.*
2. Do you understand these rights? *Yes.*
3. Do you wish to answer any questions? *No.*
4. Are you willing to answer questions without an attorney present? *No.*

Croft signed the card. Miller filled in the time, "2035 hours," and the date, and signed it too. Miller did not question Croft. He called for a car to take Croft downtown to the homicide office at Police Headquarters.

Meanwhile, a Detective Simon was at the N.C.O. club questioning the hostess, Kathy Foster. Foster, a tough-but-fragile-looking young woman with high cheekbones and a low neckline, said that Croft, a friend of hers, had picked her up at her apartment that afternoon at 2:30, driven her to work, stayed with her until 3:30 P.M., and dropped by again at 7:00 P.M.

"You're a material witness," Simon told Foster. "You're going to have to come down to headquarters and answer some questions."

"Do I *have* to?" Foster asked.

"Yes, you do," Simon responded, lying. *He* knew that you don't have to answer a police officer's questions, and that an officer can't hold you at the police station unless he has a warrant, or probable cause to believe you've committed a crime.

Croft arrived at 300 Indiana Avenue, N.W., Police Headquarters, at 9:00 P.M. Detective Miller handed him over to Homicide Detective Luce. Miller told Luce that Croft had asserted his right to remain silent. Luce, a stocky, greasy-haired man, took Croft to one of the six- by ten-foot windowless interview rooms in the rear of the homicide office on the third floor of the Municipal Building and handcuffed him to a chain locked to a desk. Croft asked Luce to get his lawyer's business card, which was in his wallet. Luce did not comply with the request. He walked out of the room, leaving Croft alone. Downstairs Kathy Foster was being questioned by detectives. Frightened and confused, she quickly broke down and admitted that Croft had not been with her that afternoon. The first time she'd seen him was at 7:00 P.M. He had looked upset. When she asked him why, he said he had "a lot on his mind" and asked her to say he had been with her from 2:30 to 3:30 P.M. if anyone inquired.

Croft sat alone for several hours, except for a few minutes while an officer took biographical information on him—isolating the suspect is a standard technique of interrogation. At 1:15 A.M., Detective Luce, accompanied by a Detective Gennetti, walked into the interview room and asked Croft, "Do you understand your rights?"

"Yes," Croft said.

"Do you know Irwin Sales?"

"No."

"Where were you late this afternoon?"

"I was with my girlfriend."

"We know you're lying," Luce said. "We have your girlfriend outside." Luce told Croft he'd be better off to say what really happened. "It can't hurt you. It can only help you, if it was self-defense." Croft said he wanted to think about it.

The detectives walked out of the interrogation room. They returned at 2:35 A.M.

"Did you kill him?" Luce asked.

"Yes, I did," Croft replied.

Luce, a veteran detective, had just made a kindergarten-level mistake. Croft had filled out a rights card with Detective Miller, asserting his right not to be questioned; and he had done nothing to retract that assertion when he acknowledged to Luce that he "understood" his rights.

After Croft answered, "Yes, I did [kill him]," Luce reread Croft his rights and had him make out a new rights card.

Croft filled it in "Yes. Yes. Yes. Yes," and signed it at 2:42 A.M. Luce spent the next half hour questioning Croft about the shooting, getting as much out of him as he could before Croft might change his mind. At 3:10 A.M., after Croft had been over everything once, Luce told him to repeat it all, one sentence at a time, while he typed it out.*

The written statement began "Q: Mr. Croft, did you shoot Irwin Sales on November 14? A: Yes."

Asked what led up to the shooting, Croft explained that, back in August, his wife told him she was having an affair with Sales. Croft decided to "question" Sales, so, having located his workplace and his car, he followed him one August evening. Sales suddenly pulled over, jumped out of his car, ran back to Croft's car, stuck "a large caliber pistol" in his face, said "If you ever come around me again, I'll blow your fucking brains out," and told Croft to drive off, which he did.

On the afternoon of November 14, Croft told Luce, he went over to the office where Sales was a clerk, intending to talk to him. "I wanted to know why he was messing with a married lady, and why he would want to destroy my family.

"I walked into the building. Sales was sitting at his desk. When he saw me, he reached down, walked out from behind the desk, pointed a gun at me, and said, 'I told you if you brought your ass around me again I'd blow your head off.' I grabbed for the gun, and the gun discharged once into the wall. We both froze for a second, in shock, and I was able to take the gun from him. I started to back out the door. He kept coming toward me. I was in fear of my life, so I shot him."

At this point, Croft interrupted himself and asked Luce if he could leave the next thing out of the statement, because "it wouldn't sound good." Luce agreed and stopped typing. Croft then confided, "I put two shots in him after he was on the floor." Luce left that out of the signed

---

* Unlike many big-city departments, the D.C. police do not have tape recorders or stenographers for taking statements.

statement but, unbeknownst to Croft, noted it down later in his "running résumé" of the investigation.

(Luce's testimony about Croft's verbal statement could be as damaging as a signed statement. There's a widespread, erroneous belief among defendants that only what is written down and signed can be used against them, as though the written word had some substance that invisible, spoken words lack. The law doesn't see it that way. Anything said by the defendant to anybody is admissible against him in court, unless it was a response to an in-custody interrogation that violated his *Miranda* rights.)

The signed statement continued, "Then I backed out the door, and ran to my car, and drove toward home. Then I realized I still had his gun in my car, so I threw it out the passenger window over a bridge into the river. Then I went home."

"What did you do at home?"

"I took a shower and changed clothes."

Croft said that he fired three or four times, and that he didn't really look at the gun, but he thought it was a .38. Later that evening, he said, he phoned his wife, who had moved with their kids to Illinois, but he didn't tell her about the shooting. She told him about it, having heard from friends. (Mrs. Croft told the police that Peter "sounded surprised" when she told him that Sales had been shot.)

Croft said he had never owned a handgun. The statement concluded in the ritual fashion: "Q: Mr. Croft, can you read and write the English language?

"A: Yes."

Croft signed it at 4:54 A.M.

§6-02

It was my day to pick up cases. I looked over the mimeographed assignment list: "Name: Peter Croft. Charge: Homicide. Attorney: Kunen." All right! A *heavy* case.

(Croft, an airman charged with killing another airman on an Air Force base, should have been processed through the military justice system, but, in the confusion following the shooting, he was turned over to the D.C. police, who took him to D.C. superior court, where he claimed indigency and his case was assigned to the Public Defender Service.)

I went down to the cell block and called out my client's name. Over to the window came a man, about thirty years old, in a nicely tailored three-piece gray suit—the first three-piece suit I had ever seen on that side of the lockup. I introduced myself, handing him one of my business cards, which, atypically, I had remembered to take with me that morning. "I'm really glad to see you, man," he said, showing more appreciation than was usually evident amongst my clientele.

"I have to write down your description today," I said: "Medium-length brown hair, light complexion, tortoise-shell aviator glasses, gray tweed three-piece suit, blue tie with white checks, cream shirt—stand up, please—five foot nine, one hundred fifty pounds, brown shoes, digital watch with steel band."

(The description has to be just right, not only because it may be important identification evidence, but to satisfy the client. "Maroon sweater," I once said to a juvenile purse-snatcher. "Burgundy," he said.)

Croft's clothes looked better than he did. He had dark circles under his eyes, sweat glistened on his brow, and he needed a shave.

"Ever been arrested before?"

"Never."

"Well, then, we may be able to get you out today. Now, how come you're in there? Did the police tell you why they arrested you?"

"The cop said that witnesses saw me leave the place where it happened,"* Croft said wearily. "They described me and my car to the cops. I've had trouble with this man before. He pulled a gun on me in August. The cops have a sworn statement from his best friend that he—"

"Who?"

"—the guy who got shot told his best friend that if anything ever happened to him, it would be me that did it. Man, can you get me something to eat? I haven't had anything to eat since yesterday afternoon."

I never did like clients' calling me "man." Very few did. "I'm sorry, I can't help you there. The marshals will bring you a sandwich around noon. Did you know the victim?"

"His name's Irwin Sales," Croft sighed, his eyes focused on a far-off sandwich.

"Where'd the incident happen?"

"The headquarters building at Bolling, building twenty. It was on the first floor, near the front door. Man, I'm *really* hungry."

---

* In fact, no witnesses were able to identify Croft. It's common police interrogation technique to lie to the suspect, telling him that he's been identified, his fingerprints have been found, his partner's confessed, and so forth. Courts have held that this does not constitute impermissible coercion.

A whiner. "I'm sorry about that, but right now the best thing I can do for you is get down this information. Did you make any statements to the police? I mean, tell me anything at all that you said to them. Any words that came out of your mouth."

"I told them that he pulled a gun on me again, we struggled, and I shot him." Croft rubbed his nose.

"When did you say that?"

He turned his gaze upward, as people do when they try to remember times. "The shooting was about three P.M. yesterday. I was arrested at about eight o'clock last night. I gave the statement at about four A.M. I was questioned until six o'clock this morning. And they never gave me anything to eat."

Croft's innards were being gnawed at by the *injustice* of his hunger as much as by the hunger itself. "They searched you, right? Did they take anything from you?"

"My wallet. And they swabbed my hands with some kind of chemical, to see if there was gunpowder on them."

"Did they find a gun?"

"No. Except a shotgun in my trunk."

"What was the situation when you gave that statement?"

"The detectives at the Homicide Bureau took the statement. I hadn't had anything to eat. I was handcuffed to a desk—too tight. My wrist still hurts," Croft said defensively, sensing my displeasure at his having talked. "I told Detective Luce that I wanted to talk to my lawyer. I had a lawyer for a car accident I was in. He wouldn't let me. He told me that if I called him, he'd just tell me to keep my mouth shut, and then the judge would think I had something to hide. If I talked, because it was my first offense, and it was self-defense, he said, the case could be thrown out."

I found Croft's account of what Detective Luce did amazing, if it was true, not because he had violated Croft's right to counsel, but because he was so blatant about it. It was as though there were no tomorrow, no court review. Detective Luce wouldn't play by the rules, but acted impulsively, and destructively to the interests of the state, which he apparently did not see as his own interests. He just wanted to exert his power right at that moment, with no view to consequences. No system can function with men like that. Luce had jeopardized the government's whole case.

What wasn't so surprising was that Croft had gone along with the cop's "advice." What Luce said did seem to make sense, after all, and the circumstances had a certain persuasive force, too: you are in a bad situation. You are handcuffed to a desk. It's the middle of the night. You are somewhere deep in the labyrinth of police headquarters. The only people in

the room with you are police. The only people in the next room are police. The only people in the room after that are police. The only people in
the world who even know where you are, are police. This is a bad situation. It is a static situation. God only knows—besides the police—how
long you're going to be in this situation. What will end it? You have tried
not talking, for hours, and it hasn't done you any good. There is only one
other thing you can try—talking. So you try it.

Croft held out a long time. The cops played him well, though. They
never had an unkind word for him—just the opposite.

"The detective said he talked to Master Sergeant Merritt, Sales's boss,
and he said Sales was a cocky smartass and no one liked him," Croft said.
"The cops showed me Merritt's statement and the statement of Sales's
friend, saying that I would be the one that did it."

I told Croft that the statement he had given might be thrown out; the
jury might never hear it. He should start all over again, and say *nothing* to
anybody. "No matter what anybody promises you or threatens you with,
just say, 'I'm sorry, my lawyer told me not to talk about it.' Okay?" He
said he understood.

In due time, our case was called. Croft and I stood before the judge. No
sooner did I state my name for the record than the assistant U.S. attorney
announced, "The government has no-papered [declined to prosecute] this
case because jurisdiction is being transferred to the military."

A picture flashed into my mind from four years back: there was Steve
Pokart, my mentor at New York Legal Aid, making a break for the courtroom door with his client the minute a juvenile court judge said she had
no jurisdiction over him because of his age.

I immediately sprang, not into action, exactly, but into words. "Well,
Your Honor, if the government has dropped the case, then there is nothing holding Mr. Croft, and I am advising him to leave."

Judge Waldorf's endless forehead furrowed all the way to the top of his
pink pate. "I believe you're right," he said.

You could feel the prosecutor's heart rising into her throat. "Your
Honor, the Air Force security police are even now on the way to pick up
the defendant. Perhaps if we could pass the case—"

"*What* case?" I said. "The government has dropped the case."

"Mr. Kunen's right," Judge Waldorf said, appearing to enjoy the mischief of it all. "Come on, let's go," I said, grabbing the startled Croft's
arm and pulling him down the aisle. His sleeve slid up, revealing the orange vinyl ID bracelet the police had riveted around his wrist. Next to the
D.A., Croft was the most surprised person there, but he trusted me
enough to follow; or, at least, he liked where I was going.

We practically ran down the aisle, burst through two sets of swinging doors, headed down the hall, made it to the central lobby, could *see* the street through the glass front doors, when we heard pounding hooves behind us. We turned to see a gigantic U.S. marshal running toward us, arms flailing.

"Hold it right there!" he said.

"What is it, Marshal?" I inquired, trying to sound calm.

"You are under arrest," he said to Croft. "I am a United States marshal. I have jurisdiction to arrest you because I have probable cause to believe that you have committed a felony. I am holding you for the military authorities." He took out his handcuffs. Croft looked at me. I made a quick calculation and decided there was no percentage in noncooperation.

"He's legally correct, Mr. Croft. I suggest you give yourself up peacefully, here, with me watching. If you run away, they can use force to apprehend you, and there won't be anyone to watch. They could even shoot you."

Croft held out his wrists. The marshal, still panting, put the cuffs on, and the three of us stood there, uncertain, coming to grips with a new situation. Just then three youngsters wearing blue berets arrived—the Air Force security police. The marshal handed Croft to them. They said they had orders to transport him to the stockade at Fort Meade.

I told them that I was his lawyer, and that I did not want him questioned. I told Croft to remember to say nothing to anyone—a simple enough instruction—that he would have a military lawyer appointed for him, and that I would contact that lawyer.

"Can't you represent me, man? I'd like to have you."

I said I doubted it, but I would look into it. "Remember, don't say anything to anyone."

They took him away, out the door, out of sight—I thought, out of my life. I didn't realize what an impression our little escape attempt had made on him. "Now, here's a lawyer who really wants to get me *out.*"

The security police took Croft to the stockade, my last words to him— "don't say anything to anyone"—no doubt ringing in his ears. But he was not through talking. When he was brought that afternoon to his commanding officer to be informed of the charges against him, he said, "I didn't kill him. He pulled a gun. It was self-defense." While trying to deny culpability, Croft had succeeded in admitting *again* that he was at the scene of the shooting, and, one might infer, fired the shots—"it was self-defense." Without his own words, the government would have had an uphill battle proving he was even *there,* since witnesses were able to provide only a general description of a man running away; none were subsequently able to identify Croft at a lineup; contrary to what the homicide detective had told him, no one had seen his car at the scene; and no one had seen the shooting itself.

§6-03

The next day I got a phone call from Captain Larry Arnold, who'd been appointed Croft's defense attorney. He explained that in addition to his right to free representation by a military defense counsel, Croft had a right to retain civilian counsel at his own expense, and Croft wanted me, though he had no money.

I was able to arrange things at work so that soon I was riding up to Fort Meade in Captain Arnold's ancient red Eldorado to talk to our client, Peter Croft.

Captain Arnold, a man about my age, thirty-three, had slightly protruding blue eyes and buck teeth, which combined to give him the appearance of being perpetually on the verge of saying something startling. During our forty-five-minute drive he restricted himself to briefing me on military procedure. He stressed that I, as civilian counsel, was chiefly responsible for the conduct of the defense, a fact he didn't seem to mind at all.

We agreed that we had to get down every detail surrounding the incident before Croft forgot—everywhere he went, everything he did, everyone he saw. Then everybody who had seen him would have to be interviewed before they forgot and, ideally, before men with badges and guns got to them and discouraged them from talking to the defense. (It is perfectly proper for either side to talk to the witnesses of either side, but the police often tell witnesses not to talk to the defense, and we always remind witnesses that they don't *have* to talk to the police.)

The Fort Meade stockade was an unimposing one-story brick building, secured only by a single chain-link fence topped with razor concertina wire. A fatigue-clad teen-aged girl at the reception desk asked who we were, looked at my lawyer's ID card, and we were in. Croft padded down the hallway in slippers and a bathrobe, rubbing the sleep from his eyes, though it was only 8:00 P.M. He and I sat side by side on a green vinyl sofa, Captain Arnold sitting on a chair opposite. We were in a large linoleum-floored recreation room, which opened onto the front reception area. It was disconcerting not to be enclosed in an interview cubicle, as at the D.C. jail. We talked softly, conspiratorially. Croft, for his part, seemed hesitant to speak within earshot of his own military defense counsel. He didn't trust officers.

On the day of the incident, Croft said, he left for work at 6:00 A.M., as always, and arrived at the Air Force office of scientific research at 6:20. He worked routinely, punching epidemiological survey data into a computer, until his noon lunch break, when he played checkers with a co-worker (who later told us that Croft was relaxed and jovial, as always. All his co-workers were fond of Croft, though none knew him well. "He's a real killer," a cleaning lady said, meaning that he told very funny stories).

At 1:45 P.M., Croft said, the cleaning lady told him that he had a call on the hall pay phone. He got on the phone and found that it was Sales. Sales, in a calm voice, told Croft that Croft's wife wanted a divorce and asked him to come see him at the headquarters building when Croft got off work. Croft went back to his console, where he remained until 2:10 P.M., when he again played checkers for fifteen minutes with a co-worker (who noticed nothing unusual about Croft's mood). He left work at 2:25 P.M.

The shooting took place half an hour later, 200 yards from Croft's workplace. Croft offered no account of where he went or what he did during that half hour. He might, for instance, have been getting whacked out on drugs and/or getting a gun. I didn't press him. I told him that at some point we were going to have to account for that time, and that he should try to remember where he had been.

Croft repeated the account of the shooting he'd given the police. After the shooting, he said, he drove home, and at 5:45 he visited a friend, a former airman named Daniels, from whom he had borrowed a five-shot .38 revolver a month earlier. He'd borrowed the gun because his house had been burglarized while he was out in Illinois trying to reconcile with his wife, who had moved with their two sons after he beat her up during an argument about her affair with Sales. The Illinois excursion turned out to be a bad trip in every way: his wife showed no interest in reconciliation, urging him to "let things be the way they are. Don't make it rough on him [Sales]." He wrecked his car on the drive back, badly banging his head; and when he got home, he found an intruder asleep in his house. Croft subdued the sleeping man with a couple of whacks with an ax handle and held him for the police, but the incident left him feeling nervous and in need of a handgun, so he borrowed Daniels's.

Croft had, in turn, loaned Daniels a shotgun, and on this evening, after the shooting, Croft asked for it back. Daniels gave it to him. Croft stayed at Daniels's for half an hour, talking about sports and the weather, and playing with Daniels's little children. (Croft seemed perfectly normal to Daniels.) Neither he nor Daniels mentioned the five-shot revolver.

From Daniels's, Croft went to see some friends at Bolling's Blanchard barracks. They told him that the police had been looking for him. "The police are nuts," Croft responded. After fifteen minutes he left to see Kathy Foster at the N.C.O. club, where he was arrested.

It had been very tedious, reconstructing every minute of a day that was thoroughly unremarkable but for one explosive moment, and I thanked Croft for his help. (I often thought in terms of the client helping me, rather than the reverse.)

"That's okay, man," Croft said as he arranged his features into an appreciative look. "I appreciate what you're doing for me. Tell me, how do our chances look?"

"Anything can happen at a trial," I said.

§6-04

We were going to trial. The only alternative was to eat the whole beef—plead guilty to murder and possession of an unregistered firearm (the shotgun), as charged. Under Article 118 of the Uniform Code of Military Justice, murder is not broken down into first- and second-degree. Provision is made for imposition of the death penalty where the killing is premeditated, but the Air Force had decided not to seek capital punishment for Croft. He faced life imprisonment. In the alien world of the Air Force, there was no plea bargaining, because they had time to try all their defendants and room to lock them all up.

We promptly filed a motion demanding a speedy trial. Under military law, the accused, once having demanded a speedy trial, has a right to have the case dismissed if the prosecution does not bring him to trial within ninety days. We didn't expect to be ready for trial within that time, but we had to make a record of wanting a speedy trial so that we could demand that the case be dismissed if the prosecution wasn't ready.

I had a number of other matters in the pipeline and was preoccupied with them, even as Croft's trial crept closer. Out of your whole caseload, you tend to address yourself not to what's most important, but to what is coming due soonest. There was nothing unusual about my being busy trying to get one client's watch back from the police and preparing for another client's petit larceny trial while letting Croft's murder case "ripen."

I drove up and saw him alone every so often to discuss the information my student investigators were bringing in.

"I can tell you right now where we're going to run into problems—" I told him a couple of weeks after his arrest, "—the gun."

His features assumed a pensive look.

"Sales was shot with a thirty-eight-caliber handgun," I said. I was looking at the brown and white linoleum tile floor, thinking it looked like the farms of Iowa viewed from 30,000 feet on a partly cloudy winter day. "People heard *five* shots. You say it was Sales's own thirty-eight, and if you can prove that, you're a free man. So you throw it in the river. His friends say Sales's thirty-eight, a *six-shot* revolver, was stolen out of his car last summer while he was in the Good Times Video Arcade playing Pac-Man. Now, it just so happens that you borrowed a thirty-eight *five-shot* revolver from Daniels and never returned it. You say you sold it in Philadelphia, to the bouncer at an after-hours joint called the Cannery Row Club, but you don't know the bouncer's last name or the exact location of the club. And your friend Kathy Foster told the police she saw you with *some* gun a couple of weeks before the shooting. You say you sold Daniels's gun the weekend before the shooting, for a hundred and fifty dollars. You never told Daniels you sold the gun and never gave him the money. Can you see how a jury is going to have a lot of trouble believing you? They're going to think you used Daniels's gun to kill Sales and then threw it into the Potomac."

Croft pursed his thin lips and ran his fingers through his blow-dried hair. "I could get a friend from Illinois to say that I sold it to him," he offered.

"For chrissake, Croft, don't say things like that to me! I'm an officer of the court! I've got professional rules I have to work under. And one of the main ones is I can't participate in the creation of false evidence. Do you understand what I'm telling you?"

He understood, and reverted to the story about the bouncer at the Cannery Row Club. I said I'd send an investigator to look for him.

§6-05

When Croft's trial was suddenly just weeks away, an insanity defense grew more appealing to us. At first we had dismissed it as hopeless. Every witness who had encountered Croft on the day of the incident described him as behaving normally before and after the shooting, and he acted like someone who knew right from wrong and was in control of his actions when he disposed of the weapon and tried to construct an alibi. But as we became more familiar with the evidence and realized how shaky the self-defense case was, we decided to explore insanity. Maybe Croft was acting *too* normally. How could a sane person shoot someone and then go relax at a friend's house, talking about sports and the weather?

I broached the subject delicately—insane people tend to take offense at any suggestion that they are insane—but I needn't have worried. Croft was up for it.

"There is a complicated legal definition of insanity," I explained, "and shrinks will come in and offer expert testimony on both sides, but it's up to the jury to decide, and it really comes down to whether they think that you should be held responsible and punished, or that you were so fucked up at the time that it wouldn't be fair to punish you."

We would move for a "bifurcated trial," in which the merits of the case (whether Croft wrongfully killed Sales) would first be tried in front of one jury, and then, if and only if that jury found him guilty, the question of his sanity would be tried in front of a second jury, which wouldn't have heard his self-defense story and wouldn't have reached any conclusions about his credibility.

"In other words, it's a fallback position. You've got nothing to lose. You can swear it was self-defense; and then, if you're found guilty, you can swear that you hated Sales so much it drove you nuts, and you were beside yourself when you shot him. I mean, you have to tell the truth, of course. But then, both those statements could be true. Insane people have a right to defend themselves, too.

"Now, it seems to me, from what you've told me, that things happened like this: You loved your wife and your two little boys. You had great plans: you were going to work in the computer field when you got out of the service. The sky was the limit. Then along comes Sales. He's screwing your wife, and she tells you about it, and it's public knowledge. The humiliation is almost more than you can bear. Are you with me so far?"

"Yeah, man, I'm with you."

"Okay. You can hardly bear it, but you do bear it. But then your wife announces she's moving with the kids back to Illinois. You start to crack. Sales has taken your *kids* away from you.

"You drive out to Illinois to try to convince Arlene to come back to you. You get into a wreck and bump your head. And you've had migraine headaches ever since. And you're on *medication* for those headaches. Maybe the medication kind of spaces you out?"

"Not really."

"Okay. You come back to D.C., and you find a burglar asleep in your house. The whole house has been trashed. You whack the guy in the head with an ax handle and hold him for the cops. The cops tell you you should have used the other end of the ax, but that's not the kind of guy you are. All your co-workers say you wouldn't hurt a flea. Still, it makes you nervous that your house has been burglarized, so you borrow a handgun from your friend Daniels.

"Then on November fourteenth Sales calls you up and tells you that Arlene wants a divorce. You're out, he's in. You don't want to hear that, especially from *him*.

"So you go over to see him, and you just *go off*, you know? Maybe the last thing you remember is him coming at you. From then on, it's like a dream. It's like it happened in a different world, or didn't happen at all. That's why you're able to act so cool and collected afterwards. Get the picture?"

"Yeah, I see." He turned his lips down and nodded his head in thoughtful affirmation. My eyes were drawn to the cotton in his ear, yellowish with the discharge of an inner infection, which he blamed on conditions in the stockade. I looked away.

"Good. What we need to do now is think of reasons why you would be likely to crack. The shrink who's working for us—what he likes to see is deterioration, a guy falling apart: you're brooding, you start making mistakes at work, your apartment turns into a mess. And we need a background. You ever do anything kind of crazy before? You have some kind of drug history, or history of mental illness in your family?"

"Well, my father used to get drunk, kick the door down, and beat up my mother. He died when he was forty, of cirrhosis of the liver and hardening of the arteries," Croft began.

". . . the arteries," I scribbled. "Okay, go ahead."

"As a juvenile, when I was twelve, I shot a close friend of mine with a twenty-two. I had told him he could have some amphetamines. He took a couple, but because he was going over to his parents' house, he asked me to hold the rest for him. He didn't come back, so I gave the rest of the pills to another friend. The first friend felt like I ripped him off, so he attacked me a few days later. He punched me. So I went home and got a gun. I shot him in the stomach. He didn't die, and he testified it was an accident. I did seven months for it." Croft told me this story with all the feeling one might put into listing one's past addresses and phone numbers.

"I had *piles* of amphetamines when I was a kid," he continued. "My mother worked for a doctor. She had grocery bags full of pills."

"Did you use any drugs on the day you shot Sales?"

"That day I drank a half pint of brandy at about noon. I drank that much daily, at lunchtime. My friend Crockett and me would smoke four or five joints, polish off a six-pack or a pint of brandy, snort half a gram of coke, and go back to work. I didn't have lunch with Crockett November fourteenth, but I did have a gram of coke with me that day and it was all gone by six P.M."

I thought that was enough to give our shrink something to work with.

When, as required, we filed a notice of intention to assert the defense of insanity, that triggered the convening of a "sanity board" by the Air Force. Three military shrinks would deliver an opinion as to Croft's sanity and report it to all parties—the defense, the prosecution, and the judge. (The reports to the prosecution and the judge would be "sanitized"—that is, only the conclusions would be reported, not the personal history on which they were based.)

Croft was put through psychiatric interviews by the shrinks, a neurological examination, laboratory tests including electroencephalogram and CAT scan, and a battery of psychological tests.

We received the board's report four days before the trial date:

The clinical psychiatric diagnosis is antisocial personality disorder. This diagnosis is associated with repetitive and continuous antisocial behavior without apparent genuine regret or remorse to include: polydrug abuse, pattern of aggressiveness characterized by physical assaults, recklessness indicated by recurrent speeding tickets, failure to accept social norms manifested by drugs such as marijuana and cocaine and extramarital affairs.

Onset of this condition was before 15 years of age, and was manifested by fire-setting, cruelty to animals, truancy, thefts, delinquency, polydrug abuse, suspension from school, and detention in a juvenile home for assault after shooting his best friend.

The subject did not at the time of the alleged criminal conduct have a mental disease or defect. . . . The accused was not substantially under the influence of alcohol or other drugs at the time of the offense.

Our own shrink had come to the same conclusion. Croft was "a classic sociopath."

What is a sociopath?

Psychiatric experts agree that sociopaths are people like Peter Croft, and that people like Peter Croft are sociopaths. (At least, they are now. They used to be "psychopaths," but the American Psychiatric Association changed the term in 1952.)

People with "sociopathic personality disturbance, antisocial reaction" crave immediate gratification and are highly impulsive; they are aggressive, feel little or no guilt, and don't empathize with, much less love, other people.[1]

Nobody knows for sure what engenders this syndrome, although one thing most sociopaths have in common, aside from being *called* sociopaths, is that they were neglected or rejected as children. Their parents (or the institution replacing them) responded inconsistently and arbitrarily (and often brutally) to them; rewards and punishments had nothing to do with their behavior, so a sense of right and wrong, or even cause and effect, was not instilled.

Many people who are considered sociopaths are good artists or writers, as well as charming conversationalists. I'm sure no one knows why. Gary Gilmore, whose execution in Utah got the death penalty back on track, showed talent at writing and illustration. Jack Abbott's writing helped him win parole. My own client Roberto Lewis, with his lovely portraits and repeated impulsive crimes, seems to fit the bill.

Whatever sociopaths are, the one thing they are not, *by definition*, is insane, because they are not suffering from an identified "mental disease or defect." Section 4.01 of the American Law Institute's Model Penal Code, after propounding the definition of insanity subsequently adopted in the District of Columbia,* goes on to state:

(2) The terms "mental disease or defect" do not include an abnormality manifested only by repeated criminal or otherwise antisocial conduct.†

---

* See pages 154–55.
† The comments appended to the code explain: "6. Paragraph (2) of section 4.01 is designed to exclude from the concept of 'mental disease or defect' the case of so-called 'psychopathic personality.' The reason for the exclusion is that . . . psychopathy 'is a statistical abnormality; that is to say, the psychopath differs from a normal person only

Of course, the concept of "mental disease or defect" is itself a matter of definition. What else could it be? It's a definition with a history, though, and it's been adjusted and readjusted with a view to bringing some people in and leaving some people out, and Croft, by design, was out. He might have been "crazy"; he definitely was "abnormal"; but "insane"? No way, José.

We gave up on insanity. Self-defense was the only way to go.

§6-06

Captain Arnold and I decided that we were not ready for trial. No one had been up to Philadelphia to look for the Cannery Row Club. We had not yet interviewed all the witnesses, let alone rehearsed ours. We had just obtained a long-requested item of discovery from the prosecution: Sales's address book. It contained the names of forty-three women, all of whom we wanted to interview. Any number of them might have had husbands whom Sales had roughed up. (Evidence of prior acts of violence by Sales would be admissible on the issue of who was, in fact, the aggressor in the showdown with Croft). We had a lot to do.

We filed a motion for a continuance, which, we assumed, would be routinely granted. I had never had a trial in D.C. superior court actually begin on the first date scheduled even if I wanted it to.

On Monday, February 25, 1981, I strode into the "courtroom" at Bolling and didn't like what I saw. The linoleum-floored, hospital-green-painted room contained barely enough furniture to set the stage for a third-rate school play. There was a raised platform along one wall for the jury, but some used office chairs, no two alike, grouped around a couple of beat-up little wooden tables, which were not even attached to the floor, were all that was provided for the lawyers. There were no pews for the audience—and no audience—just a few old bridge chairs. It was not my idea of a courtroom. *Anything* could happen in a place like that.

Captain Arnold and I took seats flanking Croft and looked at the prosecutors seated at their little table a few feet away. Captain Elizabeth

---

quantitatively or in degree, not qualitatively; and the diagnosis of psychopathic personality does not carry with it any explanation of the causes of the abnormality.'"
(Comments to the Fourth Draft, p. 160, quoted in United States v. Brawner, 471 F. 2nd 969, 993 footnote 41, U.S.C.A. [D.C. Cir. 1972].)

Biscket, a stocky young woman in an ill-fitting uniform, glanced at us, turned, and whispered into the ear of her assistant, the diminutive Captain Ed Hooton, who pushed his gray plastic glasses up on his nose, stared into the distance, and rubbed his hands together. They'd be no competition, Air Force image-wise, for the lanky Captain Arnold with his Vietnam campaign ribbon and wings.

The judge burst in, pulling a black robe over his uniform as he barked, "Don't get up!" He, at least, was a familiar type: short, scrappy, craggy-faced, gray crewcut, throws away the tuna and eats the can.

The first order of business was our motion for a continuance. I rattled off all the important work we had yet to do, noting that we had made a "good faith effort" to be ready. The prosecutors stated that they did not oppose a continuance.

"The motion is denied," the judge said.

"Excuse me, Your Honor," I said. "I think you said 'denied.' Did you mean to say 'granted'?"

"The motion is denied," the judge repeated. "Are there any other motions?"

"Your Honor," I said, forcing my words through a suddenly constricted throat, "we have other motions, but we're not prepared to go to trial. This is a very complex case, as well as a very serious one. It involves about forty witnesses and scientific evidence. I've been in trial until a couple of weeks ago, and we didn't have investigators available until recently."

"The motion is denied. The defendant has a right to a speedy trial."

"Exactly, Your Honor. It's the defendant's right, and he wants to waive it. He's incarcerated, Your Honor, so a continuance doesn't put the community at risk."

"The motion is denied."

During the time it took to take a deep breath, I decided to go ahead and say, "Very well, Your Honor. I don't want to be argumentative, but I will state, on the record, that if we go forward at this time, I will not be rendering effective assistance of counsel; I will not be a competent defense counsel, and Mr. Croft's Sixth Amendment right to counsel will be violated."

"Do you have any other motions, counsel?"

Tears welled up in my eyes. "Now you've really done it, Kunen," I thought. Larry Arnold had told me that, in the unlikely event that the judge denied our motion, I could *force* a continuance by simply *leaving*, because Croft had a right not to proceed without civilian counsel, and the military judge did not have the power to hold me in contempt. An awareness bomb went off in my stomach: *Larry Arnold was wrong.* To leave would not only be a humiliation verging on dishonor, it would be *absurd;* no game in the world includes within it the tactic of *refusing to play.*

There was nothing to do but get on with it. We made a motion to be provided funds for the employment of an investigator. Denied. We moved for severance of the unregistered weapon charge from the murder charge, since the possession of the unregistered shotgun had nothing to do with the murder and might be prejudicial—the jury might think that since Croft was carrying the shotgun, he was the sort of guy who would commit the murder. Denied.

The case was adjourned for the day so that the judge could finish off some other matters.

Croft was given a moment to talk to me before he was hauled back to the stockade. He looked sick. "I'm kind of worried, man—what you said about not being ready."

"Oh, don't pay any attention to *that*," I said. "That was just talk, to try to get the continuance. It's always nice to have more time, but we're ready, don't worry."

"Okay," he said. He looked worried.

That evening I went with my student investigator Amy Strader to the modest row house on a neat, tree-lined street in northwest Washington that was the home of Joan Davis, the decedent Sales's fiancée.

A pallid-faced young woman with a short henna-red punk rock hairdo opened the door. I noted that she was braless under her Led Zeppelin T-shirt. We explained exactly who we were (so that she wouldn't be able to disavow anything she said later on the basis that she had somehow been tricked) and said that all we wanted was to find out the truth about what happened. We weren't lying. We did want to hear the truth, *outside* the courtroom, the better to manage what would be heard *inside* the courtroom.

She silently beckoned us in with a wave of her hundred-millimeter slim cigarette.

We were uninvited, unexpected, but not entirely unwelcome. People who have been victimized by crime have a desire to talk about it and to have attention paid them. Frequently they have been alienated by bureaucratic, insensitive treatment from the police and prosecution. Only the defense seems to *care.*

Joan Davis invited us to join her at the dining table in her L-shaped living room, where she was eating Popeye's Fried Chicken in front of a blasting color TV.

I let Strader do the talking. A raw-boned twenty-year-old with a sort of Beatles' haircut, Strader bore a striking resemblance, from certain angles, to a fourteen-year-old boy. As a result, her particular cross to bear in life was that people tended not to take her seriously. This made her a devastatingly effective investigator. She seemed so sweet and innocent that people trusted her immediately. She didn't like to betray people's trust, but she had developed a way of interpreting precisely what she had said and not said so that she could see that, really, she had not misled anybody. Most of our interns picked that up quickly, from the lawyers.

(The defense has to be resourceful in its investigative techniques. It can't scare witnesses into cooperating, with badges and guns. Nor can it buy their help with a thirty-dollar fee per office visit, as U.S. attorneys can. Indigent defendants are allowed court funds for witnesses only when they are subpoenaed to a court proceeding.)

I grew restless as Strader engaged in vapid small talk with Joan Davis. Even I couldn't tell she was working. But when the dust settled, Davis had said that Croft's wife Arlene had once dropped in on Sales when Davis was with him. After shooing Arlene away, Sales told Davis that Arlene was in his Toys-for-Tots volunteer group. (Sales, we learned, was in no such group. Dishonest. Sleazy. Worth knowing by the jury.) *And* Joan Davis had seen a handgun in Sales's glove compartment *after* the night when his .38 was supposedly stolen from his car parked outside the Good Times Video Arcade.

§6-07

The court reconvened at nine o'clock sharp the next morning. That's considerably earlier than I was used to getting to work in the civilian courts. I was able to arrive on time by broadly construing red lights as the equivalent of stop signs, a transgression that seemed inconsequential to me at the time. The harshness of the hour was ameliorated by my favorite aspect of military law: coffee cups were allowed in the courtroom, and we'd recess frequently to refill them. I did the whole trial caffeinated to the sky.

We made a motion to suppress all physical evidence (notably the shotgun seized from Croft at his arrest), as well as any statements allegedly made by Croft, since, we argued, there had been no probable cause to arrest him; therefore his arrest was illegal; and the evidence and statements must be suppressed as the "fruit of an illegal arrest." That Croft fit the general description of a man seen fleeing the scene; that Sales had been involved in an affair with Croft's wife; and that Sales had once said that if anything happened to him, Croft would be responsible, we suggested, were grounds to suspect Croft, but probable cause to *arrest* him? Hardly.

The Fourth Amendment provides that "the right of the people to be secure in their persons, houses, papers, and effects, against unreasonable searches and seizures, shall not be violated, and no Warrants shall issue, but upon probable cause . . ." The Supreme Court has held that warrants are not constitutionally required for felony arrests in public places,[1] but "probable cause" is *always* required. Volumes have been written on the question of what "probable cause" means. The U.S. Court of Appeals, D.C. Circuit, explained it this way: ". . . a peace officer has probable cause to arrest 'when he has reasonable grounds, in light of the circumstances of the moment as viewed through his eyes, for belief that a felony has been committed and that the person before him committed it.' "[2] * Whatever probable cause means, reasonable minds can differ about whether a particular police officer making a particular arrest had it.

The prosecution argued that there *was* probable cause, but that, anyway, Croft had given permission to the arresting officer to go into the trunk and even handed him the keys, so that the seizure of the shotgun did not result from a "search" at all.

We insisted that Croft did not consent to the search—that it was impossible for him to consent freely to anything, lying on the ground surrounded by policemen.

The judge ruled that the arrest *was* based on probable cause and was, therefore, legal, so the shotgun would be allowed in evidence, and that statements made by Croft were not the product of an illegal arrest.

Croft's statements to Detective Luce at the homicide office had to be suppressed anyway, we argued, because they were obtained in violation of Croft's *Miranda* rights. When Croft filled out a rights card with Detective Miller indicating that he did not want to answer questions, there should have been no further attempts to question him. The police can't just wait a few minutes and read a person his rights again to see if he'll change his mind.

The Supreme Court has held, however, that there are certain circumstances in which a suspect *can* be questioned after he has asserted his right to remain silent. In *Michigan* v. *Mosely*,[3] the defendant told one police officer that he did not want to answer questions about a robbery for

---

* To arrest for a petty offense without a warrant, the officer must catch the offender in the act.

which he had just been arrested. Two hours later, a different officer read him his rights again and questioned him about a homicide, which had not been the subject of the first interrogation. The defendant waived his rights and confessed. The Supreme Court held that the confession was admissible because of its unrelatedness—two hours later, different crime—to the interrogation in regard to which the defendant had already asserted his rights.

Some knowledge of *Michigan* v. *Mosely* had evidently trickled down to Detective Luce. The notation "military arrest for possession of shotgun" had been scrawled across the rights card Croft made out with Miller at 8:35 P.M. in an apparent attempt to relate that card to a crime other than the murder. Luce testified at a pretrial hearing that he thought the first card pertained only to the shotgun possession charge, and that he thought Croft wanted to remain silent only about that misdemeanor, but was willing to answer questions about the homicide.

Even if that bit of creativity had not stunk up the courtroom, Luce would still have had a problem because, according to his own pretrial testimony, he started questioning Croft about the homicide, and obtained an admission, *before* he reread him his *Miranda* rights, pausing only to ask, "Do you understand your rights?," which is only one of the Four Questions. Luce testified that when Croft asked him to get his attorney's business card, he did not think Croft wanted to contact the attorney. "I thought he just wanted the card, that's all." The prosecution did not oppose our motion to suppress the statements to Luce.

We argued that Croft's subsequent statement to his commanding officer—"I didn't kill him. He pulled a gun. It was self-defense"—should also be suppressed because it would never have been made if not for the first, illegally obtained statement: Croft thought the cat was out of the bag. He thought he had no reason to remain silent anymore. Thus, the second statement should be suppressed as a product of the first one. Not only that, but, under military regulations, his commanding officer should not have had Croft brought to him without his lawyer present, if the C.O. *knew* that Croft had a lawyer; and the C.O. had heard from the military police that Croft *did* have a lawyer (me).

You could tell by the judge's furrowed brow that he knew he had a problem here. He obviously *had* to suppress the statements to Luce, but that meant the statement to the C.O. should be suppressed, too, and then the defendant would go free. What to do?

The judge decided to think about it for a while and adjourned for the day, after denying our renewed motion for a continuance. The next morning he announced that he would suppress the statements to Luce, prohibiting the prosecution from using them in its case, as they had been obtained in violation of Croft's *Miranda* rights. Those statements were not "coerced," however, the judge ruled, and therefore not inherently unreliable, so the prosecution could use them to "impeach" Croft—attack his credibility*—if on direct examination he testified to something clearly inconsistent with his prior statements. That is, the jury would never hear the damning "I put two bullets in him after he was on the floor" *unless* Croft offered an inconsistent account of the shooting, in which case the prosecution could confront him with the portion of his earlier statement that he had contradicted. As the judge put it, the suppression of illegally obtained statements is not "a license to lie." If we wanted to be sure the admission to Luce stayed out of evidence, we could simply not have Croft testify.

As for Croft's statement to his commanding officer, the judge decided it was admissible. It was not "tainted" by Croft's thinking the cat was out of the bag, because it was made about ten hours after the statements to Luce, in a different place. As for the C.O.'s violation of regulations by bringing Croft in without his lawyer, the judge decided that the C.O. didn't really *know* Croft had a lawyer; he had merely heard some talk to that effect.

Even as we sat in the courtroom haggling over motions, the defense case was being constructed by our investigators. Under military procedure, in contrast to the procedure at superior court, we had been provided not only with the names and addresses of all government witnesses but also with copies of statements they had given to the authorities. Our investigators interviewed all those witnesses and all the people that those people mentioned. We learned what all the witnesses' testimony would be. And it almost doesn't matter what they're going to testify to, as long as you know what it is. All news is good news: Sales had said Croft was going to kill him? Fine—that's a good reason for *Sales* to have been carrying a gun. Everybody knows Croft beat his wife? Great—we'll have Croft "voluntarily" confess to that on the stand—it will show how *honest* he is. Facts are like atoms. Many different things can be constructed from the same facts.

As a matter of fact, some of what the witnesses had to say was splendid for our side. Investigator Bert Meyers brought back a gem of a signed statement from Staff Sergeant J. B. Jones, one of Croft's co-workers who

---

* To "impeach" a witness means to attack his credibility either by specifically contradicting what he has said or by showing that he is generally unworthy of belief because, for instance, he is a convicted felon or has been caught lying before.

was also a friend of Sales's. Jones recalled that, sometime back in September or October, Sales asked Jones to point out Croft to him.

"I asked him why he wanted to see Croft," Jones said. "He said he just wanted to know who he was. I asked him, 'What you doing, messing around with his wife or something?' He just started smiling, chuckling. He said, 'You know what happens if you don't take care of your homework.'"

Nice guy, right? *Sleazo.* It got even better: "A couple of times after this incident, I mentioned this woman to Sales, and what her husband might do, and he said, 'I ain't worried about nothing. I keep my piece [gun] on me.' Irwin Sales always bragged about his piece. He said he owned a .38 and a .357 Magnum."

Jones's testimony would support the defense theory that Sales died by his own gun. Equally important, the picture he'd paint of Sales would help make the jury *want* to believe it.

Meanwhile, investigator Amanda Perwin, a student intern from Wellesley College, was getting a million-dollar signed statement from Sales's supervisor, Technical Sergeant Ken Yates. Perwin felt slightly queasy about the enterprise in which she was engaged, but she believed in hard work—that was the main thing—and she did her job well.

Yates was loath to speak ill of Sales in particular, or the dead in general, and had a profound aversion to involvement in legal proceedings or anything else that he could more readily imagine doing him harm than good. Yet Amanda got him to sign this:

Irwin Sales was a lady's man. To be frank with you, he used women. He saw them as just a piece of ass, and he'd do anything to get inside their pants. He had a lot of girlfriends, and he told everybody about them, and he'd tell you all the details. He'd tell me about it, he'd tell you about it, he'd tell the guy in the hallway about it. I mean, the bad thing about it is that if he went to bed with you tonight, tomorrow morning, everybody would know about it.

Last summer was the first time he told me about Arlene Croft. Sales was concerned. He said, "I have a problem, and I need your advice." He said that Arlene had told her husband she was seeing this guy Irwin Sales. Not only did she tell his name, but where he worked, and where he lived, and everything. At that time, I told him I'm a little concerned about a person who tells a spouse that they're going out with someone, and gives the person's name and address. I view that as possibly destructive behavior. I told him to stop seeing her.

The next morning he came in and told me that he and Arlene had talked, and they agreed they weren't going to see each other again. I asked him why, if he had so many girlfriends, why did he care so much about this lady. I mean she's married and has five [*sic*] kids. What was so special about her? He said he hated to give her up because she was just the "best lay" he had ever had, just the "best piece of ass."

Yates also remembered that Sales had once told him that he had an unregistered pistol.

And an airman on duty at the headquarters building on the day of the shooting told Perwin that Sales reported to work that day carrying a gym bag with *something* in it.

§6-08

After three days of motions, we got down to the business of jury selection, right after our renewed motion for a continuance—we wanted more time for investigation—was denied. We exercised our right to have at least one third of the jurors be enlisted men—the defendant's peers. We thought enlisted men, the military equivalent of blue-collar workers, might be more sympathetic to shooting your wife's lover as a mode of resolving marital difficulties than would the "white-collar" officers.

Each side was allowed one peremptory challenge. We bumped the jury pool's highest-ranking officer, a colonel. "Get rid of the weight," my co-counsel Captain Arnold said. Sergeants have a hard time holding their own against colonels in deliberations.

Any number of jurors could be challenged by either side for cause. The judge let us get rid of three who said that they did not believe in the right to use deadly force in self-defense.

I challenged a recently divorced enlisted man, on the theory that the prosecution, thinking they had missed something, would object to his removal, instead of insisting on it themselves. When they offered no objection, I said, weakly, that I had changed my mind.

"Oh, come on!" the judge barked. "You're a lawyer, aren't you? This isn't a game." The most promising juror was whisked away. Croft looked at me with a combination of disgust and amazement. He sighed audibly. I shook it off—chalk it up to experience. Onward.

A jury of eight was sworn—four enlisted men, three male officers, one woman officer. Our military justice system, based on the code of Gustavus Adolphus, a seventeenth-century Swedish king, requires only two thirds of the jury to concur in a conviction. The prosecutor would need six votes to win; we would need three.*

Captain Biscket delivered the prosecution's opening statement, the purpose of which is to give the broad outlines of the government case, alleging facts sufficient to prove the elements of the offenses charged. I was busy writing down everything she said, with a view to moving for a mistrial if she later failed to present evidence that she said she was going to, when I noticed that I had written, "Sales's friend Dave Johnson will testify that Sales told him, 'If anything ever happens to me, you'll know it was Peter Croft that did it.' "

That's hearsay! I realized—an out-of-court statement offered as the equivalent of testimony: "Sales told me . . ." Oh, well. There's not much point in objecting to something after it's already been said. All the judge can do is tell the jury to disregard it, which has the effect of searing it into their memories. Then she started saying it again. "I object!" I heard myself say, finding myself on my feet. "That's hearsay," the judge said. "The jury will disregard it."

(My P.D.S. supervisor said later I could have moved for a mistrial and probably gotten it, so serious and prejudicial was the prosecutor's breach.)

As she outlined the government's case—Croft had the motive, the means, and the opportunity; fled; deep-sixed the evidence; and fabricated an alibi—Biscket spoke in an unvarying tone of what was probably supposed to be righteous indignation, but sounded more like personal annoyance. It was as though the thought of the shooting gave her a headache, and she was going to give everyone else a headache, too, until she got a conviction, until she got some *relief.*

My turn. As a civilian, I faced the jurors across a cultural chasm, as well as a physical one: they were seated in one long row along a dais, their faces two feet above my head. I was foreign to them, but therein lay an advantage: I aroused their curiosity. I set out to exploit that curiosity in the most ancient and proven of ways—by telling them a story. Everyone prefers a story to a statement. Everyone prefers a story to anything.

* Historically, unanimous verdicts have been required to convict in American courts generally, and twelve-person criminal juries have been the rule. Defense attorneys argue that a less than unanimous verdict necessarily means that there was a reasonable doubt about the defendant's guilt; and that twelve jurors are necessary to ensure that the will and wisdom of the community are adequately represented (and to maximize the chances of getting at least *one* juror who won't vote to convict). The Supreme Court, however, has upheld 9–3 convictions in noncapital cases in state courts (Johnson v. Louisiana, 406 U.S. 356 [1972]), and has found six-person criminal juries constitutionally permissible, at least where the requirement of unanimity is retained (Williams v. Florida, 399 U.S. 78 [1970]).

I eased into it with a stock defense attention-grabber:

"In the opening statement, I have the opportunity to outline for you what we expect the evidence will show. As you listen to the evidence, I'd like you to remember this [I held up my hand, palm toward the jury]: Have you seen my hand? [Pause.] No, you haven't seen my hand. [I turned the back of my hand toward them.] *Now* you've seen my hand. There are two sides to this story. As you listen to the government's case, remember to keep an open mind until you've heard Peter Croft's case."

Good. The jurors hadn't heard that one before. You could see just the hint of a smile on their faces from the satisfaction of "getting it." Hand. Two sides. Clever. We're all clever here.

"As you listen to the evidence, you will hear the story of a nightmare, Peter Croft's nightmare. As nightmares often do, it started out as a pleasant dream."

The pleasant dream began with Croft and his wife-to-be meeting, as teen-agers, at a country picnic. It floated along through their wedding, the birth of their two little boys, Croft's enlistment in the service of his country.

"When the Crofts moved to Washington, their future looked bright. They were happy. Then things started to go bad; and they went bad for a reason; and the reason had a name; and the name was Irwin Sales." The prosecution had neglected to acquaint the jurors with Irwin Sales, referring to him simply as the victim, never fleshing him out. So I took care of it. Predicting exactly what various witnesses would say about him, I introduced Sales the womanizer, Sales the homewrecker, Sales the liar, Sales the gun-toting macho man. I did strike one sympathetic note: "Sales is *afraid*. He's afraid because of what he is doing. He's looking over his shoulder all the time. He's so afraid that he always carries one of his handguns."

Although I didn't explicitly say so, it was perfectly clear that Sales, by having an affair with a married woman, had violated the moral order of the universe, thus assuring his own destruction—only the details of time, place, and manner remaining for God to work out. By this account, precisely what transpired on November 14 was the *least* important aspect of the story—it was just unfortunate for Croft that he was selected as the divine instrumentality. Nonetheless, just to tie up loose ends, I concluded the story with the struggle for the gun, the accidental shot into the wall, Croft wresting the gun away. "Peter falls back and, fearing for his life, starts firing. The first shot knocks Sales's tooth out and passes into his brain—Sales is falling dead as Peter's last two shots hit him.

"Peter flees to his car and starts driving home. He realizes he still has the weapon. He throws it in the Potomac. He feels he's in big trouble—he's a murder suspect. He visits friends, tries to create an alibi. But the police suspect him, as well they should. He is the man who fired the shots. And the truth will out. And the truth will set him free. Because Peter Croft fired the shots with Sales's weapon, in self-defense."

§6-09

The prosecution called its first witness, Sarah Joswick. The prim military wife testified that as she waited outside the headquarters building for her husband, she'd heard shots and seen a man run away.

"By saying 'bang' for each shot, could you demonstrate for the court *exactly* the pattern of shots you heard?" Captain Arnold asked on cross-examination.

She lowered her eyelids for a moment as she called up that instant from three months ago.

"BANG—BANGBANG—BANGBANG," she said.

What we were interested in was the pause after the first shot—the gun was changing hands.

"One other thing," Captain Arnold said. "I'd like to show you what's been marked defense exhibit A, and ask you if you recognize it." He showed her a beautiful pencil sketch of the headquarters building, which Bert Meyers had drawn the day before when it occurred to me that our case could use some art—we hadn't found time to take photos.

"Yes. That's the front of building twenty."

"There's a sign on the door, isn't there?"

"Yes."

"That same sign was there on November fourteenth, wasn't it?"

"Yes."

"What does it say?"

"It says, 'Warning: This Building Is Under Continuous Surveillance by Closed-Circuit Cameras.' "

"Thank you."

We would argue that no one would choose to commit a murder on videotape, so it must have been self-defense. As it turned out, the video system was out of order on November 14. Croft didn't know that. Sales might have.

The next two government witnesses, like Mrs. Joswick, testified that they had heard shots and seen someone run away. The government was establishing a boring but necessary element of its case, the *corpus delicti*—"the body of the crime"—the objective proof that a crime was committed. You can't prove the defendant committed the crime unless you prove a crime was committed. Somebody shot somebody.

One witness remembered the shots as we liked them: "BANG—BANG-BANG—BANGBANG." The other thought he heard "BANGBANGBANG—BANGBANG," but he was standing right at the door of the building and may have been confused by echoes.

Officer Straus, a Metropolitan Police Department crime scene search officer, identified the photos he had taken of the scene. He was then shown a floor plan of the building, which the prosecution had prepared. Asked by Captain Hooton the routine question for getting a picture accepted into evidence, "Is it a fair and accurate representation of the entrance area as it appeared that day?," he answered, to our delight, "No." It seemed that what was depicted as a wall was actually an opening to a hallway, and that a piece of furniture was misplaced.

Even though these details were of no significance, on cross-examination we had Officer Straus stand up and meticulously draw in and initial the corrections. Every time the jurors looked at that chart it would deliver a *defense* message: the prosecution is slipshod.

We also had him point to, identify, circle, and initial a little item visible in the background of one of the photos, on a chair behind Sales's desk: an open gym bag. We would argue that Sales carried a gun to work in it. And, since Officer Straus had participated in a search of the decedent Sales's house, he was also able to tell us what he had found lying on the living-room table there: a .38, in a holster; a .357 Magnum, in a holster; and an empty holster for a .38.

"That's how many handguns?"

"Two."

"And how many holsters?"

"Three."

"Two handguns, but three holsters?"

"Yes."

"And the empty holster was for a thirty-eight?"

"Yes."

When the trial resumed the next morning, the prosecution called Metropolitan Police Department crime scene search officer Stahler, who described the recovery of five slugs: two in the body, one in the wall, one on the floor, and one from the ambulance's stretcher. He admitted that he had no way of knowing whether these were all the bullets that had been fired.

Special Agent Boston of the Air Force's Office of Special Investigations added to the government's floor plan a curved line denoting blood droplets which made a seven-foot path from a point in front of Sales's desk to a large puddle of blood—the path Sales staggered before hitting the floor, presumably. He also marked the spot where he found "an apparent tooth" on the floor in front of the desk.

On cross-examination, Boston acknowledged that he had written in his notebook (which we had seen, through discovery) that there "appeared to have been a struggle," a conclusion he based on the presence of the bullet hole high up the wall behind the desk. Boston had made no mention of a struggle in his direct examination by the prosecution.

Our objection to the introduction of Sales's jacket, complete with bullet holes and blood, was sustained. It was kept out of evidence because it was likely to "inflame the passions" of the jury and it didn't prove anything new. The guy was shot.

Detective Haviland of the security police was called to describe the apprehension of Croft and the recovery of the shotgun from his trunk. Captain Arnold got him to admit, in cross-examination, that Croft had been cooperative—he didn't struggle or attempt to flee, and he volunteered the information that the shotgun was in the trunk and gave Haviland permission to open it, pointing out the proper key.

At the pretrial motion to suppress the shotgun, we had argued that Croft was coerced into helping Haviland find the gun, because we were trying to show that the seizure was illegal. Now it suited our interests to argue that Croft had voluntarily turned over the gun. Conversely, at the suppression hearing the prosecution wanted to prove that Croft had consented to the search; now it was in their interest to downplay his helpfulness as they tried to paint a picture of a guilty man. This sort of nimble dance is perfectly proper and takes place all the time, but it does have an effect on how lawyers think of "the truth": the truth is what the evidence proves, and the evidence proves what you want it to.

Kathy Foster, Croft's barmaid friend, could have been the prosecution's star witness. The jurors, heavy-lidded with crime scene search stupor, sat up with a start when jeans-clad Kathy strode into the room. She gave her long dark hair a brave toss, but you could tell by the way she clutched her purse that she was scared. Here was the first witness with a stake in the action.

The prosecution blew it. Captain Hooton tried, at embarrassing length, to get Ms. Foster to admit a sexual relationship with Croft—"He used to come by and see me sometimes" was as far as she would go—as though the jury would hold it against Croft that he slept with somebody after his wife had left him, rather than hold it against Hooton that he was bad-gering the young lady to talk about stuff that was nobody's damn busi-ness. (We, of course, would argue that Croft's having a girlfriend showed he was well-adjusted and not likely to murder Sales.) If Hooton insisted on going into it, it would have been worthwhile for him to bring out that Foster herself was a married woman (her husband was overseas), but either this fact had escaped his attention or he failed to appreciate its po-tential for shifting "the equities" in a love-triangle murder case.

Foster, turning away from the prosecutor and speaking over her shoul-der to the judge in a voice hoarse with resentment, admitted that Croft had asked her to lie to the police for him. She was less angry at Croft for that than at the police for lying to her about having to come down and answer questions, and at the prosecutor for making her recount it all in public. She couldn't see the fairness in it.

Everybody always wanted something out of Foster. What I wanted was for her to remember that when she saw Croft carrying a pistol, it was right after his house had been burglarized. Captain Arnold and I reminded her of that when we visited her at her home, and investigator Bert Meyers re-minded her when he drove her to court to testify.

Captain Hooton got Foster to admit, reluctantly, that she had seen Croft carrying a pistol in October; but she added that his house had been burglarized just before that, and that he needed the weapon for self-defense.

Croft's commanding officer, Colonel Brand, repeated Croft's blurted-out declaration: "I didn't kill him. He pulled a gun. It was self-defense." We could live with that.

The prosecution next called Dave Johnson, Sales's best friend. The bailiff went out to the hallway to get him, but no one came in. People in the courtroom started looking at each other. The bailiff returned and said that Johnson was not there. "He was here earlier," Captain Hooton stammered, enduring a moment that was easily worth five bucks from the *Reader's Digest*. Captain Biscket decided to put Johnson over until after lunch and meanwhile call Dr. Richard Korzeniewski, deputy medical ex-aminer for the District of Columbia, to describe the autopsy on Sales.

An autopsy is the ultimate examination of a witness, everything laid bare. Dr. Korzeniewski was prepared to put on a slide show of the au-topsy, but we objected that the sole purpose of showing the slides was to appeal to the jury's emotions. All the pictures prove to a layman is that when you cut into a human body, it looks just like a steak. We insisted that Dr. Korzeniewski could explain everything perfectly well to the jury using words alone. The judge agreed with us. The photos were kept out, and the shooting of Sales remained an abstract proposition, a theoretical puzzle. The jury would see only the autopsy diagrams, which showed the wounds marked as dots on a standard, universal male figure, which looked more like a shop-window mannequin than a slain human being. The penciled-in arrows, denoting bullet trajectories, could as well have marked the direction of the flow of water through plumbing. The diagrams lent themselves to cool, rational analysis, which is what defense attorneys strive for.

As Dr. Korzeniewski testified, the jurors shifted their weight forward, concentrating, expectant. Here, at last, might be something Perry Mason-esque—entertaining and revelatory. The prosecution, having billed Korzeniewski's testimony in their opening as "a revealing analysis of events," hoped to ride him to victory—an expert, a doctor, someone not likely to be fooled, someone who "ought to know" and ought to be believed. It was false billing, as the jury must have realized. What Korzeniewski had to say was this: The man died from multiple gunshot wounds. There were four entry wounds and two exit wounds. There was no gunpowder residue or singeing of the skin, so the shots were most likely fired from more than eighteen inches away. Arbitrarily numbering the wounds 1 through 4—he had no way of determining in which order the shots were fired—Korzeniewski said shot number 1 entered above the left lip, traveling from the victim's left to his right, front to back, and sharply upward. It penetrated the brain and would have killed Sales even if no other wounds had been inflicted.

Shot number 2 entered the left shoulder and passed through the armpit, traveling left to right and slightly upward. It lacerated the trachea and subclavian artery and dropped into the chest cavity. It caused massive bleeding and, it, too, would have been fatal by itself.

Shot number 3 was an "in-and-out" wound, causing no serious harm. The bullet entered on the left side of the chest, traveled left to right and sharply upward, tunneling through the musculature without penetrating the chest cavity, and exited the left back. The exit wound was peculiar, somewhat oval in shape and ending in a four-centimeter linear abrasion; that the bullet had trouble getting out suggested that the decedent's back was against a hard surface, like a wall or floor, when this wound was inflicted.

Shot number 4 entered the side of the left upper arm, traveled left to right, front to back, and slightly upward, passing through muscle and exiting out the side of the left shoulder—a minor flesh wound.

"Do the wounds show that the decedent had his left arm stretched out to the side?" Captain Biscket asked, mentioning that particular position because it would mean that Sales had not been lunging at Croft. I didn't object to the leading question because I didn't want to appear frightened of the answer, which I knew from interviewing Dr. Korzeniewski was nothing to be afraid of. "It could have been, it's consistent," Dr. Korzeniewski replied.

Larry Arnold cross-examined. "Dr. Korzeniewski, you testified that the wounds were *consistent with* the decedent's having had his left arm stretched out to the left?"

"Yes."

"That just means it's *possible*, doesn't it?"

"Yes. I can't determine what particular position his arm was in."

It was clear that Dr. Korzeniewski was not purporting to describe Sales's position when he was shot or to offer any "revealing analysis" of the events leading to his death. The prosecution had promised something it could not deliver.

§6-10

Sales's buddy Johnson finally showed up twenty minutes after court reconvened in the afternoon—twenty minutes during which the court sat waiting for him. He lumbered down the aisle, unshaven, in dirty blue jeans and a leather vest, and sank down in the witness chair. When the judge upbraided him for being late, Johnson explained that he had been in a traffic accident.

Johnson testified that Sales's relationship to Arlene Croft was that of "mutual volunteers" in a Toys-for-Tots group; Sales's only sexual relationship for several months preceding his death was with his fiancée, Joan Davis.

Why the prosecution would put on testimony that Sales and Mrs. Croft were *not* having an affair was a mystery to me, since the affair was supposed to be Croft's motive for murdering Sales.

Mrs. Croft could have clarified matters, but the prosecution made no attempt to put her on the witness stand. We wouldn't have let them, anyway. In common law, spouses were "incompetent" witnesses—they could not testify for or against each other in criminal cases under any circumstances. Under modern rules, in the majority of American jurisdictions, a spouse is competent to testify, but the defendant can assert a privilege to prevent his spouse from testifying against him. We talked to Mrs. Croft, by telephone, about testifying *for* Peter—she'd often seen Sales carrying a gun—but her loyalties were hopelessly divided. "I'm on the fence," she said. "I stand to lose two men out of this deal."

Johnson maintained that he, himself, was not aware that Arlene Croft was married. He said that he had seen bruises on "Mrs. Croft's" face on two occasions, but before he could answer the question "What do you think caused them?" (beatings by Croft) our objection that he was not a medical expert was sustained. Finally, Johnson testified that Sales had owned a .38 Ruger Security Six, but it was stolen from his car sometime during the past summer; and, during the time Johnson knew him, Sales never carried a weapon into work.

Johnson could not have been more beautifully set up for the impeachment of his credibility. He was not just ripe to be plucked. He was overripe, and fell all by himself.

"Are you the same David Johnson who was convicted of embezzlement in 1976?" I began. The answer was yes.

(You are allowed to bring out a witness's convictions for felonies over the preceding ten years to aid the jury in evaluating his credibility. It is absolutely elementary that the prosecution should have asked Johnson about his convictions on direct examination, so it wouldn't appear that they were trying to hide anything.)

"Didn't you just testify under oath that you did not know that Peter Croft and Arlene Croft were married?" I continued.

"That's right," he said.

"Do you remember giving sworn testimony at an Article 32 hearing* in December?"

"Yes."

"Do you remember being asked this question and giving this answer: 'Q: How did Mrs. Croft meet Irwin? A: They started talking about each other's problems. Irwin tried to help Arlene get back to her husband.' "

"Right. I meant to say I didn't know whether they were still married or broke up."

"Didn't you just testify that the relationship of Irwin Sales to Mrs. Croft was one of 'mutual volunteers'?"

---

* Article 32 of the Uniform Code of Military Justice provides that no charge may be referred to a general court-martial until a thorough impartial investigation has been made. At an Article 32 hearing, an investigating officer conducts a pretrial investigation at which witnesses (including those requested by the defendant) testify under oath. The investigating officer recommends whether there should be a court-martial.

"Yes."

"Didn't you state under oath at the Article 32 hearing, 'I do know they were having an affair'?"

"I guess so."

"You guess so?"

"I did."

Johnson was not squirming. He was sitting there, sluglike, unphased by the fact that he was being shown up as a liar.

"Didn't you just testify that Sales's only female companion for several months before his death was his fiancée Joan Davis?"

"Yes."

"Do you remember being asked this question at the Article 32 and giving this answer: 'Q: Was Irwin involved with women other than Arlene Croft and Joan Davis? A: Yes. One was named Evelyn McDonald. There was a girl named Laura. Another was named Dorothy. Another was named Lois. There were a few others.' "

"If that's what it says there . . ."

"You swore to that?"

"Yes."

After that, I had Johnson say that Sales carried a gun in his car and once pulled it on Croft. Then I let him go, with thanks.

Johnson had stained both the prosecutors and the decedent with his broad brush. The prosecutors were passing out of slipshod and into sleazy, not bothering to head off Johnson's lies before presenting him to the court. (The government's client is Justice, remember.) Sales, meanwhile, was becoming familiar to the jury by the company he kept. What kind of guy would have a goon like Johnson for a best friend? The same kind of guy who would two-time his fiancée with a married woman and carry a .38 in his glove compartment. And use it.

Joan Davis, Sales's fiancée, followed Johnson to the stand. She was dressed in a mournful blue pantsuit, but she hadn't been able to resist decorating her face with mascara, eye shadow, eye liner, lip gloss, and that brown "blush" stuff that gives you cheekbones. It *was* a public appearance, and she was eye-catching. Ms. Davis could only help us. If she seemed like a low-life character, then Sales probably was, too. If she seemed like a nice person, then Sales was a son of a bitch for cheating on her with Arlene Croft.

Davis testified that she had never seen Sales carry a gun on his person, but she did see one in his glove compartment, but that was stolen outside the Good Times Video Arcade; but she did see *a* gun in the glove compartment *after* the Good Times theft, but she couldn't precisely describe the first gun, the second gun, or the difference between them. Both the prosecution and the defense had her say that Sales told her he was "afraid" because Croft was following him around (although Sales didn't tell her why). Davis was hostile and argumentative, and despite her sympathetic position, when she was through testifying, there wasn't a wet eye in the room.

The prosecution's next witness was Rawley Daniels, a big, bearded man in his thirties, with a good ol' boy's country accent. Daniels was a loyal friend of Croft's. That in itself, I thought, would appeal to the jurors. It appealed to me. There is something moving, in a phone-company-ad way, about the relationship of military buddies.

Daniels came across as the sweetest, gentlest guy you'd ever want to meet. He was extremely upset about being called as a prosecution witness and had shown up at the defense office the night before he was to testify, seeking some combination of reassurance and absolution. "I don't believe Peter could've possibly killed a man," he said.

I, somewhat disingenuously, assured him that all the defense wanted was for the truth to come out, and we were sure he would tell the truth, and it didn't make any difference whether he was called a "prosecution witness" or a "defense witness." Every witness is everybody's witness. I went over his testimony with him, pointing out the parts that were most helpful to Croft—like the fact that Croft borrowed Daniels's revolver *right after* his house was burglarized. (*Post hoc, ergo propter hoc* [after this, therefore because of this] is a fallacious but ever-popular principle of logic.)

My homily on the majesty of the adversary system turned out to be true, regarding Daniels. During his testimony it was hard to remember that the defense case had not yet begun.

On direct examination Captain Biscet asked whether he and Croft socialized together.

"When I saw the accused on a social basis, we would work on cars, or his wife and children and my family would all get together on Sunday and have dinner sometimes. We didn't go out 'jukin',' if that's what you mean." It was impossible to listen to this without thinking of a Norman Rockwell illustration.

Getting down to it, Biscet asked how many weapons Daniels owned. He said he owned three, but only two were in his possession. "I have one Hawkins, black powder, a replica; and I have a 1945 Craig nine-millimeter; and then I have a thirty-eight revolver. I don't have any idea where the thirty-eight revolver is. It was a very cheap weapon, cheaply constructed." Daniels clearly found it hard to believe that such a cheap weapon could be at the bottom of all this high-priced trouble. "It was manufactured by RG Industries; I think they are out of Florida. It is a thirty-eight special, plastic handle, with a snub nose. Five rounds would go in the cylinder. I think most of them hold six rounds, don't they?"

And what became of that .38, the prosecutor wanted to know. Everybody wanted to know. It was a question Croft would have to answer. But he could listen to Daniels's answer first.

"I loaned that thirty-eight to Specialist Croft, I guess it must have been around the middle of October. We were to go out target practicing. Or we had made plans to, but I got sick, so I wasn't going to get to go. So I loaned him the weapon."

On cross-examination I asked Daniels how he remembered that the loan of the thirty-eight to Croft was in mid-October.

Ah, yes. "It seems like shortly before that, he had had some type of a break-in in his home," he recalled. Had the prosecutors been on their toes, they could have confronted Daniels with his statement at the pretrial Article 32 hearing: "I really don't remember whether I gave him the pistol after the break-in or before." But by the time of the trial, he honestly "recalled" that the loan followed the break-in, either because it did or because he wanted it to. Daniels didn't stop there, unfortunately. "There was no reference to the break-in when I loaned him the weapon," he continued. "It was just we wanted to go target practicing."

As to what had become of the weapon, Daniels testified that shortly after the loan, sometime in October, Croft told him that someone had offered him $150 for the .38. "I told him he should've took it. I don't think the weapon cost me more than thirty-five dollars originally, but a lot of people up here don't know the value of weapons."

Redirect examination is normally limited to explaining, rebutting, or qualifying new facts brought out in cross-examination,[1] but the judge, in his discretion, let Captain Biscket stand up again and ask Daniels some important questions she had simply forgotten to ask on direct. It turned out that Daniels had caught a glimpse of his pistol lying in a drawer in Croft's desk at work one day in late October.

Biscket also wanted to hammer home the fact that Daniels never got any $150 from Croft, but she got burned for her trouble.

"Did you ever receive the one hundred fifty dollars from this 'sale'?" she demanded.

"No, but I didn't worry about it," he replied. "I figured Croft needed the money more than I did, and I knew he'd pay me as soon as he could—*that's the kind of man he is.*"

We couldn't have asked for a better parting thought as the court adjourned for the weekend.

* * *

The government's final witness, Philip Strickland, a police department firearms expert, took the stand first thing Monday morning. Strickland obviously *loved* guns, which kind of made you wonder about him, yet he was the sort of sturdy, reliable fellow you hope to find at a gas station when you are lost.

The prosecution had saved him for last, and they kept him on the stand a long time, just as though he had been able to determine whose pistol had killed Sales. But all he said was this: he had examined prosecution exhibits 5, 6, 9, 10, and 11 (the five recovered slugs) and concluded that each was fired from a .38 special or a .357 Magnum revolver having a barrel with eight grooves and eight lands (the raised areas between the grooves) with a right-hand twist. A rifled gun barrel, he explained, has spiraling grooves cut into it, which leave marks on the slug as it spins out of the barrel. These slugs' marks showed that the barrel had eight grooves and eight lands spiraling to the right.

Strickland said that weapons with those "class characteristics" were manufactured by Ruger (like Sales's "stolen" gun), RG Industries (like the gun Croft borrowed from Daniels), Rohm, Charter Arms, Dickson, Burgo, Liberty Arms, and Omega.

On cross-examination, Strickland readily conceded that there might be other manufacturers of weapons with these class characteristics, that each manufacturer he had named made more than one model with these characteristics, and that each model had a production run of a large number of individual weapons, so that he could not set any limit to the number of pistols in the world which could have fired the recovered slugs. Because the slugs were too badly bashed up to determine the "individual characteristics" of the firing weapon—the unique irregularities that form its "fingerprint"—he could not even say whether they all were fired from the same gun.*

Having gone over the evidence with Strickland at his office before the trial, *I* wasn't surprised that he hadn't solved the mystery of the gun, but the *jury* seemed to be. They looked disappointed. To them, Strickland's testimony looked like a prosecution failure. Therefore it *was* a prosecution failure. Instead of saving him for last, when the jury expects to hear

---

* Even when restricting themselves to the findings that they can realistically hope to make, firearms experts, like all forensic technicians, are far from infallible. In a 1977 Law Enforcement Assistance Administration test, given a slug fired from a .38 Smith & Wesson special revolver, and asked to identify the possible manufacturers of the firing weapon, 10 of 121 forensic labs did not list Smith & Wesson. Given a slug fired from a Beretta nine-millimeter Corto .380 auto, 31 failed to mention Beretta. (*Crime Laboratory Proficiency Testing Research Program Report*, Law Enforcement Assistance Administration, United States Department of Justice [Washington, D.C.: October 1978].)

something important, they should have explained in their opening that the ballistics evidence was inconclusive and slipped Strickland in early. The only reason to put him on at all was to show the jury that the prosecution had been thorough, leaving no stone unturned, and to keep the defense from arguing, as we would have, "Why wasn't a ballistics test done? What is the government trying to hide?"

On that inconclusive note, the government rested its case.

§6-11

It was our turn.

The defense case began inauspiciously. Richard Casey, an FBI agent, had left the defense investigator who interviewed him with the impression that Casey's analysis of the nitric acid swabs taken from the right hand of the decedent had turned up sufficient traces of antimony and barium (gunpowder residue) to prove that Sales had his hand on a gun as it discharged, a conclusion that would support Croft's story that the first shot went off as he grabbed the gun in Sales's hand. On the stand, after testifying that the swabs from Croft's hands were negative (not surprisingly, since he had taken a shower before his arrest), Casey said merely that the test results on the decedent's hand were *consistent with* Sales's having had his hand on a gun, but could also be consistent with his standing in the same room with a discharging gun, perhaps as far as four feet away. I never should have put Casey on without interviewing him myself. We dropped him as quietly as we could and tiptoed on to our next witness.

Staff Sergeant Stan Olson, who shared duty with Sales on November 14, testified that Sales arrived at 2:30, carrying a gym bag with *something* in it. Olson left to get some food at 2:40, and when he returned at 3:10 he found a crowd staring at a body. Asked about Sales's reputation for violence, Olson said, "I think"—*Objection! Opinion!* the prosecutors failed to say—"it was crucial to Sales's ego to 'conquer' women"—*Objection! Irrelevant!* the prosecutors failed to say—"because he would say things like, 'I slept with five different women this week.' "

We asked the manager of the Good Times Video Arcade, outside of which, Davis and Johnson said, Sales's .38 was stolen in the summer of 1980, just one question: Did the Good Times Video Arcade *exist* in the summer of 1980? Answer: "Good Times did not open until 1981."

Ruth Cunningham, a sixty-year-old black woman who spoke like a librarian or schoolteacher but was in fact a cleaning lady in the building where Croft worked, testified that she had indeed answered a phone call at work that afternoon and been asked to put Croft on the line. We would argue that this call was from Sales.

Captain Hooton threw her a high, hard one on cross-examination: "You can't really be sure, can you, that the phone call you remember took place on November fourteenth and not some other day?"

"Actually," she said, "I am absolutely certain that it was on November fourteenth. November fourteenth stands out clearly in my memory because it was that evening that I saw on television that there had been a shooting, and that the authorities were holding Peter Croft, and I *couldn't believe it* because I knew he could *never* do such a thing."

We followed Mrs. Cunningham with a parade of character witnesses to acquaint the jury with the *real* Peter Croft, Croft the peaceful, Croft the honest, before Croft the murder defendant took the stand. Then Mrs. Carolyn Ianini, ill at ease in a murder court-martial, but glad to be doing her civic duty, gave the jury one last review of the crucial instant that had flashed in and out of existence three months before, while she waited in a car for her husband: "BANG—BANG—BANGBANGBANG."

The shots echoed overnight.

§6-12

When court reconvened for the fourth day of testimony, Croft's co-worker Airman First Class Jess Gilmour, a jive-talking street dude who somehow kept every joint in his body moving even as he sat testifying, said that Croft "was a chump. He wouldn't fight. He'd talk his way out of a situation, or step aside." Sales, on the other hand, "would sell a lot of wolf-tickets," Gilmour said, explaining that meant he would "talk loud and stern." "Sales had a fight at the craft shop once," he said, "and I've been told"—Ding! Ding! Ding! HEARSAY! But Biscket and Hooton just sat there—"he pulled a pistol on somebody *before,* between six months and a year and a half ago."

We followed with Staff Sergeant J. B. Jones, who told about Sales's asking him to point out Croft; and Sales's slimy remark about "what happens if you don't take care of your homework"; and Sales's boasts that he kept his "piece" on him.

Then Technical Sergeant Yates hesitantly repeated his observation

that Sales "used women." By hemming and hawing and expressing re-
luctance to quote crude language in the courtroom, Yates greatly increased the impact of Sales's immortal line about Mrs. Croft, when he
finally said, "Sales said, 'She was the best piece of ass I ever had.'"

This statement was not hearsay. Hearsay is an out-of-court statement
offered as the equivalent of testimony, to prove a fact asserted in the
statement. It is inadmissible because the maker of the statement was not
under oath and is not subject to cross-examination. Here it didn't matter
whether it was true that Mrs. Croft was "the best piece of ass" Sales ever
had, so it didn't matter that Sales was not under oath when he said it or
that he was unavailable for cross-examination. What mattered was *that*
Sales *said* it. Yates was swearing to that in court and could be cross-
examined on the point. The fact that Sales uttered those words tended to
prove that Sales was involved with Arlene Croft, and thus had a reason to
fear Peter Croft, and thus had a reason to be carrying a gun. Our *sub rosa*
reason for putting the statement in was simpler: it showed that Sales was
a miserable scumbag who deserved to die.

Defense investigator Amy Strader, looking more childlike than ever in
a tweed sports coat, white shirt, and necktie, took the stand to testify that
she had taken pictures of the scene of the shooting. (She had taken pictures of the scene so that she could testify. In my trial notes I had written,
"Have Strader testify about *something*." How could *she* possibly be associated with a guilty person?) The pictures themselves, gorgeous eight-by-
ten color glossies, besides lending pizzazz to our case, actually showed a
couple of very important things: the sign on the building door warning all
entrants that they were being monitored by closed-circuit TV; and the
rear of Sales's desk, which had six shelves beautifully designed for concealing a pistol. Dark and deep, they *cried out* to have a pistol put in
them. It was difficult to look at that picture without *seeing* a pistol lying
on one of those shelves.

Then came that moment toward which we'd been working, that moment toward which we had been thrust, for three months. It was the sort
of moment when everything seems sharper, more distinct, less real, the
sort of moment when you feel more intensely than ever that your life is a
story with a plot and a resolution, the sort of moment that is known as the
Moment of Truth.

"The defense calls as its final witness Peter Croft."

Of course, this was really just the epilogue to Peter Croft's Moment of
Truth, which had occurred on November 14. He had come through that

one on top, one way or another. His testimony at this moment was my Moment, and perhaps not that, either, but at least a denouement in a drama in which I had cast myself in the lead role, not only in my mind but in the courtroom. I had tried to shift the focus from Croft to me. The question for the jury, I hoped, had become "Does this defense attorney win?" And the jury's answer would be "He *has* to. How could he not?"

We were reluctant to have Croft testify, since the prosecution had done such a poor job of carrying its burden of proving beyond a reasonable doubt that the shooting was *not* self-defense. There seemed little to gain from putting the *real* Croft on display after our witnesses had painted a picture of such a fine character. And he might say something that contradicted his statement to Detective Luce. If he did that, the prosecution would be able to "impeach" him with that part of the earlier statement which he had contradicted. But we figured the jury *wanted* to hear Croft and would draw negative inferences if he didn't testify, especially because the judge would instruct them not to. Anyway, we really *had* to put him on now because in my opening statement I had said that the jury would hear his side of the story.

(It is generally considered unwise for the defense to outline its case with much specificity in its opening statement, for just this reason—you paint yourself into a corner, losing your ability to shape your response to the case the prosecution puts on.)

Now we would find out whether my preparation of Croft the night before had been too little, too late. I had left that task to the end because I wanted Croft to hear what all the other witnesses said, so that his memory would be refreshed and his testimony would be more likely to comport with, and appear corroborated by, the testimony of the others.

I had had my hands full that last night with Gilmour, Jones, and Yates. Captain Arnold actually prepped them, but I acted as host, expressing all kinds of gratitude for their patience and cooperation while they waited their turns with him in the military defense counsel's office. I felt it was crucial to keep them happy and on our side. For some reason, I also spent a lot of time chatting up Croft's guards, who were on overtime, waiting for us to finish so they could return him to the stockade. Even unimportant dealings with people present have a way of taking precedence over dealing with "abstract" concerns, including anything, however important, which lies in the future, however near. Maybe I preferred these tasks to sitting down, finally, with Croft.

When I'd run out of other things to do, I invited Croft into an empty office and shut the door behind us.

We went over the day of the shooting minute by minute. I would remind Croft what he had said to Detective Luce, and to me at our first interview, and what others had said at the trial. Then he would repeat what he'd heard, and I would write down what he said. It would have been more efficient, eliminating the middleman, simply to write out his testimony and hand it to him, but that would have been unethical.

It wasn't long before we hit a major stumbling block: What exactly did Sales say to him on the telephone?

"He said that Arlene wanted a divorce and he wanted me to come over and talk to him."

"Croft, that doesn't make any sense! If he *asked* you to come see him, why would he pull a gun and say, 'I told you if you brought your ass around here again I would blow your head off'? You must be remembering it wrong."

He sat there, dumbly searching his memory.

"Could this be what happened?" I asked. "Sales called you up and said Arlene wanted a divorce. Period. You just said 'Oh' or 'I see' and hung up the phone. Then *you* decided to go talk to him at his work."

Croft said, "Now that you mention it, I think that is the way it went down." We made steady, if arduous, progress until I asked, "What were you doing from two-thirty P.M. to three P.M. on November fourteenth?"

Croft sat staring at the floor like a recalcitrant schoolboy in the principal's office.

"What were you *doing*?" I repeated.

Croft looked up, stared blankly into the distance beyond me, and *shrugged his shoulders.*

"For chrissake, Croft! I *told* you to think about this!" My pen narrowly missed him as it bounced off the desk.

"Some days I'd wash my car. Maybe I was washing my car?"

"Oh, Jesus! Give me a break!" I said. "You weren't washing your car." Croft looked sorry.

"Look. Isn't this what happened? You tell me. Didn't you leave work and go for a long, solitary walk, a walk somewhere nobody would have seen you? You were brooding. Sales had told you he was in and you were out. You were hurt, sad, angry. You walked along, staring at the ground in front of you, thinking. Then you decided you were going to talk to Sales. Try to remember. Is that what happened?"

"Yeah. That's what happened."

"*What?* What happened? You tell me."

"I went for a walk by myself for about half an hour. Then I drove over to see him."

I wrote that down. "Where'd you park?"

"Behind the building."

"Good. See, if you were planning to shoot him you would have parked near the door, to make a quick getaway."

The rest of what happened we knew from his statement to Detective Luce. I wrote it all down. Then I wrote out nonleading questions framed to elicit the story. Then I asked him the questions and drilled him on the answers. Then Captain Arnold came in and, playing the role of the prosecutor, cross-examined him. We went through it all several times until, at 1:30 A.M., I handed Croft a copy of the written questions and answers and suggested he read himself to sleep with them.

§6-13

Croft's chair grudgingly harumphed back, its legs scoring the linoleum. He swore to tell the truth, the whole truth, and nothing but the truth, so help him God, and took the stand. He was completely calm. He answered my questions coolly—a little too coolly, in fact. He didn't have the proper affect. He should have been a little upset that his wife was gone, maybe a little sorry that a man was dead, certainly a little nervous that he was facing life imprisonment. He was none of these, nor was he, on the other hand, cocky or bitter. He was nothing. (The one adjective that perhaps fit him was "rehearsed," as one observer put it. Maybe we had fallen into the trap of overpreparation. On the other hand, we didn't want any screw-ups.)

We eased into the testimony in the traditional manner: What's your name? Age? Job? Where do you live? How long have you lived there? Do you live with anyone? And that brought up the story of his life with the lovely Arlene Croft, and a touching story it was.

"Did you ask her out the first time you met her?"

"No."

"Why not?"

Croft hung his head for half a beat. "I was bashful, I guess. I had to get my courage up."

And on to the happy marriage, the two children, and then the *crime.* The *crime,* of course, was Sales's affair with Arlene. That was well-established.

That crime ruined Croft's life. It had led inexorably to his sitting in this court, accused of murder. How Croft had suffered! He was so upset that he raised his hand against his wife, actually *struck* her, on three different occasions.

He was telling everything. He was making a clean breast of it. He testified that he really *had* carried Daniels's pistol around, because he was nervous after the burglary of his home. And yes, he kept the money for himself after he sold the pistol to the manager of the Cannery Row Club five days before the shooting because he was in debt, because of his auto accident.

On November 14, Croft said, he got a phone call from Sales, went for a brooding walk, and went to talk to him. "Sales said, 'I told you if you brought your ass around me again I'd blow your fuckin' head off!' "

Croft described how he took the gun from Sales, exactly as he had explained it to me and to Detective Luce. Then, "He lunged at me, and I was afraid he'd get the gun back and kill me. I fired."

"How many shots did you fire?"

"I don't know, two or three."

Two or three? Well, he didn't *exactly* contradict his statement to Detective Luce about putting two shots into Sales on the floor, and the prosecutors didn't attempt to impeach him with that prior inconsistent statement.

Captain Biscket didn't lay a glove on Croft in cross-examination, so the judge tag-teamed with her. It's unfair, but common, for the judge to conduct examinations for the prosecution. It gives the jury the idea that the judge, in his wisdom, wants the prosecution to win, for some reason. But judges call it "assisting in the search for truth," and appellate courts aren't offended by it unless the judge goes completely overboard.

"How come Sales ended up on his back if he was lunging forward?" the judge wanted to know.

"I don't know. Maybe it was the force of the shots."

Plausible.

"What was the pattern of the shots?" The judge was leaning over the bench looking down at Croft.

"BANG." Pause. "BANGBANGBANG." The pause was the important part. That's when the gun was changing hands.

"If it was Sales's gun, why didn't you keep it?"

"I was afraid. I wasn't thinking." Croft was sitting forward in the witness chair, looking straight up at the judge, three feet away.

"This man you said you sold Daniels's gun to—did you try to find him to come and testify?"

"I've been in pretrial confinement since November fourteenth, sir."

"Did you have your lawyers try?"

"I object, Your Honor!" I said as I leapt to my feet. "As the court knows, the defense asked for a continuance and for funds for investigators . . ."

"All right. All right," the judge said and left off questioning.

Captain Hooton, wandering around the room like a loose cannon on a pitching deck, fired off a few questions whose aimless nature was only emphasized by the ruthless-and-clever-interrogator's look he put on his face: "Why didn't you throw the gun aside, instead of firing it?" he demanded, scowling. "Why didn't you call an ambulance?"

When Hooton couldn't think of anything else to ask, he sat down, and Croft returned to the defense table, where I touched his shoulder and whispered a word or two in what I hoped looked like a casual sign of collegial respect, such as one senator might vouchsafe to another during a break at a subcommittee hearing. *Nobody here but us stalwart citizens.*

We introduced into evidence police records proving that a burglar had, in fact, been arrested in Croft's home on October 15, giving Croft a reason to carry Daniels's gun. We introduced Arlene Croft's phone bills, proving that she had continued to call Irwin Sales right up to the time of his death, which suggested that he was still involved with her and therefore had a reason to arm himself against Croft. We introduced a police accident report verifying Croft's auto wreck in July, to show that Croft really did have big expenses and that it was therefore understandable that he pocketed the $150 for Daniels's gun. We introduced these documents *to* introduce documents, pile up evidence, *prove* something, prove anything, and prove that things said by Croft were true.

The defense rested.

The jury was excused, and we argued about what the closing instructions to them should be. In his closing instructions the judge tells the jury what they're supposed to decide and how they're supposed to decide it. He explains the elements of the offenses with which the defendant is charged, and the requirements of any affirmative defenses, such as self-defense or insanity, which have been raised; he explains what is evidence (all of the testimony and exhibits admitted) and what is not evidence (stricken testimony, anything said by the lawyers or the judge); he explains the presumption of innocence, the burden of proof, the concept of reasonable doubt. He reads most of these instructions from a book of standard instructions, so that every defendant will be judged according to rules couched in exactly the same language, rather than have his fate influenced by the pet legal explanations of a particular judge.

I share the commonly held belief that it generally doesn't make much difference which instructions are read to the jury, for the simple reason that jurors usually pay no attention to them, because committees of lawyers have written and rewritten the instructions to a state of stupefying turgidity. (Paradoxically, meaninglessness often results from lawyers' attempts at precision in meaning. Everything that is *not* meant to be meant is carefully excluded, until nothing is meant, for fear of meaning too much.)

An instruction that clearly counts, though, is the one that tells the jury what they can find the defendant guilty of. It's binding—the jury can't improvise. In Croft's case, the judge could decide that, as a matter of law, the evidence supported either a murder conviction or an acquittal, period; or he could instruct the jury to consider the lesser included offense of manslaughter. If the jury had to pick murder (a life offense) or nothing, it would make it harder for them to convict. On the other hand, it would make it very hard on Croft if they convicted. If the judge gave the jury the manslaughter instruction, it would give them an out to avoid a murder conviction, but it would decrease the chance of an outright acquittal, as they would have the easy option of a "compromise verdict"—guilty of manslaughter, which carried a maximum sentence of ten years, with parole eligibility after one third of the sentence. Both government and defense are entitled to submit proposed instructions to the judge, who makes the final decision. We were tempted to roll the dice by asking for the all-or-nothing murder instruction, but we got cold feet and asked that the manslaughter instruction be added. Biscket and Hooton took no position.

For a homicide to amount to murder, it must be perpetrated with *malice;* that is, the act must be done with a wicked state of mind, a heart "fatally bent on mischief." If the act of killing was committed not with malice, but in the heat of sudden passion produced by a provocation sufficient to provoke an ordinary man to an ungovernable rage, then the killing is manslaughter. Actually *seeing* a spouse in the act of adultery, for example, has historically been recognized as sufficient provocation to reduce killing to manslaughter, *provided* that the killing is done within a reasonable amount of time after the provocation, say a half hour or so, before the killer has time to "cool down" and consider the wickedness of what he is about to do.

The judge at first said he would not give a manslaughter instruction because the evidence didn't support the necessary finding that Croft acted in the "heat of passion."

We insisted that just because *we* had said Croft acted in self-defense, that didn't mean the jury couldn't pick and choose from all the testimony on both sides and find that he acted in the heat of passion. The defendant is entitled to have instructions given on any theory of defense for which there is any foundation in the evidence, however weak, even if the theory conflicts with the defense he has presented. For instance, a defendant who has presented an alibi—claiming not to have been present at the offense—is still entitled to an instruction on self-defense, if some evidence supporting self-defense has been presented by either side. Here, admittedly, it was hard to think of anything suggesting that Croft had been provoked to sudden passion, but the judge, realizing that a conviction might be reversed if he didn't give the instruction but would never be reversed if he did, said he'd sleep on it.

I didn't sleep on anything. I had to write a closing argument. When court adjourned at six o'clock, I said to one of my investigators, "I predict two things: one, at one A.M. tonight I won't have written the first word; two, I'll be amazed that I haven't written the first word." Both predictions came true.

We were so exhausted that the simplest tasks, like eating, seemed almost beyond our capacity and took forever to accomplish. Captain Arnold and I finally got together at my office at 9:00 P.M. He gave me a concise review of what each witness had said, in the order in which they had testified. It took us two hours. It would have taken me two days, and I still wouldn't have gotten it right. Then he left, and the last few P.D.S. lawyers left, and I found myself alone in a hollow, darkened building. I decided to make some coffee. It took me a long time to find the pot. Then I couldn't find the coffee for a while. Then I knocked over the pot of coffee and had to clean it up and start all over again. The coffee project took me one hour. It was 12:30 A.M. I was sick to my stomach from tension and exhaustion. I fought back tears.

The more I reviewed the evidence, the more despondent I became. We had an insoluble problem, and it was the same problem we were aware of on day one: Croft's story was inherently incredible. He borrows Daniels's gun, which is the type of gun which fired the fatal bullets, and that gun is nowhere to be found. He says he sold it *five days* before the shooting, but he never told Daniels he sold it, never gave him the money, and the buyer can't be found. He says he pulled Sales's gun away from Sales and fired in self-defense, but the autopsy suggests at least one shot went into Sales as he lay on the floor. Then he threw Sales's gun, the one piece of evidence that could exonerate him, into the Potomac. As against that pyramid of improbabilities, the government's theory was simple and had no loose ends: Croft brought Daniels's gun with him, blew Sales away, and threw the gun into the river. All the jury had to decide was, *whose gun was in the Potomac?* And the answer seemed as obvious as it was damning.

Even as I realized that the events of November 14 did not look good, I was swept over by another realization: the events of February 25 through 28, in the courtroom, *had* looked good. We had put on a much slicker presentation than the prosecution had.

"Put the government on trial!" I exclaimed aloud. Get the jury to *forget* about November 14, and concentrate on the events that had transpired in the courtroom, the events that they had *seen,* the events that were most *real* to them. The prosecution had been slipshod; the prosecution had not done its job; the prosecution did not *deserve* to win. Couple that with our theme from the beginning—that Sales deserved to die—and we just might win.

I put together an overview of the trial from that perspective. By 3:00 A.M. I had eight yellow legal pad pages filled with an outline. I was as prepared as I was going to be. I drove home and slept two hours.

§6-14

The judge announced that he *would* instruct the jury to consider the lesser included offense of manslaughter.

The jury filed in. From the grave expression on their faces it was apparent that today they felt less like spectators and more like people sitting in judgment of a fellow man.

Captain Biscket presented a rambling, monotonal closing argument, which lasted seventy-five minutes. Recounting, with no particular emphasis, the testimony of every single witness, she failed here, as she had failed throughout the trial, to present a "theory of the case," that is, *to explain what must have happened.* As I listened, my adrenaline and caffeine levels plummeted, and I had trouble staying awake (a condition I did not try to hide from the jury). Only one thing she said really sat me up: "Dr. Korzeniewski, the medical examiner, testified that when Sales was shot, he was not lunging forward; his arm was stretched out to the side." Dr. Korzeniewski never said that.

We broke for lunch before I had to speak. I spent the hour walking alone. I went through my argument repeatedly, compulsively, distracted only occasionally by thoughts of myself: "Here I am, about to argue my first murder trial; soon it will have been decided, it will be a long time ago, I'll be old, this will always be the day of my first murder verdict, a clear, cold, sunny day. I'll remember 'I won,' or 'I lost' ..." Self-absorbed, beyond embarrassment, I spun about in front of an antique cannon, practicing how I would act out Sales's movements as the slugs tore into him.

The time came that I was standing in the center of the court, spectators behind me, the jury towering over me. I heard my quavering voice. I had begun.

"Your Honor, ladies and gentlemen of the court: first of all, we want to thank you for your attention during what has been a long, and not always fascinating, trial. I think we all know better now what is meant by 'a trying experience.'" Clunk. *God, where is my judgment? But seriously, folks . . .*

I went into the standard burden-of-proof rap, with a little extra emphasis on the patriotism angle. "This is the last opportunity I'm going to have to speak to you on behalf of Peter Croft. I talk only once. The prosecutor gets to speak again. And there's a reason for that. It's not just some technicality or rule of procedure. The government gets to speak again because of a principle which is the very foundation of our whole system of law; a principle upon which this nation was founded; a principle which distinguishes our country from most of the nations of the earth [the jurors sat taller and seemed to fight back the urge to salute], and that is, that the government has the burden of proving, beyond a reasonable doubt, that the citizen accused is guilty of each and every element of the offense. Peter Croft is presumed innocent. He didn't even have to testify."

(I'm of two minds about emphasizing the presumption of innocence/burden of proof. It's a rule that gives the defendant an advantage, as it was intended to, if the jury adheres to it; so it makes sense to call it to their attention, logically. But theatrically, would an innocent man talk about whether his guilt has been proven *beyond a reasonable doubt?* Theatrically, I want to say it isn't even *close.* Hey, *we'll* take the burden. By *any standard,* this guy just *didn't do it.* I tried to resolve the dilemma by relating the proof-beyond-a-reasonable-doubt standard to the government's miserable performance in the courtroom, while sticking to the it's-not-even-close posture regarding what happened out in the world.)

"The government is *accusing* Peter Croft of murdering Sales." (I had decided to use Croft's first and last name every time I mentioned him, and to use Sales's last name only, in order to humanize the one, dehumanize the other, and most important, to try to keep myself from calling one by the other's name, which I had done at least once a day from the beginning.)

"There's no question that Sales is dead, and there is no question that

Peter Croft fired the shots that killed him. The question is, was the killing wrongful, that is, was it murder? Or was there legal justification for it, that is, was it self-defense?

"How will you decide that question? The one way you will *not* decide it is the way the prosecutor said." A few jurors followed my example as I cast a sidelong glance at Captain Biscket, who was pretending to be busy writing. "She said, 'We can only *speculate* as to what happened.' [She actually said that.] As the judge will instruct you, *speculate* is one thing you will not do. We do not decide issues on speculation, but by considering the evidence.

"What did the evidence show? Remember, we presented an opening statement in which we outlined for you what we expected the testimony would be, *before* the first witness took the stand." I recapitulated the opening statement, painting yet again the picture of the gun-toting Sales, home-wrecker, braggart, sexist, a man "looking over his shoulder" because he knew what he deserved. "And isn't that exactly what the testimony was? How could Peter Croft have known what all those witnesses would say before they said it? There's only one way: Peter Croft knew what they would say because he knew they would tell the truth, just as *he* told you the truth." (This was one inference supported by the evidence, and it was permissible for me to argue it to the jury. I was under no obligation to point out other, equally permissible inferences, such as that our investigators had interviewed most of the witnesses, or that we had the prior sworn statements of all of them.)

So much for the trial of Peter Croft; now for the trial of the government.

"The government, in its closing, misstated Dr. Korzeniewski's testimony. The prosecutor said that Dr. Korzeniewski said that Sales's arm was stretched to the side, not lunging forward. You remember what Dr. Korzeniewski *really* said. He said, 'I can't determine what particular position his arm was in.' The government tried to distort the testimony, tried to fool you. And I ask you, as calmly as I can, with all the control over my voice that I can muster, 'Isn't that *reprehensible?* Don't you have the right to expect better than that from your government?' " To my own surprise, my voice shook with genuine rage as I pointed an accusing finger at Captain Biscket. She looked down at her notepad.

I had my own plan for the coroner's testimony. "Let's pretend for a moment that the lieutenant colonel [sitting in the jury's center seat] is Peter Croft, backing out the door, and I am Sales." I lunged toward her. "POW!" I held my pen to my lip at the angle of the bullet's trajectory and jerked my face to the right, as though from the impact of the bullet. "The first shot enters above the lip, travels left to right, front to back, upward. It's fatal. POW! The second shot, left to right, slightly upward, penetrating the left shoulder, passing through the armpit, upward, cuts the trachea and subclavian artery and drops into the chest. Fatal." I spun to my right as I said this. "POW! Number three. Through the left arm. Flesh wound. POW! Four, left to right, through the musculature, making an oval exit as though the back were on the floor; it causes no serious injury."

Now they'd *seen* that it happened just as Peter Croft had described it.

"Finally, the government called Mr. Strickland, the firearms expert. And the government elicited testimony from him at great length, just as though he had something material to say. But he really didn't, did he? The government was trying to do it with mirrors, make it seem as though he were saying something he never said. When the smoke cleared, what exactly had he said?

"He testified that *among* the *suspect* weapons are thirty-eight and three-fifty-seven Magnum revolvers manufactured by Rohm, RG Industries, Charter Arms, Dickson, Burgo, Liberty Arms, and *Ruger* [Sales's brand]. Each manufacturer makes different models, and each model has a production run of individual weapons. If Mr. Strickland's testimony had been the same, but translated in terms of cars, then what he said would have been: 'The suspect car was a compact or a subcompact. Among the suspect manufacturers are Honda, Toyota, Datsun, Subaru, Chevy, Ford, Plymouth, or Mercury.'

"Peter Croft told you that he went to Philadelphia and sold Daniels's weapon to the bouncer at the Cannery Row Club. Did the government adduce any evidence to the contrary? Did they show that Peter Croft was on duty that weekend? That the Cannery Row Club doesn't exist?

"*Everything* happened just like Peter Croft told you. And he doesn't have to prove *anything*. The *government* has to prove, beyond a reasonable doubt, that Peter Croft wrongfully killed Sales. And the government hasn't proven *anything!*

"And why do you suppose that is? Because Peter Croft is *not guilty.*"

Captain Biscket managed to speak for another half hour in rebuttal without putting forth a prosecution theory of the case. Then the judge instructed the jury.

He explained that self-defense in a homicide is established when two elements are present: first, the defendant must actually have had a reasonable belief that death or grievous bodily harm was about to be inflicted upon him; second, the defendant must have believed that the force he used was necessary to protect himself.

Regarding the first element, the test for the reasonableness of the defendant's belief that he was in danger is *objective,* that is, the jury must decide whether a reasonable, prudent person, facing the circumstances the defendant faced, would have believed he was in imminent danger of death or grievous injury. Accordingly, such subjective factors as the particular defendant's intelligence and emotional stability are *not* relevant to the jury's determination of whether his fear was reasonable. But objective factors such as the defendant's size, and the possibility of a safe retreat,* are relevant.

The test for the second element—that the defendant believed the amount of force he used was necessary—is *subjective:* what matters is what *he* thought was necessary to protect himself, whether "reasonable" or not; so the defendant's particular intellectual and emotional makeup *is* relevant. In other words, once it is objectively established that the defendant reasonably thought he was in danger of death or grievous bodily harm, whether or not he actually *was* in such danger—some toy guns would fool anyone—the only question remaining is whether he really thought he had to do what he did. "Detached reflection cannot be demanded in the presence of an uplifted knife," Justice Holmes observed.[1]

The judge continued the instructions by drawing a distinction between direct and circumstantial evidence, and then explaining that there was no practical difference between them: "Direct evidence is the testimony of a person who asserts actual knowledge of a fact, such as an eyewitness; circumstantial evidence is proof of a chain of facts and circumstances indicating the guilt or innocence of a defendant. The law makes no distinction between the weight to be given to either direct or circumstantial evidence. Nor is a greater degree of certainty required of circumstantial evidence than of direct evidence. In reaching a verdict in this case, you should weigh all of the evidence presented, whether direct or circumstantial."

The judge continued in this vein for *an hour.* Then the jury retired to deliberate.

Captain Arnold and I went to his office and drank coffee while Croft chatted with his guards in the anteroom. I was too exhausted to feel much of anything beyond relief that the trial was over, although I certainly hoped that we'd win, so that all of our effort would not have been for nothing.

---

* Common law required a person to "retreat to the wall" if he safely could, before using deadly force to defend himself, except that—this is the "castle doctrine"—he was under no duty to retreat if attacked in his own home. The "American rule," followed in most states, imposes no duty to retreat. The military rule splits the difference, holding that the defendant's retreat, or failure to retreat, is one factor to be considered in light of all the circumstances in deciding whether he acted in self-defense.

Before we had a chance to reflect, we were called back to the courtroom. Forty-five minutes had passed. After evaluating the testimony of
thirty-three witnesses, the jurors were back with their verdict. The "president of the court" (foreman), a John Wayne look-alike lieutenant colonel, stood and, grim-faced, with a faltering voice, read the following:
"The court, two thirds of all members present concurring in each finding
of guilty, finds the defendant: of the charge, not guilty; of the specifica-
tion, not guilty; of the additional charge, guilty; of the additional specifi-
cation, guilty." Not guilty of murder, guilty of carrying an unregistered
firearm. The jury, which had been unanimous in both findings, pronounced sentence: ten days' incarceration, with credit for the ninety days
he had served in pretrial detention. Croft was a free man.

Croft smiled and shook my hand. "I never doubted for a second that
we were going to win," he said. "Can I get my shotgun back?"

Croft's guards threw their arms around him.

The judge came up to me in the hallway. "If you'd like, I'll give you
that continuance now," he said, smiling. Judges like it when the best law-
yering wins—they're lawyers, too.

§6-15

" 'Get away with murder,' " I thought, upon hearing the verdict. "I have
gotten away with murder." I was awed by the *enormity* of it. The Sixth
Commandment.* It made me feel bad—my stomach, particularly—but
not as bad as *losing* would have. To those turkeys? Yet another client of
mine locked up? I preferred to grapple with the moral problem of winning. That's the sort of problem you want to have.

Anyway, I really didn't know whether Croft had committed murder.
There was certainly some evidence to suggest that he had, but, on the
other hand, how account for the wild shot high in the wall? Why would
he pick the middle of the afternoon in a public lobby in front of a video
camera? In any case, it didn't matter what I thought.

Asked by Boswell what he thought of "supporting a cause which you
know to be bad," Dr. Johnson replied, "Sir, you do not know it to be
good or bad till the Judge determines it. . . . An argument which does not
convince yourself, may convince the Judge to whom you urge it: and if it

* Or Fifth, depending on how you count.

does convince him, why, then, Sir, you are wrong, and he is right." Dr. Johnson's observation is reprinted in the A.B.A. *Code of Professional Responsibility.*[1]

Croft was not guilty. The jury said so.

Regardless of what Croft had or had not done, there remained the problem of what I had done in preparing him to testify. A popular handbook for defense attorneys reflects the mainstream thinking of the defense bar when it suggests, "Although he should not tell the witness specifically what to say, it is certainly within the province of counsel to discuss the witness's answers, highlighting possible problems with proposed answers and suggesting ways in which they could be avoided. The witness should also be instructed as to any potential pitfalls in his testimony and how best to deal with them."[2]

What I did would have fit that description if I hadn't been so direct. I don't think Chief Justice Warren Burger himself would find fault with my saying to Croft, "There are inconsistencies in your account, and here they are . . . There are gaps in your account, and here they are . . . There are parts of your account that I disbelieve, and that I predict the jury will disbelieve, and here they are . . . Now I'd suggest that you try to remember what really happened." Warren Burger might quibble, but few other lawyers would, if I went a little further and tried to jog my client's memory: "Maybe you spent some time alone, and went for a walk or something?" But I definitely went too far when I said, "Isn't this what happened? Didn't you go for a walk?" I guess under the pressure of the moment, I just couldn't see the difference.

I do think it's better to be overzealous than underzealous. Overzealousness can be corrected by the prosecution. (They might at least have asked, "Did you go over your testimony with your attorney?," an innocent question with an innocent answer—"Yes"—but one that nonetheless communicates a certain suspicion to the jury.) Underzealousness cannot be corrected by anyone.

An hour after the verdict, the defense team—not including Croft, who'd gone back to be processed out of the stockade—sat around the kitchen table in Captain Arnold's Florida Avenue row house, drinking Scotch and champagne and smoking. We relived the trial amid gales of laughter, the responsibility off our shoulders and our hearts exultant—we were the victors.

"I couldn't believe it when you said, 'Maybe the Cannery Row Club doesn't exist'!" Arnold laughed.

"I didn't realize I said that."

"It didn't matter *what* you said. You were *rolling,* and the jury was rolling with you."

As my mood got more and more elevated, it dawned on me that my patriotic rap to the jury about the United States' being different from most of the nations of the world, because we put the burden of proof on the government, was *true*. I had thought I was being cynical and manipulative when I'd said it, but it really was true. And if the government doesn't prove its case, the accused *should* go free.

I felt proud to be an American.

It was around this stage of my career that the image of someone in my own family being the victim of a violent crime started coming to my mind more and more frequently. I imagined that the criminal would be put on trial, and that I would walk up to him in open court and shoot him dead.

§6-16

Howard Robbins had been ordered by the court, upon the government's motion, to be held under mental observation in St. Elizabeths. He'd been there six months. After the first month, the St. E's doctors reported that "although he has a factual understanding of the proceedings pending against him, he is considered incompetent for trial by virtue of not having a rational understanding of the proceedings pending against him and not being able to consult with counsel with a reasonable degree of rational understanding." He was diagnosed as "schizophrenia, paranoid type," and, the doctors concluded, "The alleged offenses, if committed by him, were the product of his mental disease; as a result of his mental disease, he lacked substantial capacity to appreciate the wrongfulness of his conduct or conform his conduct to the requirements of the law." He was insane at the time of the offense, in their opinion.

I had requested a hearing at which Howard could contest the finding of incompetency, and Judge Milmoe finally did appoint an *amicus*—an independent counsel—to argue that Howard was competent.

Howard Robbins's competency hearing was postponed many times, for many reasons, none of them having to do with Howard Robbins.

Howard, meanwhile, continued to insist that he was competent, sane, and innocent. And St. Elizabeths periodically reported that he remained incompetent.

"He thinks we don't know what we're talking about. He thinks we're relying on untrue information from his mother and you," one of the St.

E's psychiatrists told me. "He thinks we're colluding to harm him. He hates the idea of an insanity defense, because he fears he's lost his mind, which is a nightmarish feeling." Howard's insistence that he was sane was instrumental in convincing the psychiatrists that he was not. "Where there's a danger of long incarceration, only a very sick person refuses to raise an insanity defense," one doctor said.

Howard telephoned me daily, and I visited him every so often. He always had new witnesses for me to interview, who, he claimed, would tell me he was never jealous of Sheila, and would never have shot her. "I've seen her with hundreds of men. I've seen her with millions of men. It's cool." But the witnesses never knew anything about it. They hardly knew Howard. His mother called them his "dream friends."

Howard continued to profess confidence that he would win at trial, because Sheila would "hang herself" on the witness stand. "It would be easier for her to reach up and grab the sun than to come in and tell the truth," he said.

Finally the hospital shrinks, after plying him with Thorazine for six months, concluded that he had become competent. Our own doctor told me that Howard was *getting* competent, "but he may be pretending that he's incompetent, by continuing to insist that he's competent, just as he did when he was incompetent." I could see which way the wind was blowing. There was no sense destroying my relationship with Howard by arguing for incompetency when all the shrinks were lining up against me. I did not contest the findings of the St. Elizabeths doctors. The court found Howard Robbins competent and set his case down for trial in four months.

I could see that Howard really was coming around, gradually. Fissures were appearing in his delusional system, though he tried to shore it up.

"For a while, I thought, 'I'm in trouble. I better face up to it,' " he told me. "I thought the paperboy saw me shoot them. But then I realized that he was lying.

"And my friend Lenny can't testify that I gave him the gun," Howard reasoned, "because he got rid of it, and that's a crime, destruction of evidence."

"Who said you gave Lenny the gun?" I asked, taken aback.

"You told me that," Howard said.

"I never told you that, Howard. This is the first I've heard of it."

He frowned thoughtfully. "Well, it must've been somebody else."

One day he called me up and told me he was "ready to tell the truth."

I drove over the bridge onto the small-town main street that is Martin Luther King Boulevard in Anacostia, past the World's Largest Chair

(19½ feet tall, 4,600 pounds, mahogany, presented to Curtis Brothers Furniture Company for their outstanding leadership and service to the public, 1959), to the top of a hill, where a nine-foot brick wall on the right side of the road and an iron fence on the left signified that I was traversing the St. Elizabeths grounds. I continued by three gates, until the wall on the right gave way to normal society's border crossing, a forlorn frontier outpost whose vandalized sign read

> nald's
> RGERS
> LION SERVED

I hung a left into gate number 4 and parked. I walked along Dogwood Street (the sign said), between a number of gloomy, forbidding Victorian brick buildings with orange tile roofs. A faint odor of disinfectant wafted on the spring breeze.

An elderly man with spindly white legs, in denim shorts and a rumpled checked sports shirt, walked by me without appearing to see me. He seemed to be concentrating on putting one foot in front of the other, as though counting his steps. Several other old men sat on park benches, one to a bench, silent, still. A young man lay half-asleep in the shade of an oak tree, his hands in his pants. A crewcut fellow walked over, and, smiling amiably, sat down beside him. "You got a hard-on?" he asked. A little orange Cushman work vehicle puttered by like a lunar explorer.

> *Don't you want me, baby?*
> *Don't you want me, o-o-o . . .*
> Another thirty-minute free ride from
> D.C. 101!

I could hear a radio blasting in the John Howard Pavilion. A six-story brick building which looks like a phone company office, it holds defendants undergoing pretrial mental observation, as well as those who have been committed following verdicts of not guilty by reason of insanity. As I drew nearer, the radio was joined by the solitary thump-thump-thump of a one-man basketball game inside.

Entering, I was frisked, and walked through a metal detector, then through a turnstile. (Another turnstile would count me on the way out.) An electronic lock was activated, and I shoved open a steel door. It clunked shut behind me. A steel door ahead of me was buzzed open. I was met by an attendant holding a big ring with about fifty keys on it. He walked me through a twisting course, unlocking doors and locking them behind us, to an elevator operable only with a key. After the elevator, there were more doors, more locks. Altogether, I had passed through seven locked doors when I arrived on Ward 7. A dozen pajama-clad lunatics shuffled up to me in zombielike Thorazine trances. They all appeared to have poorly fitted glass eyes—too large, and too dull. Howard and I went into an empty office, shut the door, and sat down, alone. There I was, with a homicidal maniac, and seven locked doors *behind* me. *He won't hurt me. You'd have to be crazy to hurt your own lawyer.*

Howard solemnly announced that he had decided he could trust me, and he was going to tell the truth. I played a drum roll in my head.

"It was an accident," Howard said. "Sheila had got me five hundred dollars' worth of drugs, and I owed her the money. I kept telling her I would get it soon. Then, that night, I bumped into her and David on the street. David was drunk. He started arguing with me about the money. Then Sheila said she was going to kill me if I didn't pay up right then. She pulled a gun. I grabbed it, and while we were struggling for it, it went off three times."

This story wasn't true; or, I should say, I didn't believe it. The paperboy saw Howard fire at Sheila. But the interesting thing was that Howard was now using *facts* to construct his story, very much as a lawyer does. The paperboy said that David did appear drunk—he stumbled off a curb; and he did hear an argument in which one of the men—he didn't know which—said, "Give the lady her money." And he did hear just three shots, not the fusillade Sheila had said was fired at her on the ground.

(Still more of what Howard had said from the beginning turned out to be true. To my surprise, the Citizen Complaint Bureau ultimately found complaints by Howard against Sheila in its files, which had resulted in two face-to-face hearings. The hearing officer had concluded, "It is quite clear to me that the complainant [Howard] hates the defendant, but why, I could not make out. I could not tell who was telling the truth.")

"Howard," I said gently, "I have to advise you that, in my professional opinion, a jury will not believe that the gun went off accidentally three times. And the paperboy will testify that he saw you stand there and shoot Sheila."*

"Well, it's obvious the paperboy's lying," Howard explained with a shrug.

Howard's partial reconciliation with reality led him to compromise. He agreed to let me move for a two-stage trial. We would proceed with the

---

* I found out later that the government was unaware of the existence of the paperboy.

defense of "accident," and then, if and only if he was found guilty, we would advance the defense of insanity. The judge denied that motion, however. We would get only one trial and only one jury. We could choose between accident or insanity, or we could argue both to the same jury—"he was insane at the time of the accident"—an undesirable way to proceed, since the jury would be skeptical of our insanity defense once we had squandered our credibility on the accident theory.

Howard had no trouble understanding the problems this ruling raised. He modified his plan: he would plead not guilty by reason of insanity outright *if* there were nicks on the sidewalk at the crime scene, corroborating Sheila's story that he had fired at her on the ground.

There weren't any nicks on the sidewalk. I considered lying to him— saying that there were. That one little lie might avert a twenty-to-life sentence. But I had never lied to a client, at least not about anything important.

I decided to tell him the truth and persuade him to go with the insanity plea anyway. I thought the truth might have a special aura, visible to the insane, which would cause him to accept it.

I fortified myself with Wild Turkey—trying to get on Howard's wavelength—and drove out again to see him, and to test the power of truth.

The moment I walked in, he said, "I've been thinking this over, and I've talked it over with some people here, and I think I better go ahead and go along with that insanity plea. I mean, if they're going to be making up evidence, there's not much sense trying to fight it."

You may be crazy, but you're not dumb.

The government, in a last-ditch effort to develop evidence that Howard was sane, obtained a court order to have him evaluated by the city's most prosecutorial psychiatrist. ("They roll back a stone and pull him out of his cave for situations like these," my supervisor said. "He *never* finds *anyone* insane.") But even this doctor reported, "Schizophrenic behavior is not necessarily completely disorganized. If Mr. Robbins' behavior showed indications of reflection on the consequences of his behavior, it would not be inconsistent with schizophrenia." He concluded that the shooting was a "product" of Howard's mental disease.

The government decided not to oppose our insanity plea.

I felt afterward that I probably really shouldn't have given Howard a big smile and handshake when the judge, on the basis of the shrinks' reports, without taking any testimony, pronounced him not guilty by reason of insanity.

§6-17

The U.S. attorney finally closed a deal with the snitch who had information on the bus murder. The man said that it was B.J. who did it (just as we'd thought), and that he did it with a white-handled five-shot revolver, and that the revolver belonged to a certain individual, whose name he supplied. A Detective Kanjian, who told me there was "a lot of resistance" in the police department to his reopening a closed case, found that the police already had that revolver in their possession. It had been recovered from under a car near the scene of a Fourteenth Street drug bust two weeks after the bus murder. Ballistics tests indicated that it *was* the gun that fired the slug that killed the man on the bus. The gun's owner said that B.J. had borrowed it one day in July, and returned it with one less bullet.

The prosecutor dropped the charges against Buie just before his trial, eleven months after his arrest. A warrant was put out for B.J., but he was shot and killed by a policeman in an unrelated incident before he could be brought to justice.

§6-18

I was sitting in court, waiting forever to do a two-minute preliminary hearing, when something caught my attention. Someone was accused of murdering Richard Joe Madison, one of my first juvenile clients—the one who was committed by Judge Quinn even though he got a part-time job and went to tutoring and counseling, the one whose brother died in a sewer. The homicide detective who was testifying was an unctuous, evasive type, whom I had come to dislike, just from seeing him testify before. Suddenly I found myself rooting for him, yet the only difference between this case and all the other cases was that I knew the victim, which was no difference at all.

"A witness near the alley," he was saying, "heard the defendant say,

'I'm going to kill you for robbing me.' Then the witness heard Mr. Madison screaming, 'Help! Help! He's killing me!' followed by several shots."

The defendant's lawyer, one of P.D.S.'s best, asked, "Isn't it true that Mr. Madison had an extensive robbery record?"

Walking down the aisle after the hearing, the defendant smugly smiled at a friend in the audience.

I went and talked to my boss. "I think my feelings are irrelevant, but there comes a point . . ." P.D.S. got off the case. We had a conflict of interest. We could be accused of not trying hard enough to defend a client who was accused of killing another client of ours.

A few days later, I opened the Washington *Post* and saw pictures of 175 local people killed by gunfire in the past year. There, right underneath Richard Joe Madison's picture, was a photo of Yeats Moore, my kid who was arrested for smoking on a bus. He'd been found in an alley with a bullet in the back of his head. I pulled out their files and marked their cases "closed."

AFTERWORD

"If the courts were organized to promote justice," Clarence Darrow told the inmates of the Cook County Jail in 1902, "the people would elect somebody to defend all these criminals [sic], somebody as smart as the prosecutor—and give him as many detectives and as many assistants to help, and pay as much money to defend you as to prosecute you."[1]

Darrow's vision will probably never be fully realized, as justice is never as popular as order. Still, Darrow would have been impressed by the system in Washington, D.C., where the courts operate in a reasonably just fashion: most of the guilty are convicted, and nearly all of the innocent go free.

By no means should one conclude that justice prevails in Washington. Ninety-nine percent of the injustice associated with crime occurs before the principals come into contact with the criminal justice system: the victim has already been victimized; the defendant, more often than not, has been subjected to every kind of abuse, from inadequate prenatal care to exclusion from the work force. The police, courts, and prisons are just mop-up operations.

"Now, no intelligent physician would consider treating an ailment without trying to discover its cause," Darrow wrote,[2] yet that is how we treat crime, concentrating on the symptomatic relief we think the criminal justice system should bring—fast, fast, fast.

In 1981, state governments alone spent $2.5 billion on police and $5 billion on corrections.[3] We are setting new records for the number of people imprisoned, which rose 12.1 percent in the one year from 1980 to 1981. The only limit on the number of people in prison is the space available. When we get more space, we lock up more people. New prisons generally reach capacity by the second year they are open.[4]

The courts cannot reduce crime or establish justice. They are just a sorting mechanism between the front end of the system—the police—and the back end—the prisons. To the extent that the public supports adequate judicial resources and effective representation for the accused, the sorting can be done in a just and equitable manner.

I am proud of the role I played in that process.

NOTES

CHAPTER ONE

§1-03

1. E. R. Shipp, "Manhattan Studying Washington in Effort to Lift Courts' Efficiency," New York *Times,* March 30, 1981, p. 1.

CHAPTER THREE

§3-03

1. *Crime and Arrest Profile: The Nation's Capital, 1980,* Office of Criminal Justice Plans and Analysis, Government of the District of Columbia (Washington, D.C.: September 1981), table 6, p. 10.

2. *Crime and Justice Profile: The Nation's Capital,* Office of Criminal Justice Plans and Analysis, Government of the District of Columbia (Washington, D.C.: October 1979), p. 51.

§3-05

1. *1980 Annual Report, District of Columbia Courts,* Joint Committee on Judicial Administration in the District of Columbia and the Executive Officer of the District of Columbia Courts (Washington, D.C.), p. 57.

2. *Metropolitan Police Department, Washington, D.C., Fiscal Year 1980 Annual Report,* Government of the District of Columbia (Washington, D.C.: June 1981).

3. *Statistical Report, United States Attorney's Office, Fiscal Year 1980,* United States Department of Justice, Executive Office for United States Attorneys, Prepared by Systems Design and Development Staff of the Justice Management Division, Report 1-21 (Washington, D.C.), table 3.

4. *Metropolitan Police Department, Washington, D.C., Fiscal Year 1980 Annual Report,* p. 56.

5. As of April 1, 1982. Figures courtesy of FBI.

§3-09

1. "In the Matter of an Inquiry into Allegations of Misconduct Against Juveniles Detained at and Committed at Cedar Knoll Institution," Special Proceeding M-3, Superior Court of the District of Columbia, Family Division–Juvenile Branch, Judge Kessler (Washington, D.C.: October 27, 1978), p. 20, quoting City Council Task Force on the Reorganization of the Department of Human Resources, "Report to the Council of the District of Columbia on the Operation of the Department of Human Resources" (Washington, D.C.: January 1978), p. 234.

2. "In the Matter of an Inquiry . . ." pp. 2, 20.

3. Ibid, p. 20.

4. Ibid, p. 49.

5. *Crime and Justice Profile: The Nation's Capital,* p. 117.

6. Ibid, p. 115 (total for 1978).

7. Superior Court of the District of Columbia Rules, Juvenile Rule 2.

8. Private conversation, Jerome Miller.

§3-12

1. F. C. Bartlett, *Remembering: A Study in Experimental and Social Psychology* (New York: Cambridge University Press, 1967), p. 213, quoted by Monroe H. Freedman in *Lawyers' Ethics in an Adversary System* (Indianapolis: Bobbs-Merrill, 1975), p. 66.

2. E. Loftus, in *Psychology Today*, December 1974, pp. 117, 119, quoted by Freedman, op. cit. p. 67.

3. G. A. Talland, *Disorders of Memory and Learning* (New York: Penguin, 1969), pp. 18-19, quoted by Freedman, op. cit. p. 67.

CHAPTER FOUR

§4-01

1. Disciplinary Rule 7-102 (A) (6).

§4-13

1. 21 D.C. Code 501 et seq.

2. Stack v. Boyle, 342 U.S. 1 (1951).

3. *Recommendation Guidelines,* District of Columbia Pretrial Services Agency (Washington, D.C.: June 1980, revised March 1981), p. 8.

4. *The D.C. Pretrial Services Agency, Washington, D.C., an Exemplary Project,* U.S. Department of Justice, National Institute of Justice, Office of Development, Testing, and Dissemination (Washington, D.C.: May 1981), p. 7.

5. *Report of the D.C. Pretrial Services Agency for the Period January 1, 1981-December 31, 1981,* Government of the District of Columbia (Washington, D.C.), p. 15.

6. *Recommendation Guidelines,* p. 9.

§4-14

1. *Crime and Arrest Profile: The Nation's Capital, 1980,* table 10, p. 16.

§4-20

1. Marquis James, *The Life of Andrew Jackson* (New York: Bobbs-Merrill, 1938).

2. *Public Defender Service for the District of Columbia, Tenth Annual Report,* Fiscal Year 1980, Public Defender Service (Washington, D.C.: 1981), p. 20.

3. Private conversation, David Powell, Ph.D., Chief, Post-trial Branch, St. Elizabeths Hospital, May 6, 1983.

4. Private conversation, Ross Dicker, Esq., Public Defender Service, May 5, 1983.

5. Private conversation, Philip Baridon, Ph.D., Chief, Program Evaluation Branch, Forensic Division, St. Elizabeths Hospital, May 9, 1983.

6. Bethea v. United States, 365 A.2nd 64 (D.C. Ct. App. 1976).

7. McDonald v. United States, 114 U.S. App. D.C. 120, 124 (1962).

8. United States v. Brawner, 153 U.S. App. D.C. 1 (1972), *dissent.*

9. H.R. 6716, introduced June 24, 1982, quoted by Bruce J. Ennis in "Straight Talk about the Insanity Defense," *The Nation,* July 24-31, 1982, p. 70. Mr. Ennis provides a lucid analysis of the issues involved in reforming the insanity defense.

10. Leland v. Oregon, 343 U.S. 790, 802, *dissent.*

§4-23

1. Olmstead v. United States, 277 U.S. 438 (1928), *dissent.*

§4-25

1. *Public Defender Service for the District of Columbia, Tenth Annual Report,* p. 20.

2. Information provided by the Unitarian Universalist Service Committee's National Moratorium on Prison Construction, 324 C Street, S.E., Washington, D.C. 20003.

3. Brady v. United States, 397 U.S. 742 (1970).

CHAPTER FIVE

§5-01

1. *Crime and Justice Profile: The Nation's Capital,* p. 150.

§5-06

1. Johns v. Smyth, 176 F. Supp. 949, 953 (E.D. Va. 1959).

2. Friedman, "Professional Responsibility in D.C.: A Survey," *Res Ipsa Loquitur,* 1972, p. 60, quoted by Freedman, *Lawyers' Ethics in an Adversary System,* p. 38.

3. Instruction 2.27, *Criminal Jury Instructions, District of Columbia,* Third Edition, Young Lawyers Section, The Bar Association of the District of Columbia (Washington, D.C.: 1978).

4. Lord Brougham, in his representation of Queen Caroline, *Trial of Queen Caroline* 8 (1821), quoted by Freedman, op. cit. p. 9.

5. Instruction 5.09, *Criminal Jury Instructions, District of Columbia.*

§5-09

1. Private conversation, Kirby Howlett, Esq., Public Defender Service, August 1982.

CHAPTER SIX

§6-05

1. This description of the sociopathic syndrome is drawn from William and Jean McCord, *The Psychopath, an Essay on the Criminal Mind* (New York: Van Nostrand, 1964).

§6-07

1. United States v. Watson, 423 U.S. 411 (1976).

2. Gatlin v. United States, 117 U.S. App. D.C. 123, 129, n. 6 (1963), quoting Bell v. United States, 102 U.S. App. D.C. 383, 388 (1957), cert. denied, 358 U.S. 885 (1958).

3. Michigan v. Mosely, 423 U.S. 96 (1975).

§6-10

1. Edward H. Cleary, general editor, *McCormick's Handbook of the Law of Evidence,* 2nd. ed. (St. Paul: West Publishing Co., 1972), Chapter 4, Section 32.

§6-14

1. Brown v. United States, 256 U.S. 335, 343 (1921).

§6-15

1. Ethical Consideration 2-29, Footnote 50, quoting 2 Boswell, *The Life of Johnson,* pp. 47–48 (Hill ed., 1887).

2. *Criminal Trials: A Defense Attorney's Handbook,* Public Defender Service (Washington, D.C.), pp. 14–33.

AFTERWORD

1. Arthur Weinberg, ed., *Attorney for the Damned* (New York: Simon and Schuster, 1957), p. 12.

2. Clarence Darrow, *The Story of My Life* (New York: Scribner's, 1932), p. 77.

3. "States' Income at $300 Billion for First Time, U.S. Reports," New York *Times*, October 25, 1982.

4. Jessica Mitford, "An Update on the 'Prison Business,'" *The Nation*, October 30, 1982. p. 424.

About the Author

JAMES S. KUNEN lives in New York City, where he has abandoned the law (at least temporarily) for the typewriter. He is the author of *The Strawberry Statement* (Random House, 1969) and *Standard Operating Procedure* (Avon, 1971).